GOOD AND EASY SEWING BOOK

Drawings by Jackie Dalton

Photographs by Walter Herstatt

THE *Betty Crocker* HOME LIBRARY

GOOD AND EASY SEWING BOOK

For you and your family

by Joanne Schreiber and Carter Houck

UNIVERSAL PUBLISHING INC. UPd NEW YORK

DISTRIBUTED BY CHARLES SCRIBNER'S SONS

The authors thank the following companies for their cooperation in supplying information and materials used in the preparation of this book: Armo Company; B. Blumenthal Buttons; B. G. E. Buttons; Brand Name Fabrics; Concord Fabrics; Dan River Fabrics; Franken Trimmings; Lowenthal Trimmings; The Rag Doll; The Singer Company; The Talon Company; William E. Wright Trimmings.

Dear Friend,

When it comes to sewing, there are the lucky ones who seem to have been born with a silver thimble on their finger. And at the other extreme a few, not so lucky, who will always have trouble sewing on a button. Then there are the many in-betweens (like yourself perhaps?) who would dearly love to sew . . . for both the satisfactions and the savings . . . but who lack the courage and the skill to start.

This book is meant to help you over that hurdle. It should guide you carefully, step-by-step through the maze of patterns and fabrics, cutting and stitching, fitting and finishing. The authors, who have had rich experience in the sewing field—writing, editing, teaching, and dressmaking—consider sewing not only a craft, but an art form. But it is an art, they feel, that takes something more than talent alone to master. You need patience, confidence, and a knowledge of the basics. The first is strictly up to you. For the other two, count on the pages that follow.

Even if you know the fundamentals of sewing, you'll find many new "how-to's" and tips for using the new fabrics and sewing aids and for improving your techniques. It's a book meant not just for reading once, but to keep near your sewing machine for ready reference . . . hopefully, to help make sewing for yourself and your family agreeably "Good and Easy."

Betty Crocker

CONTENTS

Introduction

YOUR SEWING TOOLS

A Friendly Sewing Machine • Which Machine to Choose? • Portable or Cabinet? • Straight-Stitch or Zigzag? • Know Your Machine • Practice Stitching • Your Sewing Machine Attachments.

Good and Easy Sewing Aids • For Your Sewing Box • Sewing Aids for Non-Sewing.

Your Sewing Center • Pick a Sewing Spot • Three Sewing Centers: Bedroom, Dining Room, and Basement Family Room.

SMART SHOPPING

Shopping Hints • The Big Pattern Catalogs • What Size Are You? • Picking a Pattern • The Pattern Envelope • Choose Your Fabric • How Patterns Are Made.

The World of Fabrics • What Is a Fabric? • Fiber into Fabric • Fabric Categories • Fabric Widths.

Know-How for Notions • Decorative Trimmings • Practical Tapes • Other Notions by the Yard • Fastenings • Thread.

The Inside Story: Fabrics for Linings, Interlinings, Underlinings, Facings, Interfacings.

THE PRE-SEWING SESSION

Make Your Pattern Fit You • The Easy Way to Pattern Alteration • A Pattern Alteration Checklist • Questions Often Asked About Pattern Alteration.

Now Prepare Your Fabric • Straighten the Grain Line • What about Pre-Shrinking? • Some Other Pre-Cutting Tips • A Guide to Special Fabric Types • Questions Often Asked About Pre-Sewing.

Layouts, Pinning, Cutting, Marking • Laying out Your Pattern • Pinning • Cutting Made Easy • How to Transfer the Markings on Your Pattern • Questions Often Asked About Pinning and Cutting.

Understanding Underlinings and Interfacings

FINISHING DETAILS 94

Trim with Bias Strips of Fabric • Cut Your Own Bias Trim • Corded Piping • Bound Edges • Double Bias.

Fasten Everything Down! • Buttoned Up • How to Make a Shank • What Kind of Thread? • It's a Snap! • Hooks, Eyes, and Thread Loops.

NOW YOU CAN TRY...

Trim with Bias Strips of Fabric • Cut Your Own Bias Trim • Corded Piping • Bound Edges • Double Bias.

Fasten Everything Down! • Buttoned Up • How to Make a Shank • What Kind of Thread? • It's a Snap! • Hooks, Eyes, and Thread Loops.

NOW YOU CAN TRY...

Secrets for Slacks • Pick a Pattern • Take a Measurement • Alter the Pattern.

Sewing with Specialty Fabrics • Double Knits • Nylon Tricot • Permanent-Press and Wash-and-Wear Fabrics • Stretch Fabrics • Bonded Fabrics • Laminated Fabrics • Vinyl Fabrics • Fake Fur.

Lingerie—Lacy and Lovely • Choose an Easy Fabric • Lingerie Patterns • Waistband Finishes.

PROFESSIONAL SUCCESS TIPS AND DESIGNER FINISHES

Trim with Bias Strips of Fabric • Cut Your Own Bias Trim • Corded Piping • Bound Edges • Double Bias.

Fasten Everything Down! • Buttoned Up • How to Make a Shank • What Kind of Thread? • It's a Snap! • Hooks, Eyes, and Thread Loops.

Alterations You Can Make • Shorten a Hemline • The Back Pleat Problem • Shorten a Coat Hem • Lengthen a Hemline • Other Lengthening Techniques • Take in a Hipline in a Skirt • Let out a Hipline • Raise a Waistline • Shorten or Lengthen a Sleeve.

Make-over Magic—Remodeling Tips and Suggestions.

Make Your Own Patchwork • How to Make a Patchwork Evening Skirt.

Checking a Ready-Made Garment.

SEWING FOR OTHERS 137

Sewing for Men • Pattern Sizes • Make a Shirt • Other Gift Ideas for Men.

Sewing for Babies and Children • Check the Pattern Books • Gift Stitchery • Make it Fit • Growth Allowance.

Special Finishes for Children's Clothes • Scallops• Ruffles • French Seams.

Decorative Stitching • Fun with Appliqué • To Appliqué by Hand • To Appliqué by Machine.

Halloween Costumes and Special Outfits.

Make a Decorative Wall Hanging for a Special Child.

A SEWING GRAB BAG OF HELPFUL HINTS AND TIPS 148

Your Sewing Calendar • Tips From the Sewing Experts • Take it Easy— Let the Professionals Give You a Hand • Questions and Answers About Your Sewing Machine • Caring for Your Clothes.

For Easy Reference 153

Your Personal Measurement Chart • Standard Pattern Industry Charts • Figure Types • Fabric Conversion Chart • Fabric, Thread, and Needle Chart.

A Glossary of Sewing Terms 161

A Fabric Glossary 166

Index 173

COLOR ILLUSTRATIONS

INTRODUCTION

If all the information in this book could be boiled down to just one tip for good and easy sewing, it would be this: Take the time to sew it right.

In spite of all the new jiffy patterns and miracle fabrics and new sewing machines, there is just one real time-saver in sewing. That is to avoid tiresome ripping out and restitching by sewing it correctly the first time. And that is where this book can help you.

It is written as a step-by-step guide, taking you logically through all the steps of dressmaking, from selecting your pattern to sewing on the final button. Pre-sewing steps are emphasized, since the accuracy of pattern alteration, cutting, and marking is the key to the fit of the finished garment. Because you tackle such details as bound buttonholes and pockets before you stitch the garment sections together (it's easier to work on a flat surface), the section on show-off details comes before garment assembly. Worked buttonholes, on the other hand, are done when everything else is just about finished, so those are discussed much later in the book.

Often it is possible to do something more than one way. In most such cases we have described only the easiest method. In a few instances, however, we have given a choice so you can select the method that best fits your skill . . . or your mood. A special section called "Success Tips" tells you how to make some details even easier by faking them or leaving them out. And there is more practical help in sections on shopping, budget-stretching, alterations, mending and makeover, gift-stitching, sewing items such as slacks and lingerie, and working with specialty fabrics.

Step-by-step photographs have been included wherever a visual presentation makes instructions easier to understand. Carter Houck worked each step for the camera so that you would have the opportunity of seeing how someone with experience handles her tools and materials while you are learning to follow the procedures described in the text.

Let this book help you complete each step carefully and correctly as you go along. You will find that you are not only getting things done quickly but that you are enjoying every minute you spend sewing things you and your family can be proud to wear.

YOUR SEWING TOOLS

Good tools are as important in sewing as they are in cooking. Your sewing machine and your sewing aids should be selected as carefully as your range and your kitchen tools, for good performance and long-lasting satisfaction. As any cook knows: good tools make easier work.

A Friendly Sewing Machine

You know how your husband feels about his car? That's how you're going to feel about your sewing machine. It is a friend, an extension of your creative self, and it's there to help you make beautiful things. It's a machine, all right, but it's a friendly machine. So choose it carefully, treat it lovingly, and it will repay you with smooth, dependable sewing, year after year.

WHICH MACHINE TO CHOOSE?

How do you decide which machine to buy? You research the market—by talking with your friends, reading consumer reports, visiting sewing centers and department stores, and asking for demonstrations. Get acquainted with the various makes, their price ranges, their service and trade-in policies.

Think of a sewing machine as an investment, not a luxury. Get a new one if you possibly can; it will repay you many times over with superior performance and will actually encourage you to sew more. And the more you sew, the easier sewing will become.

How can you be sure that you are selecting the right machine? You can rent a sewing machine for a week or so and test it under actual at-home conditions. Make a dress on it and see how many of the stitches and attachments you use.

If the price of a new machine is out of sight for you right now, you can save by buying a used machine. Be sure to get it from a reliable dealer; be sure it carries a guarantee; and be sure it has a full set of everything that goes with it—attachments, foot control and cord, instruction booklet, and a free lesson in using the machine.

Basically, there are just four kinds of sewing machines: straight-stitch, zigzag, lightweight, or heavy duty.

PORTABLE OR CABINET?

The terms portable and cabinet are misleading, because any standard machine may come in a carrying case and may be installed in a cabinet.

If you will be sewing on the run in a college dormitory, tiny apartment, or mobile home, choose a lightweight model in a carrying case. There are several kinds that do just about everything a full-size machine does, and weigh fifteen pounds or less. A full-size machine in a carrying case weighs in at twenty-five to thirty pounds, a fair load for a small woman.

If your living pattern is pretty settled, a sewing cabinet is more comfortable for long sewing sessions and offers more protection for the machine. Most cabinets have drawers to hold thread, patterns, and notions. There's good design going into cabinets. You are sure to find Early American, Spanish, modern, or traditional styles to blend with your decor.

STRAIGHT-STITCH OR ZIGZAG?

Now for the big question: straight-stitch or zigzag? There are plain and fancy versions of each, and you can select according to your price range.

A budget-priced straight-stitch machine will sew backward and forward; will offer stitch-length, pressure, and tension regulators; and will have a light and some basic attachments.

A medium-priced straight-stitch machine may also have an automatic bobbin-winder (a great convenience), more attachments, more sophisticated design and color, a better-looking carrying case, and a fitted plastic container for the accessories.

A simple zigzag machine, which does straight as well as zigzag stitching, has a mechanism that permits its needle to go sideways as well as forward and backward. This zigzag stitch is ideal for stretch fabrics and knits, and is the basis of all decorative stitches. In addition to the controls offered on a straight-stitch machine, a zigzag will have a setting to switch from straight to zigzag sewing, a setting to control the width of the zigzag stitch, and probably some discs (sometimes called cams) to insert for additional stitches.

A simple zigzag will do overcasting, blind hemming, buttonholes, decorative stitching, and of course, zigzag sewing. Since this is the stitch preferred for knit fabrics and since knits are so popular, a simple zigzag sewing machine is probably your best bet.

A more expensive zigzag will have more stitches built into it which you dial or push-button into action. It will also offer discs for extra designs. It will have such refinements as a built-in buttonholer, two-speed sewing, special non-slip fabric feeds, magnetic throat plates, five kinds of stitching—straight, zigzag, stretch, basting, and chain stitching.

All that is a bit overwhelming, expensive, and not necessary for general sewing.

Sewing machines, like cars, have trade-in value, provided you trade with a reputable dealer. You can start with a simple straight-stitch now, and trade up to a zigzag later.

If you have inherited Grandmother's treadle and if it still works, don't be in a hurry to trade it in. Millions of women have two sewing machines, believe it or not. If you have a teen-age daughter or if you will have one in a few years, she can learn to sew on the old machine while you perform on the new zigzag machine. It is nice, too, to have a portable to take traveling, or an extra machine for a friend to use during an afternoon of sewing together.

KNOW YOUR MACHINE

Though sewing machines differ in design and their approaches to setting controls, they are basically the same.

The main spool of thread is on top of the machine. The thread runs down through a series of hooks and levers until it goes through the eye of the needle. A second thread is wound on the bobbin. The even interlocking of these two threads makes the stitch on the zigzag machine as well as on the straight-stitch models.

Be sure to read your instruction manual carefully. Keep it near the machine and refer to it often. The people who write sewing machine manuals are trained in telling nonprofessionals clearly and simply how to run their machines and how to use the settings and attachments. When the machine is running smoothly, sewing is speedy, easy, and fun.

Some of the newer machines have a trapdoor at the side to show the threading sequence. This procedure is also shown in the instruction book. Be sure your machine is threaded correctly, so you can avoid skipped stitches, snarls, broken thread, and an unthreaded needle.

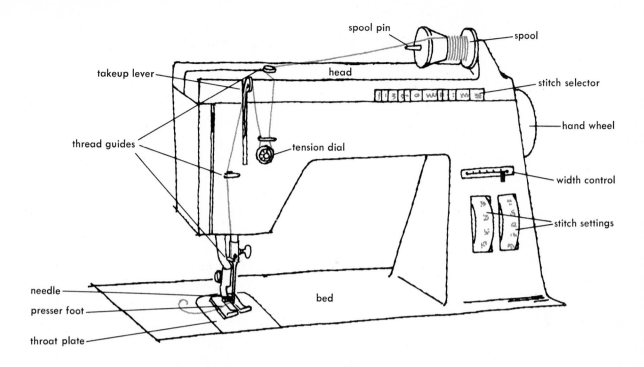

spool pin
spool
takeup lever
head
stitch selector
thread guides
hand wheel
tension dial
width control
stitch settings
needle
bed
presser foot
throat plate

The machine pictured is a composite of many different kinds to help you identify various parts that you may have on your machine. It is not a drawing of any one machine.

PRACTICE STITCHING

When you are sure your machine is threaded correctly, you are ready for practice stitching. Cut a few pieces of lightweight cotton about 8" square and select a thread of a contrasting color. Fabric and thread should contrast so the stitches show up easily.

Place a double layer of fabric under the needle, pulling both threads back away from the fabric. Leave about a 4" end on the threads. Be sure the larger amount of fabric is to the left of the needle. Line right edges up with the longest mark on the throat plate. That is the ⅝" mark, the standard seam allowance on most patterns and the measurement you will use most often. If you are sewing on an older machine that doesn't have these measured guidelines, use a strip of transparent tape to mark the ⅝" measurement.

Lower presser foot. Turn hand wheel toward you to insert needle in the fabric. Press gently on your foot or knee control and start stitching slowly, guiding fabric gently without pulling and keeping the edge even with the ⅝" guideline.

It will be easier for you to watch the edge of the fabric rather than the needle at first. When you reach the end of the fabric, stop stitching. Turn wheel to raise needle out of the fabric. Raise presser foot. Pull fabric back behind the needle and cut threads.

Continue practicing, using the other lines on the throat plate as guides. Draw a curved line on the cloth and try following the curve. Stitch backward a few stitches at the end of a line of stitching to lock the stitch. This is a technique you will use often, to anchor the end of a dart, for example. If yours is a zigzag machine, practice zigzag stitching too until you can handle your machine easily and confidently.

YOUR SEWING MACHINE ATTACHMENTS

All machines, straight and zigzag, come with a box full of gadgets and attachments. They are all described in the instruction manual that comes with the machine: some are more useful than others. The one indispensable aid is the cording and zipper foot, which slides back and forth so you can stitch very close to a raised edge. It makes zipper insertion easy! You will also need extra needles and bobbins, a lint brush, and an oil tube.

Cording and zipper foot

Your machine needs care to keep it humming. The section on page 150 gives you tips

Sewing aids: (1) press mitt, (2) needle board, (3) sleeve roll, (4) tailor's ham, (5) seam and corner board, (6) steam iron, (7) press cloth.

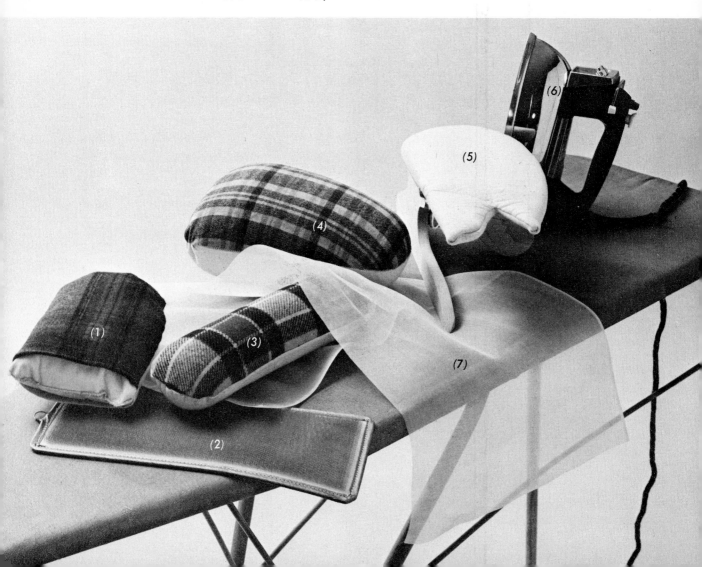

on machine maintenance and so does your instruction book. Remember to keep the machine unplugged and covered when it is not in use, and to keep small children away from it. A few such simple precautions will repay you with years of good and easy sewing!

Sewing Aids

ROCK-BOTTOM LIST	ADD-LATER LIST
Pressing equipment	
steam iron, ironing board, transparent press cloth, press mitt	sleeveboard (or seam and corner board which offers several pressing surfaces), sleeve roll (you can make your own from rolled newspaper and toweling), needle board, tailor's ham (for shaping)
Measuring equipment	
tape measure, yardstick, six-inch ruler or hem gauge	skirt marker (pin or chalk model), hem pressing gauge, scalloped rulers
Cutting equipment	
large and sharp dressmaker's shears, small trimming scissors (left-hand scissors are available), cutting board or large table, seam ripper	pinking shears, buttonhole scissors
Marking equipment	
dressmaker's carbon and tracing wheel, tailor's chalk	chalk pencil
Miscellaneous equipment	
hand needles, machine needles (assorted sizes), straight pins and pin cushion, mercerized and polyester/cotton thread in assorted colors, thimble	bodkin, tweezers, awl, emery bag, dress form, darning egg

Good and Easy Sewing Aids

Besides your sewing machine, you will need a group of items called sewing aids. These are designed to help you with sewing projects and to make sewing easier.

While there are literally thousands of items available in the sewing section of the notions counter, you need only a few aids at first. Later, as your skill increases, you can expand your collection. At left is a rock-bottom list, plus an add-later list.

Some of this equipment will be part of your regular household inventory, such as the iron, ironing board, and yardstick.

FOR YOUR SEWING BOX

If your sewing room is more like a sewing box, you will need to prune even the rock-bottom list to save space.

Minimum sewing aids:
tape measure
six-inch ruler
medium shears
small trimming scissors
chalk
thimble
pincushion
an assortment of thread, hand and machine needles, straight pins

SEWING AIDS FOR NON-SEWING

There is also a category of aids that replace sewing, to add more quick and easy techniques to your skills.

Iron-ons:
patches for blue jeans, knit patches for sweaters, corduroy and other fabric patches

mending muslin for sheets

mending tapes

fusibles (bonding agents which fuse two fabrics together)

Stick-ons:

transparent tape for pattern alteration and for anchoring pattern pieces to fabrics that should not be pinned

zipper tape, to hold zipper in place for stitching

fabric glue for hemming vinyl and flattening out seam allowances in fabric that should not be pressed

A Buttoneer: a gadget that attaches buttons with tough nylon filament. It is good for attaching buttons which can't be reached from the wrong side and for buttons on children's coats

Your Sewing Center

Now that you have your sewing equipment assembled, you need a place to put it all.

Ideally your sewing center should be in a light-traffic part of the house, yet fairly near the front door, the telephone, the kitchen, and the children's play area. You should be able to leave the sewing machine out between sewing periods. It takes time to set it up in the morning and take it down again at night. It is better to spend the time actually sewing.

We all dream of a Mom room—a pretty, sunny room with the laundry equipment, sewing center, desk, telephone, and comfortable chair all together, plus a radio to give us music as we work.

If that's not possible, you can still have a sewing center in the bedroom, the dining room, or family room, or even in the living room. The secret is storage; you really need a cabinet or closet which can be opened wide so everything is within easy sight and reach, and closed up or screened off when you are not sewing.

PICK A SEWING SPOT

Here are the points to consider when deciding where to sew.

Good natural *light* for daytime work and good general light for night are invaluable.

Three *electrical outlets* are necessary for light, iron, and sewing machine.

The best work height for a *sewing and cutting table* is 28″. It should be accessible from three sides and measure at least 56″ x 36″.

A *sewing machine table* on which you place a portable must be sturdy and allow for elbow room on the left of the machine.

A *mirror* is an important aid in fitting.

Storage shelves or drawers are required for keeping sewing baskets, boxes of supplies, thread racks, patterns, and fabrics.

An old highboy, the kind often found in secondhand furniture stores, offers good storage space. Fit the top drawer with thread racks and wicker baskets for small sewing items. Put patterns, buttons, and trimmings in the second drawer. Use the third for projects-in-work, and the bottom for fabrics. Decorate the highboy with bright paint, magazine cutout collages, or painted-on spools, tapes, and fabrics. This is the sort of sewing cabinet that is fun as well as useful.

THREE SEWING CENTERS: BEDROOM, DINING ROOM, AND BASEMENT FAMILY ROOM

Here are three sewing center designs to give you ideas for your own sewing center. One

A bedroom sewing center (courtesy of Parents' Magazine).

is set in a bedroom, one in a dining room, and one in a basement family room. Study the sketches and see which suggestions are best for you.

1. A bedroom sewing center. An attractive cabinet measuring ten feet wide, eight feet tall and eighteen inches deep holds everything you need. The end of the cutting table toward the cabinet slides up on nylon rollers. A full-length mirror is attached to the door of the cabinet holding the dress form. Sewing aids are hung handily on a pegboard.

2. A dining room sewing center. The average dining table is just right for pinning and

A dining room sewing center (courtesy of Parents' Magazine).

A sewing center in the basement family room (courtesy of Parents' Magazine).

cutting. Cabinets hold sewing equipment. A cabinet for the sewing machine can blend with decor, or a portable machine can be set on the low sideboard. Set up a portable ironing board near an electric outlet.

3. The sewing center in a basement family room. This beautifully designed unit may be closed up entirely when not in use. The two side panels are twelve inches deep and four feet wide, and hinged to swing shut on nylon casters. The cutting table is hinged and raises up to become a cabinet door. Good overhead light is provided and there is a spotlight at the sewing table. Pegboard is used for thread and scissors storage. An ironing board can be stored inside the panel at the left.

SMART SHOPPING

Just as a good dinner begins in the supermarket, so a good sewing project begins in the fabric shop with top-quality ingredients, carefully selected and lovingly assembled.

And just as there are tips and guidelines for supermarket shopping, there are tips and guidelines for shopping to sew. The fabrics are so beautiful, the patterns so enticing, the trims and notions so appealing that it's easy to get completely carried away—unless you have a plan!

Which should you buy first—the pattern or the fabric? If you stop and think a minute, you'll realize that you have to buy the pattern first, because your shopping list is right there on the back of the envelope.

But you can decide on your fabric first, then pick your pattern, and then buy all the ingredients, including just the right amount of fabric.

Shopping Hints

Before you go to the store, try to have some idea of the kind of garment you want to make, or you will find yourself hopelessly sidetracked by all the new fabrics and fashions.

Try not to shop when you are in a hurry. You will almost certainly forget something and have to return to the store—and that takes time.

It's easier if you don't have to take the children with you. Even though some places have toy areas for small fry, you will be able to think better without them.

Buy everything you need all at once, even when you think you have the right thread or zipper at home. There are two reasons for this. You will know the total cost of the garment you are making and you can estimate just how much money you are saving by sewing. Also, you will have everything you need available when you begin, so you won't be stalled by return shopping trips once you have started to sew.

THE BIG PATTERN CATALOGS

Those enormous, heavy pattern catalogs are marvelous sources of inspiration and information. But they take time to plow through. If you can't take the time in the shop to study the patterns carefully, there are a couple of alternative measures.

Sometimes, a friendly shop will let you take the big catalog home overnight or for the weekend, to study at your leisure—with your Girl Scout promise to bring it back on time.

When a new edition of a pattern book comes out, you can often buy the old one for a dollar or two.

Some of the pattern companies have small, at-home catalogs with a representative group of current styles. Pattern magazines feature the newest styles, along with worthwhile articles on sewing techniques.

Home catalogs and magazines both encourage mail-order buying of patterns, and most newspapers have mail-order patterns which are sometimes less expensive than the big pattern brands. Mail-order buying is a convenience if you aren't in a hurry.

The big catalogs are designed for your convenience, to make your selection of patterns even easier. Index tabs guide you to the right section. In the back, a page may be given to exact information on fabrics, accessories, and linings used in sketches and photographs. Each pattern is indexed in the back by its number and the page number. The standard measurement charts in the back are to help you choose your own figure type and pattern size.

The sizes break down into misses', women's, half-size, young junior/teen, junior, junior petite, young boys and men, toddlers', children's, and girls'. No matter what shape you're in, there's a pattern which will come reasonably close to your size.

As a working rule, buy a dress pattern by your bust size and a slacks pattern by your hip size. If you fall between two sizes, the smaller one will probably give you a better fit and be easier to alter. Go by your own true measurement; the moving-around room, called ease allowance, has been included in the pattern.

WHAT SIZE ARE YOU?

To determine your pattern size, look at the charts on pages 156 and 157. Find your figure type. Measure your bust, waist, and hip cir-

cumference and the important back-of-neck-to-waist length. Hold the tape snugly but not tightly—and be honest! Compare your measurements with those given on the chart. Choose the pattern size that has measurements most closely corresponding to your own.

Once you have determined your pattern type and size, stick with them. Choose your patterns from the right group, and don't try to make a misses' pattern fit a woman's figure. Pattern grading—that is, changing pattern proportions for different figure types—is a complicated and difficult business, better left to experts.

PICKING A PATTERN

Pick simple styles for your early sewing efforts, remembering that a style that is simple in fashion terms may not be simple in sewing

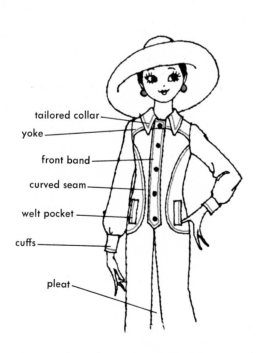

tailored collar
yoke
front band
curved seam
welt pocket
cuffs
pleat

A difficult pattern

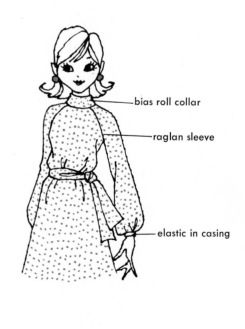

bias roll collar
raglan sleeve
elastic in casing

A simple pattern

terms. For example, a classic shirtwaist might be called a simple dress—but it has set-in sleeves, possibly with cuffs, a tailored collar, a skirt gathered or pleated onto the bodice, buttons, buttonholes—in short, a lot of time-consuming detail.

For good and easy sewing, pick a pattern with a minimum number of pattern pieces and consequently a minimum number of seams. Most pattern companies offer simple patterns called "easy" or "jiffy" or "instant." They are specifically designed for good fashion through quick stitchery. Start with one of these patterns, use good fabric, and give careful attention to sewing detail. You will have a creation to be proud of.

THE PATTERN ENVELOPE

There is a world of information jam-packed onto the back of a pattern envelope. Take the time to read it.

There will be a sketch of the back view; a detailed description of the garment with a note on the number of pattern pieces it has; a chart of the body measurements within the pattern's size range; a chart of yardage requirements for various fabric widths for all versions of the garment; yardage for interfacing, lining, and underlining; a suggestion about the suitability of striped, plaid, diagonal, napped, or pile materials; the finished back length and hem width of the garment in each size; and finally the notions list for zipper, thread, trims, fastenings, seam bindings, and the other small ingredients of the dress.

Most pattern envelopes have a choice of styles called View A, View B, and so forth, with different sleeves, collars, and necklines. Decide on the view you want and mark it on the back of the envelope. Circle the yardage for all materials required for your pattern size. This makes it easier to keep your shopping list straight.

CHOOSE YOUR FABRIC

Did you fall in love with a delicious silky print or a wild diagonal stripe? Read the pattern envelope before you buy! The pattern designers know just what fabrics are best for the pattern and list them on the envelope. A typical list calls for "crisp fabrics such as linen, piqué, satin, brocade, medium-weight wool, silk and worsted, and double knit."

There are patterns made especially for knit materials. Some patterns just won't work in a too-heavy or too-light fabric; others can't be done in velvets or plaids or strong diagonals. Take the pattern maker's fabric advice for best results.

HOW PATTERNS ARE MADE

Have you ever wondered how patterns are made? It's quite a process, bringing you the best styles for your good and easy sewing. American patterns represent the newest fashions and the best dressmaking know-how.

Pattern sizes are based on data supplied by the United States Bureau of Standards, so the measurements for a basic size 10 are the same for any pattern brand. The difference in fit comes with the ease allowance provided by the manufacturers.

Every few years the average figure measurements are reviewed and if necessary revised, to bring pattern sizing closer to ready-to-wear sizing.

A pattern begins with a designer's sketch. A pattern maker creates a basic paper pattern. This is interpreted in muslin and is draped and fitted to a dress form in a standard size. The corrected muslin is used to make a master pattern of heavy paper.

Then a dressmaker constructs the garment, using appropriate fabrics. A live model tries it on and more adjustments are made.

Meanwhile, experts work out that important back-of-the-envelope copy about yardages, linings, notions, measurements, and so forth. Other experts figure out the cutting and lay-out charts, the step-by-step sketches, and the directions for the instruction sheets to make the actual sewing as easy for you as they can.

Still other experts go through the complicated business of grading the pattern through its sizes to help you achieve perfect fit.

Finally the pattern is printed, cut into separate pieces, folded and tucked with the instruction sheet into the printed envelope. The artwork on the cover of the envelope is also used in the catalogs for a completely coordinated buying guide.

The World of Fabrics

The fabric world is a technical place, jam-packed with man-made fabrics, natural fabrics, and a combination of both. But don't worry; you don't need to know about all of them. Indeed, new ones appear so fast that any list would be outdated almost before it was printed.

What you need to know for your good and easy sewing are basic fabric types, widths, general sewing techniques, and whether to wash or dry-clean the finished garment.

A fabric glossary on page 166 will give more information. Here are the basics.

WHAT IS A FABRIC?

Fabric is a creative combination of fiber, weave, and finish. The many ways in which these elements are combined account for the exciting variety of materials you find in a fabric shop.

Color doesn't count here. It can be added to the raw fiber, to the woven yard goods, or to the finished fabric. There are really only two kinds of fiber—natural and man-made. The natural ones are silk, wool, linen, and cotton. Everything else is man-made.

In general, most linens and cottons may be washed. Most silks and wools should be dry-cleaned unless they are specifically labeled washable.

Most synthetics, such as nylon, Dacron®, Orlon®, and the like, are miracle fibers and materials made of them are truly carefree.

The blends complicate the picture a bit. Your best bet is to follow the recommended procedure for the dominant fiber. The most common blend is 65% Dacron® with 35% cotton. This blend is shrinkproof, washable, and requires no ironing. A blend of 80% wool and 20% nylon, on the other hand, should be pre-shrunk (more about that later), dry-cleaned, and treated like a wool fabric.

When you buy a piece of fabric, don't be afraid to ask the salesperson what the fabric is, how to sew with it, what kind of thread is recommended, and how to care for the finished garment. Salespeople are trained to answer these questions, and most of them are enthusiastic, patient, and willing to help you.

More and more manufacturers are shipping bolts of cloth with sewing or laundering instructions on little tags or slips to be tucked into the shopping bag. Ask whether instructions are available for your fabric.

FIBER INTO FABRIC

When the original yarn or fiber is made into a piece of cloth, it is either woven, knit, or matted like felt.

There are only three types of weaves: basic basket weave, a diagonal twill weave, and the sleek satin weave. Every other weave is a variation on one of these themes.

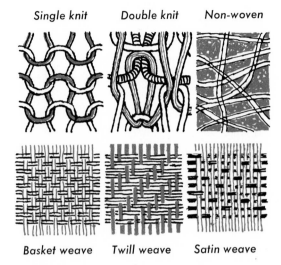

Single knit   Double knit   Non-woven

Basket weave   Twill weave   Satin weave

There are only two kinds of knits: single knit, done on one pair of needles, and double knit, done on two pairs of needles. All others are variations of these two.

Felt and non-woven lining materials, such as Pellon® or Earl-glo Reemay®* are made by matting fibers with heat, moisture, and pressure. Non-woven materials have no grain, so they can't ravel.

After the fibers have been woven or knit or pressed into a fabric, finishing takes place. Basic finishing processes include bleaching, dyeing, napping (for velvets and similar pile materials), printing, and sizing for strength and smoothness.

When the dyeing is done after the cloth is woven, it is called piece-dyed. When the yarns are dyed and the cloth woven from the colored yarns, it is called yarn-dyed. Plaids and checks are good examples of yarn-dyeing.

Other finishes include processes for crease and stain resistance, flame retardance, moth re-

* DuPont's Spunbonded Polyester.

pellency, shrinkage control, and even germ resistance.

FABRIC CATEGORIES

Pattern companies, in guiding you to the kind of fabric best suited to your pattern, tend to group fabrics by weight, describing them as sheer, soft, crisp, and so forth.

Here's how actual fabrics fit the groupings. *Sheer and soft*: batiste, chiffon, lace, marquisette, georgette
Sheer and crisp: dimity, organdy, dotted swiss, organza
Soft: challis, crepe, peau de soie, silk or synthetic jersey, tricot, satin
Crisp and light: chambray, silk foulard, gingham, shantung, lawn, percale, seersucker, taffeta
Medium firm: broadcloth, poplin, faille, flannel, gabardine, double knits, linen, muslin, oxford, piqué, sheer woolens.
Soft and heavy: chinchilla, corduroy, felt, fleece, fake fur, matelasse, velvet, velveteen, suede cloth, terry cloth, tweed, quilted fabrics
Crisp and heavy: brocade, duck, canvas, sailcloth, metallic cloth
Specialty fabrics: bondeds, stretch fabrics, vinyls, leather, fur

FABRIC WIDTHS

Fabrics range from 35 inches to 108 inches. Here are typical widths:
36": linens, velveteens, corduroys
36"–39": cottons and silks
39"–42": silks and synthetics
45": cotton/synthetic blends
54"–60": wools and wool blends
36"–72": felts
54"–60": double knits
45"–108": tricots
A conversion chart is on page 158.

Know-How for Notions

At the bottom of the list on the back of your pattern envelope, you will find the notions section.

All sorts of sewing ingredients are classified as notions—buttons, zippers, tapes, and trims. These are the little extras that help make a beautifully finished garment.

DECORATIVE TRIMMINGS

Look through the trimmings section of your store. You will be enchanted by the variety, the color, the detail, the whimsy, and the delicacy of the many trims. Just be sure when you buy them that they have the washable or cleanable properties as the fabric you are using.

Though there are hundreds of trims available, they break down into these basic categories:

Laces: pretty openwork designs in Val, Alençon, and crochet types are made in flat or ruffled versions.

Flat braids: soutache, middy, and other flat, solid-color braids are used both decoratively and functionally.

Fringes: ball fringe, flat fringe in several lengths, and loop fringes are available.

Venice laces: more deeply textured than the fine laces. Often seen in multitoned floral designs.

Rufflings: pleated, fluffy, plain, or color-edged.

Accent trims: great variety in woven braids, ribbon bands, rickracks, beaded and jeweled trims.

Eyelet embroidery: flat, ruffled, or with beading insertion, a traditional favorite.

Decorative trims are available by the package or by the yard. Look them over and try them out, but go easy. A touch of trim is usually all that is needed.

PRACTICAL TAPES

Don't be misled by this heading; practical tapes come in so many lovely colors that they can be used decoratively. They are also designed for such jobs as hem finishing, staying a curved edge, and seam finishing.

Seam binding: usually made of rayon, looks like a thin ribbon, ½″ wide. Comes in sew-on and iron-on versions. Used flat as a hem finish or to stay a curvey edge. (See pages 99, 117.) In spite of its name, it is not used to bind seams.

Bias seam tape: made of bias rayon, folded to ½″. Used to bind hem edges, seams, or curved edges on knit or woven fabrics.

Bias tape: usually made of fine cotton. Some brands are available in pre-shrunk versions. Single fold is ½″ wide; double fold is ¼″ wide; wide tape is ⅞″ wide. These are used mostly for color trim and applique detail.

Seam lace: decorative, flexible, and available in many colors. Used for hem and seam finishing. Comes in wide and narrow versions.

Hem facing: this tape is a full 2″ wide. It is used for backing a hem, or for color trim. It is available in lace, bias cotton, or acetate taffeta.

Blanket binding: satin ribbon 2″ or 2⅞″ wide. Used to bind blankets and baby buntings.

Piping: bias tape over fine cord is used to stitch into seams as decorative edging.

Twill tape: in various widths, this tough cotton tape is used as drawstrings, reinforcement for buttons, other heavy-duty jobs.

OTHER NOTIONS BY THE YARD

Cording, in weights from very fine to quite heavy, is designed to be covered with fabric.

Belting is used for backing fabric belts in waistbands. If belting is not available in the width or color you want, stiff grosgrain ribbon may be substituted.

Horsehair, in widths from ½″ to 3½″, is

PRACTICAL TAPES Left column: *bias tape, rayon seam binding, iron-on seam binding, covered cording, jumbo rickrack, medium rickrack, linen tape.* Right column: *wide bias tape, rayon hem facing, wide and narrow lace.*

used to stiffen hemlines.

Elastic is available in all sorts of versions. Elastic thread may be used on a sewing machine. Flat elastic in widths from ¼" to 1" may be stitched on or inserted in a casing. Special elastics are packaged for lingerie, pajamas, waistbands, and other specialized uses. Chlorine-treated nylon elastic is recommended for swimsuits, while rayon elastic is satisfactory for general wear.

FASTENINGS

Everything you need to make a garment open and close is listed as a notion. That includes buttons, zippers, snaps, and all kinds of fastenings.

Zippers

There are dozens of zipper sizes, and the zipper tapes come in dozens of colors, often color-matched right in the rack with threads and tapes. Here are the basic zipper types.

Neckline or skirt: 7" and 9", for shorts and slacks as well.

Dress: 12" and 14". A standard dress zipper is destined for use in the underarm seam, and has a bar tack at the top of the tape.

Neckline: in 4", 5", 6" and 10" lengths, a neckline zipper may be used for long sleeves and children's clothes as well as necklines. In lengths from 16" to 36", it may be used on dresses and robes.

Invisible zipper: with a special foot, you can hide this zipper in a seam-like closing with no stitching showing. Available in polyester and metal versions for use with sheer or heavier materials.

Separating zipper: in lightweight version, in lengths from 10" through 22". In heavy-weight version, 14" through 24". For use on garments which open completely such as jackets and robes.

Trouser zipper: constructed to withstand commercial pressing and allow double stitching.

A SAMPLER OF ZIPPERS From top: *nylon skirt zipper, nylon dress zipper, metal industrial zipper, metal separating zipper, invisible zipper, five-inch nylon neckline zipper, four-inch sleeve zipper.*

These are the most common zipper types. They come in fashion colors with nylon teeth, nylon coils, or metal teeth. Unless the package specifically says that the zipper tape is pre-shrunk, dip it in water and press tape dry before using.

Buttons

Buttons are the fashion leaders in fastenings. They get prettier every year. They can be jeweled or faceted, domed or crowned; they can be made of bone, tortoise shell, glass, horn, leather, wood, pearl, metal, and plastic. They come in all the top fashion colors, are often coordinated to seasonable fabric colors, and do wonders to accent a costume.

Another effective fastening is a double button connected by a chain. It creates a swagger-ing, military effect at the neck of a jacket or cape and makes buttonholes unnecessary.

Buttons come in specific sizes, and these are indicated on the pattern envelope.

Snap Fasteners

Snap fasteners are used in areas where there will be little strain. Use black or silver-toned ones for most jobs; fabric-covered ones for special garments, and hammer-on ones for children's play clothes.

Hooks and Eyes

Hooks and eyes are used where there will be some strain. The bar-eye is used for edges that overlap, while the round eye is used for edges that meet. Large, silk-covered ones are used on fur coats. Large, decorative brass hooks and eyes may be used for special effects. A flat metal hook is available for use on waistbands.

THREAD

Thread is one of the most important notions. How could you sew without it? If you look on page 159, you will find a chart giving specifics on both threads and needles. Select a color a shade darker than the fabric; it stitches up lighter.

Polyester/cotton threads are recommended for use on synthetics and knits, and are satisfactory for use on most other fabrics as well. Size 50 mercerized cotton thread is preferred for use on natural fibers—cotton, linen, and wool. If available, silk thread should be used on silk fabrics.

The pattern envelope gives you a complete and exact listing of the notions you need, and the pattern instruction sheet tells you what to do with them.

Trust the experts. Get what they list, and do what they say. You will find they know what they are talking about and that their advice makes sewing easier!

The Inside Story: Fabrics for Linings, Interlinings, Underlinings, Facings, Interfacings

What goes inside a dress? Should it be lined or underlined? Faced, interfaced, or just let alone?

Let's clear up a little of the confusion with a definition of terms.

A lining is made separately, and is joined to the garment at neckline and armhole and tacked to zipper.

An interlining goes between the lining and the garment, and is used for warmth in winter coats.

Top row: *Pearl buttons with shanks, size 60 (1½") to 16 (¼"). Second row: Pearl shirt buttons, size 60 (1½") to 18 (⅜"). Third row: Hooks and eyes in various sizes and types, cord-covered, black, and silver. Fourth row: Snaps in various sizes silk-covered, silver, and black. Fifth row: Grippers, hammer-on type, decorative, and utilitarian.*

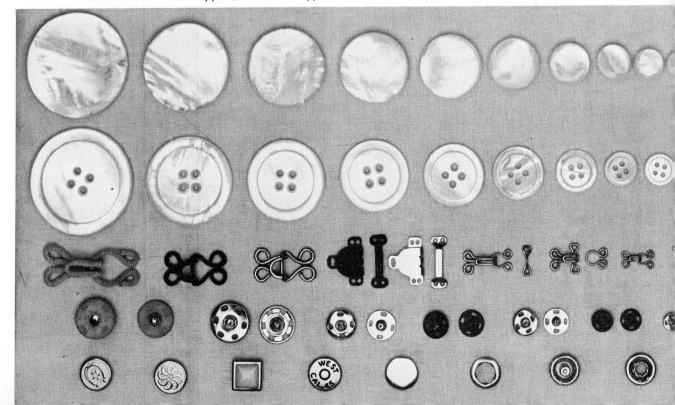

An underlining is cut and stitched right along with the outside fabric.

A facing doubles and finishes an edge, and is usually made of self-fabric.

An interfacing is placed between the facing and the garment for shaping, reinforcement, or firmness.

You will not find exact lining information on the pattern envelope. The choice of lining material depends on the choice of garment fabric.

Although there are dozens of lining, underlining, and interfacing fabrics on the market, you can narrow the choice to a very few which will serve you in most of your dressmaking.

When making your decision, remember that the supporting material should never be heavier than the original fabric, must be able to be cared for (washed or dry-cleaned) in the same way as the original material, and that it should be of comparable quality.

For most fabrics of light to medium weight, SiBonne!®, UnderCurrent®, and Bisque™ are fine linings and underlinings. They come in many colors, have been processed for shrinkage control, are permanent press and endearingly easy to handle. Besides, they are pretty in their own right.

Siri®, Pellon®, and Earl-glo Reemay®* are used for dress interfacings. Siri® is woven; Pellon® and Earl-glo Reemay® are non-woven fabrics available in several weights. Lining or underlining is generally unnecessary for knits, but if it seems desirable, the softer types, such as Ciao™, are best. Use any of the listed interfacings for knits.

For clingy synthetic materials use Ciao™ or Crepe de Chine™, all-polyester crepe linings with an anti-static finish.

These are enough to start on. As your skill increases, you may want to try other shaping materials for different effects. In the meantime, take the easy way, and confirm your selection with your salesperson.

* DuPont's Spunbonded Polyester.

THE PRE-SEWING SESSION

You have assembled the ingredients for your sewing project. Now it's time to prepare those ingredients for the actual stitching, just as you prepare foods for cooking. Pre-sewing includes pattern alteration, fabric preparation, laying out the pattern on the fabric, pinning, cutting, and marking. Work carefully, for these steps are very important to the final fit of your garment.

Make Your Pattern Fit You

You have found the pattern size closest to your measurements and you've bought a pattern in that size. Now what do you have to do to make it fit you exactly? Use your nice new tape measure to take your measurements.

Turn to the Personal Measurement Chart on page 155. Stand in front of a full-length mirror, wearing just your bra and panties. Pulling the tape snugly but not tightly, take *all* the measurements indicated on the chart and write them down. Your work will be more accurate if you can get a friend to help you. Take the shoulder-to-waist measurement by tying a string around your waist and running the tape measure from the top of your shoulder, where the bra strap comes, down to the string in front, then in back.

When you finish, you will have a complete record of your body measurements. You will need to add ease allowance. Here is a basic guide to follow.

To this measurement	Add this for ease allowance
bust	3″ for sleeved dress
	2″ for sleeveless dress
waist	1″ for fitted waist
hip (at 4″, 7″, and 10″ below waist)	2″

around upper arm	2″
around ¾ arm	1½″
around wrist	1″

Notice that you add ease only to the measurements that go around you. These ease allowances are minimum for a slim dress.

THE EASY WAY TO PATTERN ALTERATION

When you have completed your measurement chart and added your ease allowances, you are ready to tackle pattern alteration.

One of the great things about sewing for yourself is that your clothes will fit beautifully. That is because you do your alterations *before you even cut out the dress*. You do it right on the paper pattern pieces! Then, when you lay the altered pattern on the fabric, you know that you are cutting out a dress that will surely fit.

Here is an easy approach to pattern alteration. It is guaranteed to succeed, if you are honest about your measurements.

> *You will need:*
> tape measure
> tissue paper
> dark pencil or felt pen
> magic transparent tape
> scissors
> complete personal measurement chart

It is not advisable to try to fit a pattern by pinning it together and trying it on. It's almost impossible to get an accurate measurement that way, and the pattern is apt to rip. It may, however, be helpful to hold the pattern pieces against you just to see the relationship of these odd-looking flat pieces of paper to your body.

If the pattern pieces are wrinkled, press

them with a warm iron. Draw lines across the pattern pieces to correspond to the measurements you have taken. These measurement points are: on the skirt at 4″, 7″, and 10″ below the waist, on the pattern back between the armholes just above the armhole notches, across the front at the same place, and at all other places listed on your chart (page 155).

Measure the body pieces of the pattern from center back around to center front, taking your tape from seam line to seam line or fold line. Leave out darts and seam allowances, as these are not part of the finished garment when it is stitched together.

Move the tape from piece to piece, measuring each section from the previous measurement. This is much easier than trying to add up these separate measurements with their fractions. It gives you an instant and accurate total when you finish.

Be sure to double the measurement on pieces

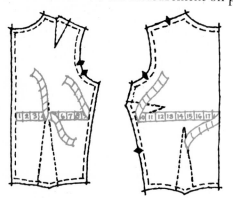

Double a width measurement.

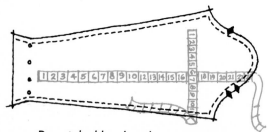

Do not double a length measurement.

that are cut double, such as the skirt and bodice pieces. Do not double for length or sleeve measurements or for single pieces such as a back cut out in one piece.

Now compare your measurements with the dimensions of the pattern. Don't try to work a pattern alteration into exact fractions. Your figure often varies slightly from morning to night, and soft fabrics will stretch slightly beyond the size of the paper pattern. Do as well as you can at this stage, and you can make final adjustments after the dress is basted together.

A PATTERN ALTERATION CHECKLIST

While some adjustments are possible after cutting, others are not. These are the alterations that *must* be done on the pattern:

1. length to be added anywhere (waist, skirt, or sleeve)
2. enlarging bustline, sleeve, or hipline
3. width added across shoulder back
4. square shoulder adjustment
5. width reduced in upper chest
6. waist shortened in princess or shift line
7. moving dart to adjust height of bust

Remember to compensate for alterations on pattern pieces that join the altered pieces. If you shortened the bodice front, you must shorten the back too.

To shorten or take in a pattern piece, lay a tuck across the pattern piece and secure with transparent tape. Don't use pins. They will tear the pattern.

To lengthen the pattern or make it bigger, split the pattern where indicated. Lay a strip of tissue paper underneath, separate the pattern till it is big enough or long enough, and tape the tissue to fill the gap.

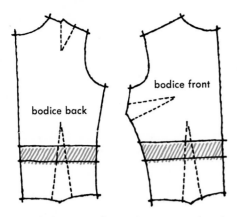

bodice back

bodice front

Shaded areas indicate tissue-paper inserts.

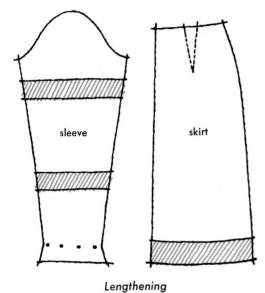

sleeve

skirt

Lengthening

1. Length to Be Added

Lengthening is the easiest alteration; most patterns have a line to indicate where to lengthen, so you can splice in the necessary amount on bodice or sleeve. Skirts are best lengthened at the bottom.

2. Enlarging

The *bust alteration* should be made by splitting the pattern on a curved line to the armhole to prevent widening the upper chest area. If extra width is needed all the way down to the

waist, split to the side of the under-bust dart (A). If the waist is to remain the same, split through the dart to make a larger dart with no more width at the waist (B). Split the side dart also to allow the pattern to lie flat while you control the spread of the curved split. Tape tissue to fill the gap.

The *sleeve* is opened in the upper arm where fullness is needed, but brought back in at the cap so there is no more to ease into the armhole. It is usually best to taper back in toward

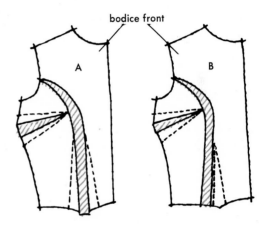

bodice front

A

B

Enlarging bust

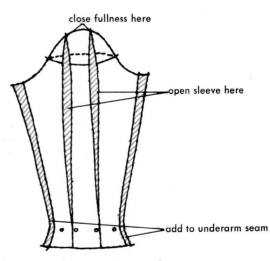

close fullness here

open sleeve here

add to underarm seam

Enlarging sleeve

the bottom of the sleeve also. This forms a small horizontal dart near the top of the pattern piece. This will not shorten the sleeve; it just gives the cap a lower, wider curve.

For further width, a small addition, not more than ⅜″, can be made on the underarm seam. Be sure the additions are equal on both sides.

Hip additions may be made on the side seam, almost into infinity. They may be tapered back in at the waist, *but must be continued downward from the hip to the bottom of the skirt.* The wider hip requires the wider lower edge to keep the original line of the design.

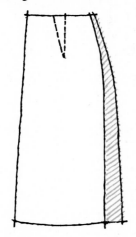

Add width to skirt at the side to enlarge hip measurement.

3. Adding Width Across Shoulder Back

Width may be increased across the shoulder back measurement as in (A), then reduced to the waist. The back shoulder is bias enough to be eased into the front shoulder, so that no corresponding width need be added to the front. Or as in (B) the width may be added only across the shoulder blades and completely reduced above and below by splitting through upper and lower darts, thereby making larger darts with no extra width at shoulder top or waist.

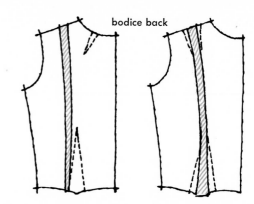

bodice back

A. *Split to side of waist dart for extra ease in waist and across shoulder.*

B. *Split through shoulder and waist darts for ease across shoulder blades only.*

4. Adjusting for Square Shoulders

If your shoulders are very square and high, you will have noticed a pull across both front and back of all your clothes, from the tip of one shoulder to the tip of the other. Sometimes just ¼″ raised at the edge of the shoulder line and reduced to nothing at the neck edge is enough to correct this. More than ½″ is never necessary. Don't forget to raise armholes and notches correspondingly on both front and back bodice pieces.

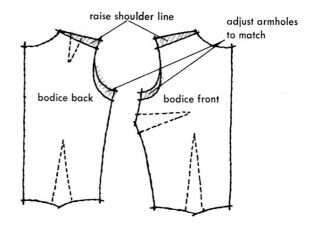

raise shoulder line

adjust armholes to match

bodice back

bodice front

5. Reducing Width in Upper Chest

The upper chest width may be reduced

through the shoulder (A). There is, however, an advantage to reducing toward the neck when the neck is wide or low (B). If the lower dart is split at the same time, the pattern will lie flat.

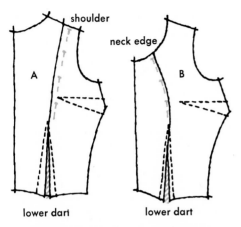

Reduce width in front at shoulder or neck edge. Note split in lower darts.

6. Shortening the Waist in a One-Piece Dress

Shortening the waist in a one-piece shift

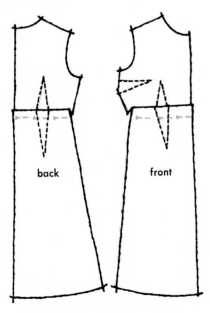

Shorten waist in one-piece dress

or princess line dress allows the waist and hip curve to fall in the proper place. If this is not done, the dress often seems too tight in the hip, and an ugly wrinkle forms around the waist. Be sure to check total length after making this alteration.

7. Moving Darts to Adjust Height of Bust

For a lower bust line, the side dart can be traced and moved down and the under-bust dart can be shortened (A). The opposite procedure raises the bust line (B).

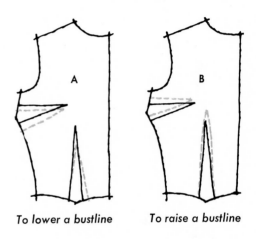

To lower a bustline   To raise a bustline

QUESTIONS OFTEN ASKED ABOUT PATTERN ALTERATION

1. Must I measure and check an entire pattern each time I start to cut out?

The *seven* places mentioned are the really important ones for any fitted dress with sleeves. Check them all on every pattern.

2. If I lengthen the front waist 1½″ and the back waist only ½″, what happens at the sides?

Compensation must be made by slanting the insert so that the two pieces are lengthened the same amount at the sides. Similar compensation must be made on any adjoining pieces.

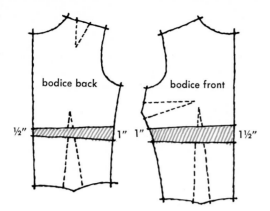

Be sure alterations match on adjoining seams.

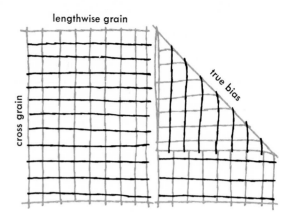

3. I'm always afraid of gaining a few pounds and not having enough seams to let out. Is there any place I can safely make a wider seam?

For safety you can always add ⅜″ on the *true side seams*. This gives you a total side seam of 1″, the kind you like to find in a ready-made dress. It gives a feeling of security even if you don't expect to gain weight.

Now Prepare Your Fabric

You have taken your measurements and altered your pattern. The next step is to get your fabric ready for cutting.

STRAIGHTEN THE GRAIN LINE

Do you know what a grain line is? There are two of them: the cross grain is the true crosswise thread of your material, and the lengthwise grain is the true lengthwise thread. The two grains lie exactly at right angles to each other, and the diagonal line between them is the true bias. Sometimes, because the fabric was stretched out of shape when originally wound on the bolt or the piece wasn't cut

straight when taken off the bolt, the grains will not lie at right angles.

To straighten a woven fabric, cut along the crosswise thread line at each end. If the weave is not obvious to the naked eye, pull up a thread with a pin and pull it gently all the way across the piece. There will be a faint straight line where the thread was; cut along it. If the thread doesn't pull easily, just start raveling along the end till one thread ravels all the way across.

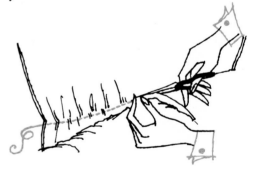

Pull a cross thread to find true grain line.

Now fold the fabric in half on the length grain, laying the selvages together the way it was folded on the bolt. If the diagonally opposite corners fall short when the selvages are evenly together, pull the two short corners away from each other. Fold again and see

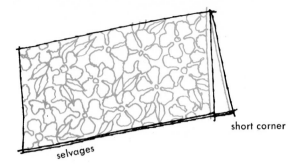

selvages
short corner

whether the corners are closer. Do this till the fabric lies square all around. Sometimes it helps to use the steam iron a little, or to wet a washable fabric, so that it will be more pliable to straighten.

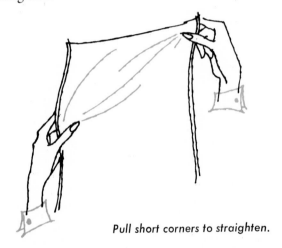

Pull short corners to straighten.

Knit is harder to straighten because it has no cross-grain thread to pull. In the right light, however, it may be possible to see a slight

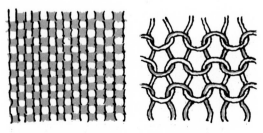

A woven fabric   *A knit fabric*

shading across the fabric, often just on the wrong side, and to cut along that. Otherwise, you just have to trust to luck that a good knit is usually fairly straight as it comes off the bolt.

Bonded fabrics cannot be straightened. They are fastened securely to the backing; if the grain line has been pulled out, there is no way to pull it back. Be sure bondeds are straight *before you buy!* Also check permanent-press or crease-resistant fabrics for straight grain as they are very difficult to straighten.

WHAT ABOUT PRE-SHRINKING?

When you bought your fabric, you found some necessary bits of information on a tag, or on the end of the bolt, or you asked the salesperson. Either way, you should know whether your fabric is hand washable or machine washable; whether it is bonded, woven, or knit of natural, synthetic, or blended fibers; whether it is colorfast; and very importantly, whether it has been pre-shrunk.

If your fabric has a tag saying that it is completely pre-shrunk and needle-ready, go right ahead and lay out your pattern.

If the label says there is even a one percent residual shrinkage, you will be wise to deal with it before cutting. Woolens and washables are most likely to need pre-shrinking. *Pre-shrink cotton knits and knit terries as they shrink more than five percent in washing.*

The simplest way to pre-shrink a washable is to dip it in warm water and hang it over a perfectly straight surface such as a shower rod. Be sure you hang it straight! If the fabric does not require hand washing you can, if you prefer, machine-wash and tumble-dry it.

To be perfectly safe, pre-shrink zippers, trims, tapes, and linings to be used with washables. You may dip them in warm water and hang them to drip dry, or you may press them dry with an iron.

Woolens and wool knits, especially imports, are apt to shrink slightly in the first cleaning unless they are completely guaranteed. The safest way to have them pre-shrunk is to ask a good dry cleaner to "sponge them for shrinkage." If he doesn't know what you're talking about, find a cleaner who does.

You may shrink short lengths of wool yourself by rolling them overnight in a damp sheet or towel and pressing them out carefully the next day. Long lengths are so unwieldy that you are apt to pull them out of shape on the ironing board.

If you are in doubt about strong colors on a print, especially a hand-screened one, cut off a small corner and test it in cool water. Often a little color will bleed out, but not run into the other colors. If it does, you may want to soak the whole piece in cool water to get rid of this excess dye. Some fabrics, such as batik, can be soaked in cool salt water (two tablespoons of salt to a quart of water) and then rinsed to further stabilize the color.

SOME OTHER PRE-CUTTING TIPS

Wools are folded right sides together on the bolt, to keep the right side clean. Nevertheless, pastels and especially knits sometimes have a soiled, shadowy line along the fold. Check carefully. If you think it will show,

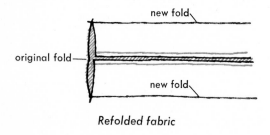

Refolded fabric

try refolding the fabric to avoid using this part. If a crease in a permanent-press fabric seems very sharp, test it by pressing. If necessary, try to position your pattern pieces around it.

You may notice some knots on the wrong side of wools. These are known as "weaver's knots" and are not considered flaws, as they do not go through to the right side. Many rough fabrics have large slubs of thread on the right side. These are considered part of the beauty of linens, silk linens, shantungs, and similar materials.

Cottons are folded right side out on the bolt. If a solid-color fabric seems to be the same on both sides, choose one side and use it throughout the garment, just in case the shading or sheen differs slightly.

If the wrong side of a fabric is especially appealing, there is no law against using it, provided you check thoroughly for flaws. In a heavily textured fabric, the wrong side sometimes provides an interesting contrast trim.

A GUIDE TO SPECIAL FABRIC TYPES

You should make your very first dresses of a solid or all-over-print fabric. It is, however, possible that you've already purchased a plaid or a napped fabric, corduroy perhaps, or a diagonal wool that looked like a plain weave to your inexperienced eye. All of these fabrics will require a little more time and thought for layout. Check your pattern carefully for any suggestions, either on the envelope or in the guide sheet, then read the instructions given here.

If a plaid is printed on and not woven in, it is very likely to be slightly crooked, and very troublesome to work with. For easier sewing, be sure to pick a woven plaid.

Below are a balanced and an unbalanced plaid, and a balanced and an unbalanced stripe. Turn the page upside down, and you will see that the balanced ones are the same either way, but the unbalanced ones are not. So—handle an unbalanced plaid or stripe as an all-one-way design, as described in your pattern instruction sheet.

Napped fabrics are those which have a soft surface that can be smoothed like fur in one direction only. They include velvet, velveteen, corduroy, velour, wool fleece, and most fur fabrics. They are always cut all one way.

Diagonals have a distinct line running at a bias angle to the grain. It is just a decorative effect of the weave. Most diagonals should run from the left shoulder to the right hip if you are using the correct side as the right side. Diagonals are exactly the same up and down, so pattern pieces may be laid in either direction,

and do not have to be cut all one way. Before choosing a diagonal fabric, read the pattern envelope. Some patterns are marked "not suitable for diagonal fabrics."

QUESTIONS OFTEN ASKED ABOUT PRE-SEWING

1. Why did my lined dress pucker after cleaning?

The lining shrank but the fabric didn't. Remember to read the labels on the bolts of *both* lining and fabric when you buy them and ask the salesperson for further information on finish and shrinkage control.

2. Why do the lines of my diagonal fabric run in so many directions on my dress?

Some of the pieces were cut on the bias, which made the pattern unsuitable for diagonals. Watch for a caution about this

BALANCED AND UNBALANCED PLAIDS AND STRIPES. Top row: (left) a balanced plaid, (right) an unbalanced plaid. Bottom row: (left) a balanced stripe, (right) an unbalanced stripe.

Me? Preshrink a lining?

What do they mean, "not suitable for diagonals"?

But the fabric looked straight!

on the pattern envelope.

3. Why do I see a slanted line running across the front of my skirt?

This sometimes happens if you forget to straighten the ends and lay the corners together when the fabric is folded. The cross-grain line often shows more than you think it will.

Layouts, Pinning, Cutting, Marking

Your fabric is ready, your pattern is altered, the great moment is at hand! It's time to pin the pattern pieces to the fabric. Work carefully; here is where you begin to see what the finished dress will look like. Take a deep breath; get out your pins, scissors, and cutting board; and away you go!

LAYING OUT YOUR PATTERN

Any large flat surface, such as a dining table, a Ping-Pong table, or two card tables put together, will serve as a cutting area. A large cardboard cutting board will improve any of these surfaces and may even be laid on the floor. You can anchor slippery fabrics to it with pins; it keeps your good table from getting scratched; and it is marked out in exact inches and yards to save lots of guesswork.

Open your guide sheet and look for the layout that matches your size, view, and fabric width. If your fabric has a nap or one-way design, look for a layout marked "with nap." It provides for all the pieces being laid in one direction.

Once you find your layout, circle it for easy reference.

You need not stick exactly to the layouts, if you make sure to pay attention to the *fold lines and grain lines* on each pattern piece. Almost all pieces are laid on double fabric. If a piece is on the fold, it opens out into one big piece with a left and right side (A). If it is not on the fold, two pieces are cut, one for the left and one for the right.

As long as pieces are to be laid double, whether on the fold or not, it makes no difference whether you lay the pattern piece right side up or right side down—the correct pieces will still be there after you have cut. But look out for the pieces marked "Cut One!" *They must be laid right side up on the right side of the fabric* (B).

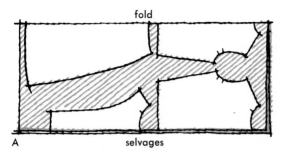

Laying out a pattern

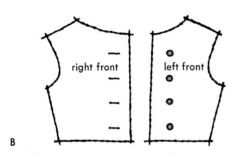

These pattern pieces are marked "cut one."

Be very careful to lay fold pieces directly on the length-grain fold of the fabric. It is often easier to see when pinning if you trim off the margin of the pattern along the fold line. The other margins should not be trimmed, because they make cutting smoother and give you a place to ink in small additions on a side seam.

Fabrics with nap or one-way design present a simple problem in that every piece must be laid in the same direction.

Here's an easy way to remember which kind of nap should stroke in which direction. Cotton (corduroy, velveteen, etc.) strokes upward as the plant grows from the ground.

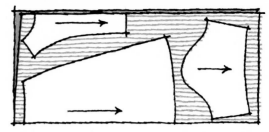

Layout for fabric with nap or one-way design

Wool strokes down, as it grows on sheep. Cotton has a deeper, richer look when worked nap up, and wool wears better when worked nap down.

Balanced plaids and stripes have definite centers, and their designs repeat to right and left, and from top to bottom, identically. Pin fabric layers together at ends so stripes fall exactly on top of like stripes. On plaids, pin the fabric every so often along the sides, too. Be sure to lay pieces so that any line marked "center" on the pattern, whether on a fold or not, will fall on one of the stripe or plaid centers.

On plaids, you must also be sure to match horizontal lines at seams. Be sure to put match-

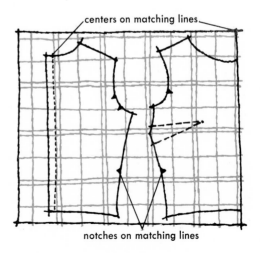

ing notches on matching lines. If you lay skirt side seam notch #7 on a red line, be sure its matching notch on the skirt back is also on a red line.

There are curved and slanted seam lines where plaids and stripes go a bit astray. There is nothing wrong with this if you keep the slipping even on both sides. Don't get too fussy. Just take a look at a ready-to-wear plaid dress, even a good one, and you will feel better.

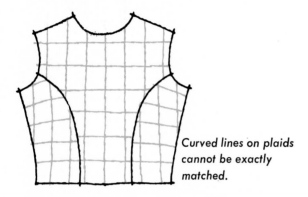

Curved lines on plaids cannot be exactly matched.

As a beginner, you will find it easier to work with solids or small all-over designs rather than with unbalanced stripes or plaids or other more elaborate geometrics. If you get brave and launch into such a project, however, remember that both the rules for plaids and the rules for one-way designs must be followed. That's twice as many things to remember, like rubbing your head and patting your tummy simultaneously!

One nice thing about having a large cutting area is that you can scatter all the pieces of the pattern on the fabric and rearrange as you like for better utilization of yardage before pinning them down. It gets to be a game called "How much fabric can I save?" which is then followed by another game called "Isn't it fun to invent things to do with leftovers?"

PINNING

Pin fold line down carefully, work out any wrinkles, pin down corners, and then pin frequently along sides, especially at curves and hard-to-cut spots. Hold fabric flat with one hand while pinning with an up-and-down motion with the other hand. Pin on a surface that you don't mind scratching. If you worry about scratching, you will find yourself lifting the fabric, and that will pull everything out of line.

Measure from selvage to grain line for a perfect parallel. Pin grain line in place, smooth pattern pieces, and work outward to corners. Proceed as before, always pinning inside cutting lines at frequent intervals.

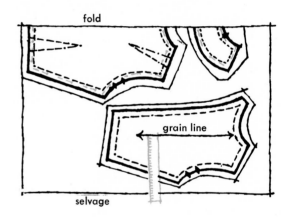

When some pieces have to be pinned on double fabric and some on single, check against your layout to make sure that you have room for all the pieces before cutting any. Never pin a piece on, then in the heat of excitement cut it, then pin and cut another, and so forth. You will surely finish without fabric enough for some major piece. Plan ahead!

CUTTING MADE EASY

Time for a final check: Look at your fold lines, your grain lines, your pattern pieces.

Double check if you're using a plaid or a nap or a pattern with "cut one" pieces. Everything okay? Let's cut!

With good, sharp shears (*not pinking shears*), cut just outside the cutting line so you'll be sure not to have a skimpy seam. Keep the back of the shears firmly on the table, and move them along with strong, even strokes. The more hesitant you are, the choppier your edges will be—so be brave! Keep your other hand on the fabric to control it and hold it flat on the table.

Never cut more than two layers at a time even if you are using electric scissors. There's a temptation to cut four layers when you are planning to cut out lining pieces just like the dress pieces. But this usually causes slipping of at least one layer, and gets your grain line off. You don't save that much time, and the wear and tear on your hand is not comfortable.

Some patterns call for bias strips cut from leftover pieces of fabric. While you can still see the selvages, mark the length and cross grain with a ruler and chalk on the area to be used for bias strips. After all the other pattern pieces are cut out, fold the leftovers so the length and cross lines lie together. *Then the fold is on the true bias.* Measure, chalk, pin, and cut strips in the desired width. You may have to piece them to get enough length. See page 104.

HOW TO TRANSFER THE MARKINGS ON YOUR PATTERN

Patterns have several markings that are important for correct assembly. In addition to notches there are markings for darts, button positions, pocket placements, corners, slashes, and other details that have to be transferred to the fabric. (Seam lines do not have to be trans-ferred—there is a guideline on the throat plate of your sewing machine to keep the width of seams accurate.) Notches are clipped; other markings are transferred by using tailor tacks, a tracing wheel, or chalk and pins.

Clipping

Along the edges of the pattern pieces you will find *notches*. Transfer these to the fabric by making one sharp ¼″ clip at each notch. The *ends of folds* should be clipped in the same manner as a fold serves as a marking for a center (center front or center back). You may also clip the ends of lines marking the wide ends of darts.

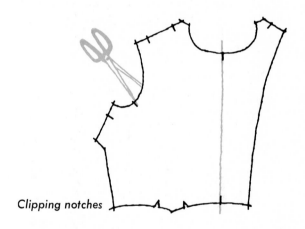

Clipping notches

Tailor Tacks

The most accurate way to transfer pattern markings is with tailor tacks, and in the end they are the least time consuming.

Tailor tacks are loops you make with needle and thread to transfer pattern markings to both sides of the fabric at once.

Here's a quick way to make tailor tacks, so they stay when you need them and come out easily when you're through. Take a few minutes to practice making them, so you can mark fine fabrics without any risk of damage.

Pick a thread that contrasts with your fabric, thread the needle, double the thread, and leave ends unknotted. On a flat surface, take a stitch down and up through pattern and fabric. Leave a long end, about 2″. Make another stitch across the first, leaving a loop of about 1″. Cut off the other end to 2″. When you have marked a whole pattern piece, take the pins out. Slip one hand between fabric and pattern to hold the thread loop tightly as you tear the paper quickly away with the other hand. The pattern will not be damaged, and the tack will be more secure than if you cut the loop.

Pull the two layers of fabric apart as far as the loop will let them go and cut the thread between the layers. If the pattern has several types of markings such as large dots, small dots, squares, and such, you can do each type of symbol in a different color.

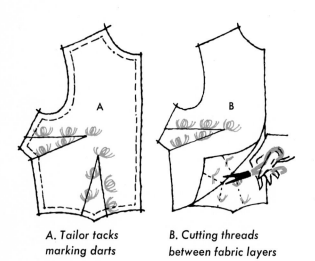

A. Tailor tacks
marking darts

B. Cutting threads
between fabric layers

An added advantage to tailor tacks is that the markings are on both sides of the fabric. The cut ends can help you identify right and wrong sides of your fabric as you're working on the garment.

Tracing

You may also mark with tracing wheel and dressmaker's carbon, according to directions on the package, but be sure you mark only on wrong sides. Even then, the marks may show through delicate fabrics. On thick and soft fabrics or fabrics with a multicolor design, the markings may not show at all.

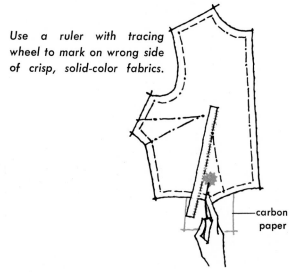

Use a ruler with tracing wheel to mark on wrong side of crisp, solid-color fabrics.

carbon paper

Chalk and Pins

With the printed, nonperforated patterns of today, marking with chalk and pins is very difficult and it's nearly impossible to be accurate. If you put your sewing away for a few days, the pins may fall out and the chalk may brush off. Chalk is great for marking fitting corrections later on, but it is not as satisfactory as a few well-placed tailor tacks at the beginning.

QUESTIONS OFTEN ASKED ABOUT PINNING AND CUTTING

1. Why does my pattern move and get crooked even while I'm pinning it to the fabric?

Remember to hold it all flat with one

hand, and pin down onto the table, never lifting with the pins.

2. Why can't I cut a smooth edge even with sharp shears?

Either you didn't pin enough, or you failed to keep the shears flat on the table when cutting.

Understanding Underlinings and Interfacings

On page 19, you found definitions for underlinings, interfacings, and all those pieces that don't show on the outside of your finished dress.

Now let's find out what you do with them. Just to keep things simple, only the two which you will be using in simple dresses, interfacings and underlinings, are discussed here. Loose linings will be explained later.

WHAT IS AN UNDERLINING?

Underlining is an all-over shaping that is put on the back of each garment piece before the pieces are joined. It gives support and shape to a fabric which lacks firmness and makes slippery fabrics, like chiffon and lace, much easier to handle.

There are certain thin, firm fabrics made specially for underlining. You will find these discussed on page 20. And remember—while the term "underlining" may sound terribly professional, it is very easy to do. It is mostly just a matter of handling two pieces of material as though they were one.

After you have cut out your outside fabric, transfer pattern markings and remove the pattern pieces. Cut your underlining by the main body pieces of the pattern. Pin and cut as you did the outer fabric. Clip notches.

Don't mark the darts and other construction points on your underlining material. You can use the markings on the outer fabric as your guide.

Press all underlining pieces and garment pieces. Lay the underlining pieces down on a flat table. Lay the fabric pieces wrong side down on the underlining pieces. Pin around the edge. Keep underlining smooth and tight. Machine stitch all around ⅜" from the edge so that the stitching is inside the seam allowance. Leave hem free. You will have less slipping if you sew with the underlining uppermost, and you will sew faster with a long stitch.

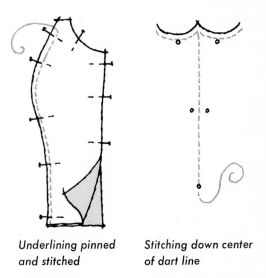

Underlining pinned and stitched

Stitching down center of dart line

For extra security, stitch down the center of the dart line, so pieces will stay together to the point of the dart.

Now, with the underlining joined to the outer fabric, you can forget about it. Just go ahead and start making that dress.

AND AN INTERFACING?

Interfacing is a bit like underlining, but used only in specific areas. It is possible to use both on the same garment, but that is done more often in tailoring than in dressmaking. Interfacing is most often necessary in shaped collars and cuffs and in the areas around buttons and buttonholes.

Not all garments need interfacing. Even when the pattern calls for it, if you think it adds too much to the bulk, you can leave it out. Better to sew light than to sew heavy.

If the dress is washable, the interfacing should be too. Remember, too, that often only the slightest extra body is needed, and a little piece of organdy or any lightweight, crisp underlining fabric might be all you need for a dress or blouse collar.

Lightweight woven interfacings work better in bias roll collars and cuffs, but non-wovens are just great where a flat, smooth look is needed.

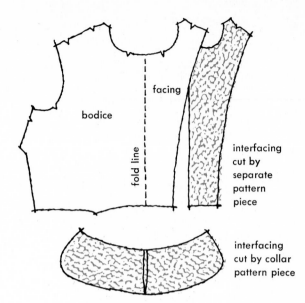

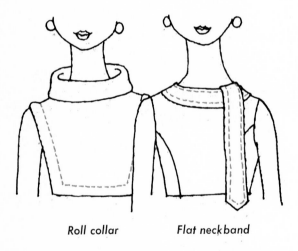

Roll collar   Flat neckband

Cut the interfacing by the pieces given on the pattern layout; some are special pieces, and some are just that same old collar piece over again. You may hand-baste these pieces to the wrong side of the proper garment pieces. The interfacing is then included in the seams, and may be trimmed later to eliminate bulk.

Does all this inside story make you feel as though you are building a dress to last through the ages? Relax! Modern dressmaking is child's play compared to the way they used to construct dresses. Take a look at some of the old dresses that have wound up in museums. They are perfectly magnificent, built and constructed, almost, rather than sewn, with layer on layer, with muslin and crinoline, with whalebone and silk, all put together by hand. So be it! Our clothes are just as beautiful today and much easier to make—even with underlinings!

Of course, there are many clothes that shouldn't be lined at all. Most knits look better if they are free and fluid. Some silks and crepes and dresses with softly flowing lines are pretty and feminine just as they are.

But, and this is a big but, don't skimp on the time for lining the tailored or molded dress that cries for shaping, or reinforcing the delicate fabric that will wear poorly without help. The work isn't difficult and it is well worth the time you spend doing it.

Decorative trims
—to add spice, whimsy, color, design, texture, glitter, delicacy, elegance, and fun to your sewing
—to accent a hem, a sleeve, a collar, a pocket
—to bring out the best in your fabric
—to inspire the designer in you.

Samples of lightweight fabrics in categories as described on pattern envelopes.

top row: *SHEER AND SOFT FABRICS* such as: rayon georgette, nylon georgette, burnt-out georgette, silk chiffon, silk crepe chiffon.

second row: *SHEER AND CRISP FABRICS* such as: border lace, cotton-Dacron® batiste, cotton leno, nylon dotted swiss, silk organza, cotton lace.

third row: *SOFT FABRICS* such as: cotton crepe, challis, rayon slipper satin, silk surah, rayon lining satin, synthetic tricot.

fourth row: *CRISP AND LIGHT FABRICS* such as: nylon surah, silk shantung, underlining, cotton voile, printed silk pongee, cotton gingham.

Samples of medium, heavy, and specialty fabrics in categories as described on pattern envelopes. top row: MEDIUM-FIRM FABRICS such as: wool double knit, linen, worsted, rayon moiré, Thai silk, wool suiting.

second row: SOFT AND HEAVY FABRICS such as: cotton velveteen, wool tweed, cotton velvet, wool fleece, sweater knit, cotton corduroy.

third row: CRISP AND HEAVY FABRICS such as: pure silk damask, metallic brocade, wool ottoman, cotton brocade, matelassé, cotton cloqué.

fourth row: SPECIALTY FABRICS such as: reptile vinyl, terry cloth, metallic vinyl, felt, suede cloth.

Find the right button. *No matter what you're sewing, the right button will make it distinctive. Choose buttons to glitter and sparkle, to harmonize or contrast, to show off a perfect buttonhole, or to serve as a purely decorative accent.*

Four kinds of buttonholes shown clockwise from top: *Double-breasted closing with bound buttonholes; front closing with loop buttonholes and ball buttons; shirt-type front closing with vertical machine-worked buttonholes; corded buttonholes.*

Imaginative fastenings: A trio of tiny buckles for a front shoulder closing, a chain-and-buttons arrangement to control a deep V-neckline, a braided frog to add elegance to a simple Peter Pan collar, and a cardigan closing joined by a pair of chained dinosaurs.

A variety of pockets shown clockwise from top: Top-stitched curved welt pocket, patch pocket with lined flap, bias welt pocket, tailored and top-stitched patch pocket with zipper, buttonhole pockets.

Zippers can be decorative, too. A tiny tassel accents the crisp white windowpane check; a yard of crisp grosgrain ribbon converts a zipper into a colorful decoration to be top-stitched on a sweater; short sleeve zippers accent the lines of a raglan sleeve; the invisible is betrayed only by a distinctive oval tab; elegant brocade trim edges the zipper and goes on to shape a handsome mandarin collar.

FIRST STEPS IN STITCHING—STAYSTITCH, EASE, AND GATHER

You're on your way! Now you have a pile of cutout fabric sections properly marked. You also have a pattern instruction sheet to give you your step-by-step guide to completing your garment.

Obviously, you must now join those pieces of fabric to shape your dress. But before you can start joining pieces, there's some preliminary stitching you will have to do to make the fabric behave and to make one piece fit the way it should against its partner.

It's easy to visualize if you think of making a garment as being a bit like sculpting. Then you will see the need for molding and shaping that two-dimensional piece of cloth to fit your definitely three-dimensional figure.

Staystitching Comes First

Staystitching does just what it says it does: it stays, or holds, the edge of a fabric in place. Staystitch along edges that may stretch out of shape, either because the fabric is soft or because the grain is bias along that edge.

Staystitching is done with a straight, medium, machine stitch just inside the seam allowance. Don't use a zigzag stitch here, because that is a stretchy stitch and won't hold the edge firm.

The areas most likely to require staystitching are the neckline, especially if it is deeply scooped or V-line, and the armhole.

If the fabric is extremely soft, like some wools and most sheers, the machine stitching itself may pucker the line. To prevent this, cut a piece of tissue paper by the pattern piece, pin the fabric to it, and stitch through fabric

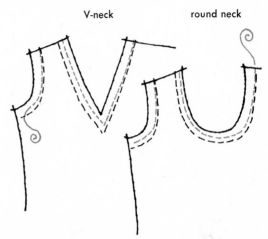

V-neck   round neck

Staystitching around neckline and armholes

and paper. Tear paper away, and the edge will hold its shape through handling and fitting.

For further ways to deal with areas which may stretch, see taping (page 117).

Most pattern directions call for staystitching around corners which are marked "clip" or "slash" on the pattern piece. *Be sure you have marked these corners precisely before removing the pattern from the fabric.*

On the "clip" corners, stitch for an inch or two directly on the seam line, pivot on the needle exactly at the corner, and continue directly on the seam line for another inch or two. Now you can make your clip. Be brave,

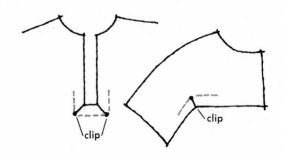

clip   clip

37

use very sharp scissors, and clip right to the corner.

On long, narrow slashes, your job will be easier if you make one stitch across at the point instead of pivoting around. This separates the two lines of stitching just enough to get the scissors between. For more information on re-inforcing narrow slashes, see page 77.

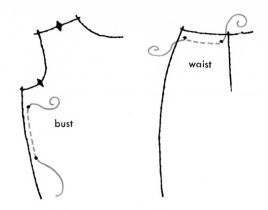

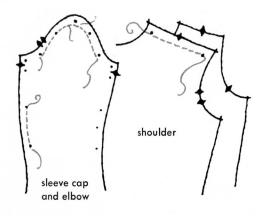

Neck slash   *Gusset slash*

Ease Is Easy

You ease a piece of fabric when you shorten a seam edge a bit so it will fit nicely against its shorter adjoining piece. That gives a little ease in the piece you have shortened. Use a longer machine stitch to ease than to staystitch.

Easing is usually called for in the sleeve at

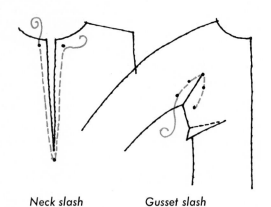

sleeve cap and elbow   *shoulder*

the cap and the elbow, in the back shoulder, at the side of the bust, and in the waist.

You may also find ease useful on the front curve of a sleeveless armhole and the lower front curves of a scooped neckline. In both cases, easing shapes the fabric in toward the

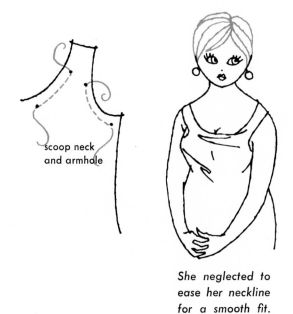

scoop neck and armhole

She neglected to ease her neckline for a smooth fit.

body and prevents unattractive gaping. The more full-busted a person is, the more apt she is to need this neck and armhole easing.

For ease allowance, place the stitching (about six stitches to the inch) along the seam line, between the marks indicated. Since the bobbin thread pulls more easily than the top thread, make a habit of doing ease stitching on the right side of the fabric. You will always be able to pull the threads appearing on the wrong side.

Pin the seams together at the markings and pull the ease thread gently until the longer piece fits the shorter piece. Tie off the thread ends. In the description of set-in sleeves, you will find more detailed information on handling and stitching ease (page 85).

Gathering Together

One step from easing brings us to gathering. It's the same idea, but in gathering you are pulling in an even longer piece of fabric to fit a short one.

This time you will need two rows of long machine stitching, about six stitches to the inch. Place one row on each side of the seam line, at ½″ and ¾″ from the edge of the fabric. Leave a good length of thread at each end, and be sure not to get the ends tangled. To gather, take both bobbin threads together, and slide fabric gently along, pulling the bobbin threads.

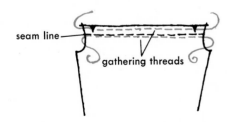

When the piece is gathered to match the adjoining piece, tie off the ends of the threads and distribute the fullness evenly.

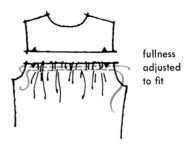

fullness adjusted to fit

To sew a gathered section to another section, pin seams right sides together and baste if necessary. Arrange sewing so that the gathered piece is uppermost; it's easier to control that way.

Stitch right along between the rows of gathering stitches. It's an easy line to follow. After stitching, pull out the row that shows below the seam line. This little trick gives you tiny, fine, smooth folds of fabric. There is no lumpy gathering this way!

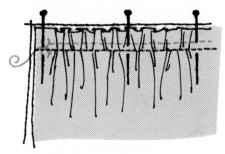

Other Helpful Hints

Don't try to work with more than a yard of gathering at a time. If a skirt is two yards around, use two sets of gathering threads.

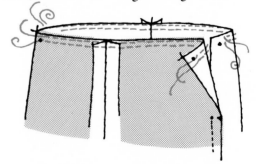

If fabric is very heavy, try using heavy-duty mercerized thread and a slightly looser tension.

If you have a very short area to gather, don't break off the stitching at the end of the first row. Instead, pivot the needle, make one stitch, pivot again, and stitch back along the row so there will be only one set of thread ends to deal with.

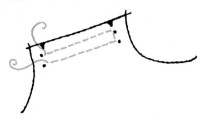

Always gather by machine. It gives a much smoother finish than hand gathering.

QUESTIONS OFTEN ASKED ABOUT EASE AND GATHER

1. Why does the ease look fine until I sew that piece to the adjoining piece, when it turns into a series of ugly little puckers?

You didn't put the ease thread near enough to the seam line for proper control.

2. When I seam the gathered piece to the next piece, why are there great awkward folds where there should be nice fine gathers?

In stitching the seam you got outside the well-defined path between the two rows of gathering thread.

3. Why does my ease or gathering thread sometimes lock tightly when I'm pulling it?

You pulled both the bobbin and the top thread. Pull the bobbin thread only.

Basting and Fitting

Time for a first fitting already? It certainly is. Baste together the main body pieces, so you can see how the finished garment will look.

Now you can mark and adjust those little areas that couldn't quite get worked out in the pattern alteration.

Don't skip this step; it's very important to the final fit. Besides, it's the only time you will have a big needle-and-thread basting job. Pin basting takes care of other jobs very well.

There are two reasons for basting, even though you altered the pattern with great care. One is, simply, that it is impossible to take into account every little variation and bump and hollow of the human frame when measuring with a tape measure. The other is that fabrics behave differently from pattern paper and even very differently from each other. Make a dress in firm cotton and it will fit you about the way the pattern measured. Try the same pattern in a soft wool, and you will discover that it grew a bit and the seams all need to be made deeper.

BASTING HOW-TO

Enough for the whys of basting for fit; now the hows. Hand basting is easy and relaxing, especially if you do it while chatting with a friend or half watching TV. Use any odds and ends of mercerized thread, in a color different from the fabric. Use *single thread* and a nice long needle. Knot the thread with a big knot that can't pull out when you try on. Baste on the seam lines and dart lines for true fit. (If you sew through the basting, it still pulls out quite easily. A pair of tweezers will

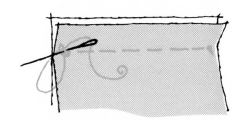

help.) Use a long running stitch, and fasten off with several small stitches, running the needle back through the loop of each.

MACHINE BASTING

The newest machines have a true basting stitch, very long and very easy to pull out. If you own one of these, by all means get out the instruction book and learn how to set the dials. On most machines, the long stitch suggested for basting (about six to an inch) seems more trouble than it's worth for most basting. Unlike hand basting, it gets pretty scrambled in the final stitching and is hard to pick out. Furthermore, some fabrics, such as taffeta, needle-mark when machine stitched so that machine stitching twice is more dangerous to the fabric.

RIGHT SIDES TOGETHER

Remember that nearly everything you will ever sew is *seamed and darted with right sides*

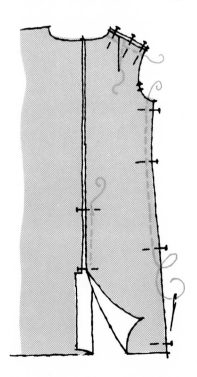

of the fabric together. Of course, then, that is the way you put everything together when you baste. Before you baste, you should pin all matching points, such as notches and important tailor tacks, together. Put the ends of the seams together also, then pin a few times in between these several points on long seams. In this way you will avoid stretching one layer of fabric as you baste and you won't arrive at the end of a seam with an inch left over on one piece.

MAIN PIECES ONLY

The main body pieces that you baste together do not include all sorts of facings and trims and such, and no set-in sleeves—just fronts, backs, tops, and bottoms. If a dress or even just a skirt has panels (such as center front and two side fronts, and possibly the same kind of back), put the whole front together and the whole back together. Then do

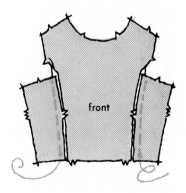

front

the side seams and shoulder seams last. In this way you get a much clearer picture of what you're making, and you're far less apt to come out with two necklines and three armholes or something of the sort.

If there are darts, baste them in first. Then baste seams. It is easy to run a basting stitch behind a dart, instead of over it, leaving the

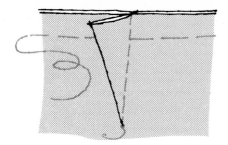

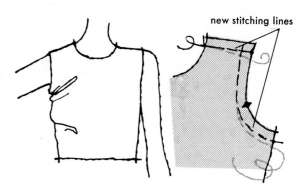

new stitching lines

Raise shoulder seam and lower armhole.

dart standing free from the seam for easy stitching.

If the dress has a waistline, that is, a separate skirt and bodice, baste and try on the two pieces separately. You may want to baste them together later for a final fitting of waist length and the hang of the skirt. The only other things you're apt to want to baste and try on further along in the dress are set-in sleeves.

WEAR THE RIGHT UNDERGARMENTS

One small concession that you must make to this fitting process is to wear the correct undergarments every time you try on. This is especially important in dresses with elaborate bodices or necklines. The proper bra, strapped, strapless, padded, or whatever the dress seems to call for, may alter dart placements and depth of neckline. It seems needless to speak of what girdles or the lack of same can do to a fitted skirt. Of course, a really unfitted or gathered skirt doesn't even need to be tried on.

TRY-ON TIME

Try the dress on *right side out*. This is a precaution in case one hip is larger or one shoulder higher. If the dress is put on wrong side out, the sides will be reversed. If one shoulder is low, one side of the bodice will slump down in folds, and taking a bit larger shoulder seam on that side will help. Just remember to lower the armhole and notches

when you are ready to set in the sleeve.

Side-bust darts can be moved up or down, and under-bust ones raised or lowered at the point. Just stick one or two pins in where you want the dart to go and you will then be able to get it realigned before you stitch. This is the time to start using chalk to transfer the pin markings from outside to inside.

It is, of course, nice if you have a sewing friend who will help with fittings. But if you don't, learn to estimate for yourself. Often, without even pinning, you can judge that taking in or letting out a skirt seam about ¼" one each side seam (a total of 1" on the entire hip measure) is all you need. Waists that are too tight are easily remedied by making each dart a little bit smaller, and vice versa if you're lucky and the waist is too large.

You can pin in seams or darts from the outside, tapering off where you need to. When you take the dress off, turn it wrong side out and chalk against the pins. Then you can remove the pins and use the chalk lines as a stitching guide.

QUESTIONS OFTEN ASKED
ABOUT FITTING

1. Why did my basting pull out when I tried on my dress? Should I make smaller stitches?

You didn't fasten the thread securely at the ends; the stitches were probably fine.

2. Is it really necessary to do so much basting, when all I found out was that the dress fit me perfectly?.

You're lucky if it did, but think what a thrill you got seeing what it was going to look like. You may have learned a few things about how to assemble the pieces that made the actual sewing easier.

SHOW-OFF SEWING—BUTTONHOLES, POCKETS, PLEATS, AND TUCKS

Anyone who sews is always proud of the show-off details that make a dress so special—the well-done buttonhole, the perfect pocket, the special details that the really experienced sewers look for.

It's time for those now. You're well along—past the first fitting. That was done before the detail sewing just because you might have decided that you needed to change the position of a buttonhole or pocket after seeing how the dress will look. Short people, for instance, often have to raise the pocket markings on a skirt. You may have to change the buttonhole lineup, if you altered the pattern.

If you marked fitting lines and changes when you tried on the basted dress, just be sure they are clearly marked now. You may want to take out the bastings so you can get at the buttonhole or pocket area more easily, but you can repin or rebaste later when you are ready for final stitching.

Before You Start

Be sure everything is where it should be before you start your show-off details. The underlining is in place; the interfacing, if you used it, is firmly and smoothly basted in. The watchword is "measure and mark!"

You will find here only one way to do most of these details. The ones given are the easiest, and they will work on just about any kind of fabric. Right now, learn one system and stick to it. Later, when you have had more experience, you may try out more complicated methods and add them to your repertoire of sewing techniques.

How to Be a Show-off Without Really Trying

If you would like to save time, or if you find you need more experience before you attempt to work on real pockets and buttonholes, just turn to page 116. You will find ways to skip the more time-consuming details and achieve the effect without work. Faking some details now will give you more practice time, so your next dress will be a real example of show-off sewing.

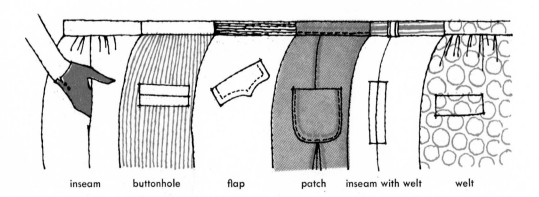

inseam   buttonhole   flap   patch   inseam with welt   welt

A variety of pockets

Buttonhole Lineup

It may seem unfair that buttonholes, which are so precise, always appear in such obvious spots as right down the middle of the front of your dress. The placement and size of buttonholes are, however, almost more important than the technique of making them, because at least the button hides one end of the opening. Nothing hides the fact that there's a great variance in alignment or spacing.

Remember that a woman's garment buttons right over left, a man's left over right. If you can't get it figured out any other way, hold the right front up to yourself to be absolutely sure. If a dress buttons in the back, it is still usually right over left.

You probably made one tailor tack or dressmaker's carbon mark for each button and buttonhole at the center front and maybe another one at the other end of the buttonhole. Now it is necessary to measure and mark with even more accuracy. Run a chalk or hand-basting line down the center front. Run another line parallel to this one ⅛″ closer to the garment edge. This second line represents the actual starting point of the buttonhole and should never be moved. There will be a third parallel

line on the opposite side of the center front. Its distance from the starting line is determined by the size of the button.

Most buttons require a buttonhole about ¼″ longer than their diameter. If the button is small and slick, perhaps only ⅛″. If the button is very thick or rough, test it through a slit in a piece of fabric to make sure that ¼″ is enough. Always move the third line (the buttonhole end line) only to change the size of the buttonhole.

Remeasure carefully between buttonhole markings and draw a line across at each one with chalk or basting. These lines should be directly on the cross-grain line and perpendicular to the other three lines.

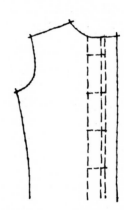

Markings in place on bodice front

On a double-breasted dress, the center front line falls between the two rows of buttons. Placement of buttonholes is clearly marked on the pattern. You are not expected to make buttonholes for both rows of buttons, but only for the ones closest to the edge. The other row of buttons is sewn on the outside of the garment, and there is sometimes a snap underneath the top layer of fabric.

— center front line

— starting line for buttonholes

— buttonhole end line

— cross lines for buttonholes

If a dress has a very narrow band, like a man's shirt front, then the buttonholes are marked to run vertically.

Only one row of button-holes for a double-breasted closing   *Up-and-down buttonholes for front band closing*

Take your time with the marking, measure carefully, and try for absolute accuracy no matter what sort of buttonhole you are making.

Bound Buttonholes— Easy Patch Method

Bound buttonholes, which are simply buttonholes finished with self-fabric, must be done at this early stage in the construction. They are desirable on good wools, linens, heavy cottons, and heavy silks. Avoid them on ravelly fabrics, sheers, and nubby materials. On any fabric, it takes practice to do bound button-holes neatly. It may be wise to choose a pattern without them until you feel confident enough to tackle this special technique.

Machine-worked and hand-worked buttonholes are done later in the construction process, and you will find instructions for these on page 94. Use these for sheers, for children's wear, and for casual clothes.

There are several ways to make a bound buttonhole. The patch method is the easiest.

A BUTTONHOLE SAMPLE

Always make a sample buttonhole before applying it directly to the garment piece. The sample must be layered exactly as the garment is. To make a buttonhole sample piece, cut a six-inch square of the garment fabric, and back it with exactly the underlining and interfacing used on the garment. Duplicate the buttonhole markings on this piece, basting lines and all. By making one or two buttonholes on this piece, you will find out about length, proportioning, and grain line for your fabric, and whether the button you have chosen will fit through the finished buttonhole.

STAYSTITCH TO START

Staystitch a rectangle around the marked buttonhole line, by machine, exactly on the

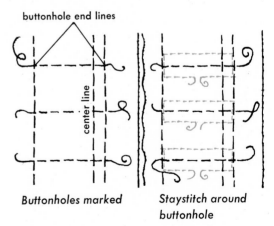

Buttonholes marked   *Staystitch around buttonhole*

grain! This makes a guideline for you to follow on the reverse side where you will do the actual buttonhole stitching. When you turn the piece over, you may find that the grain on the interfacing is not quite straight with the outer grain, but that is not really a problem.

CUT YOUR PATCH

Cut bias patches of fabric about 3″ x 4″. If the fabric is limp or porous, back the patch with an identical bias patch of light underlining. Generally a bias patch makes a more attractive and better wearing buttonhole. It is also much easier to handle and not so prone to ravel as a straight piece. Some ribbed fabrics and herringbones will, however, be more attractive on the straight grain. Try both ways on your sample to make sure.

PLACE THE PATCH

Center the patch directly over the buttonhole marking, right sides together, and pin in place. Turn to reverse side to stitch, so that you can follow staystitch guidelines. Set the machine for twelve stitches to the inch and stitch a rectangle, starting at center of long side (not at corner) and working just outside the staystitch lines. In dress fabrics the buttonhole should be four or five stitches wide and

as long as marked. Buttonholes on a heavy suit or coat fabric might be as much as six or seven stitches wide.

Stitch all buttonholes on the sample piece, then recheck size and placement with a ruler. Make any necessary changes; it's a lot easier to rip now than later. When everything is corrected, stitch once again around, exactly on first stitching, then run a few extra rows of stitching in the center of the buttonhole. This makes the buttonholes easier to handle, and impervious to wear.

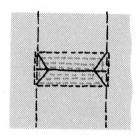

CUT, TURN, FOLD, PRESS, AND STITCH

With sharp strong scissors make a buttonhole cut, down the center to ¼″ from each end, then all the way back to the corners.

Turn patch through cut, press ends back firmly to form rectangle.

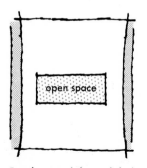

Patch turned through hole

Fold one side of patch to center of opening, forming lip or pleat, and press. Repeat with other side. Be sure that all four small seams

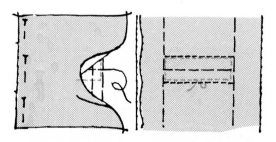

Center patch over buttonhole marking

Stitch around buttonhole. Follow stitching on wrong side.

press away from the buttonhole, so that the lips have a smooth, slightly recessed effect.

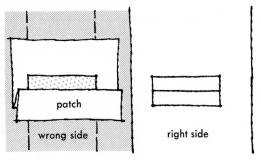

Fold lips of patch.

Tack pleats together by hand at each end of opening. Lay the patch down on the machine, turn the garment back, and stitch across the patch, pleats, and small triangle of fabric.

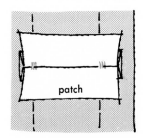

Tack pleats together.

While stitching, pull the end of the patch, so that the machine will go in very close, right over the original end stitches of the rectangle. This holds the end of the buttonhole securely and gives a clean professional look to the ends

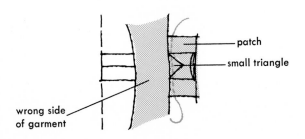

on the outside, where it counts! Trim the patch to about ½″ all around. Steam-press again.

FACING FINISH FOR BUTTONHOLE

At this stage the buttonhole only goes through the outer fabric and the interfacing. Later, when the neckline is finished and the facing is in place, you will have to complete the buttonhole through the facing.

Lay the garment on a flat surface and pin the facing in place all around each buttonhole. Watch grain lines and don't force the front of the garment out of shape! With small scissors, cut through from front of buttonhole to start the slit. From facing side, either complete the slit to the ends of the buttonhole or cut to ¼″ from the ends and back to the corners in the same way that you cut the original buttonhole. The rectangular cut is generally better for heavy fabrics.

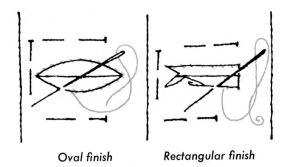

Oval finish   Rectangular finish

Starting along one side, turn the edges under with your fingernail and carefully blindstitch in place. (See page 101.) In turning the corners or ends, take a few extra stitches for added strength. Press gently on the facing, using a press cloth and steam.

QUESTIONS OFTEN ASKED ABOUT BOUND BUTTONHOLES

1. Why is my bound buttonhole stiff and bulky when I try to press it?

If you need greater flexibility, cut the patch on the bias.

2. How can I make a buttonhole lip look firm instead of limp?

   You probably should have backed the patch with a light underlining.

3. Why don't I get a really sharp clean corner on my buttonhole?

   Either you did not clip close enough to the corners, or you didn't pull the patch end when you stitched across it.

4. How can I keep a stubborn fabric in place after I've pressed the lips?

   Tack the little seams along the side of the buttonhole to the interfacing, then tack the loose patch piece to those same seams.

Loop Buttonholes— A Pretty Detail

Many patterns call for loop buttonholes. They are quite easy and very attractive.

COVER THE CORDING

The first step in making loop buttonholes is to make the fabric-covered spaghetti cord, which can also be used for straps and figure-eight closings, and in larger sizes for tie belts.

Here's the quick and easy way to cover that slender cording.

Cut a true bias strip of fabric about 1½″ wide and 10″ or more long (see page 104). Cut a piece of fine cotton cable cord, about ⅛″ diameter, and a little more than twice as long as the fabric strip. Locate the exact center of the length of cord, and stitch it to the wrong side of the bias strip as shown, working ¼″ from the raw edge. Stitch back and forth several times for security.

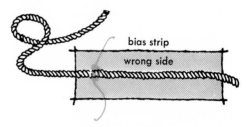

Put the zipper or cording foot on your sewing machine. Turn fabric so it lies right sides together around the other half of the cord.

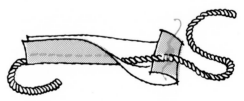

Fold bias back and stitch.

Stitch with foot *fairly close* to cord. Be sure to avoid catching the bit of fabric that is folded under and secured to the cord. Stretch fabric along the cord as you stitch, to make it slightly looser and easier to turn. Trim seams to ⅛″.

Trim seam to 1/8".

Now you have a piece of cord that's half covered and half uncovered. Start sliding the fabric gently but firmly back over itself, so that it starts to cover the other half of the cord. The trick is in the little piece of fabric that is already turned and secured to the cord,

Pull fabric back over itself.

making it possible to get the turn started. Pull up a little fabric at a time and slide it along. Never try to move too much fabric at a time. When you finish, just snip off the leftover uncovered cord.

STITCH THE LOOPS

Now lay out a plan for button-loop spacing on firm white paper. Draw two lines, representing the seam line and depth of loops. Mark

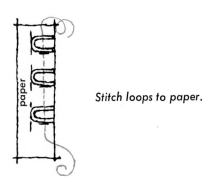

Stitch loops to paper.

out space for each loop, and for distance between. With a long machine stitch, sew loops to paper. Then sew to right side of garment, and tear away paper. Be sure loops are facing away from seam line in toward the body of the garment.

Lay facing on garment, right sides together, and pin it in place. Turn garment to the wrong side and follow the stitching line while you stitch facing in place.

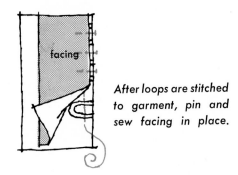

After loops are stitched to garment, pin and sew facing in place.

Turn facing to wrong side. The button loops will turn over too, and will lie along the exact edge of your garment. Understitch. (See page 76.) Press facing and finish raw edge.

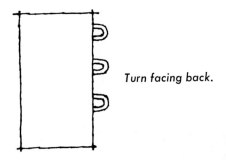

Turn facing back.

You can use this type of loop buttonhole on any dress, provided the facing is stitched on along the edge. If the facing turns under like a hem, there is no seam to hold the loop ends.

Bound Buttonhole Pocket— Five-Line Method

Any method for making a bound buttonhole can be used (two or three times larger) for a pocket. For the larger area the five-line method is easy to measure and stitch, and a bit firmer than the patch-method buttonhole.

Cut a strip, bias or straight, 3½″ wide and 1¼″ (2 seam allowances) longer than the finished pocket. Machine-staystitch the pocket line so that you can see it clearly on the reverse side of the garment. Center the strip over this line on the right side of the garment, right sides together. Pin in place. On the wrong side of the garment, machine-baste over the pocket line again. You will see this line on the strip.

Machine-baste over pocket line on wrong side.

On the strip draw two end lines with ruler and chalk. They must be perfectly perpendicular to the pocket line. Between these two lines machine-baste the strip to the garment

Machine-baste along chalked lines on the strip.

½″ above and below the pocket line.

Fold one side of the strip back along the machine basting and press it. On the wrong side of the garment, mark the end lines with chalk and stitch permanently through the folded side, exactly halfway between the pocket line and the outer basting line. Fasten the ends of the stitching, preferably by back-stitching three or four stitches.

With the strip folded along its basting line, machine-stitch between the pocket line and the two outer lines.

Fold the other side back and repeat. You will now see the five lines of stitching on the reverse side. Pull out the three basting lines. Split the entire strip down the center. Do not cut through garment at this time.

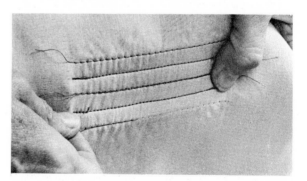

Now you have five lines of stitches showing on the reverse side. Pull out basting lines (rows 1, 3, and 5) and leave the permanently stitched lines (rows 2 and 4).

On the wrong side of the garment, make a buttonhole cut down the center to ½″ from each end, and all the way back to the corners, not including the strip. Turn the strip through. Lay the strip down on the machine, fold back the garment until the loose triangle of fabric appears. Stitch across the strip and the triangle as close to the ends of the first stitching as possible.

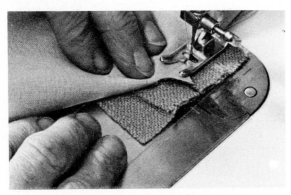

With the garment folded back so tiny triangle is plainly seen, stitch across strip and triangle.

Lay the lower (shorter) pocket piece against lower seam of pocket binding, raw edges together. Stitch straight edge of pocket to seam along previous stitching line, and fold curved edge down. Repeat for top pocket section. The two pocket pieces will meet. Pin the edges of the pieces together very flat and stitch all around.

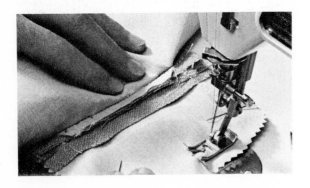

QUESTIONS OFTEN ASKED ABOUT BUTTONHOLE POCKETS

1. Why do the corners of my buttonholes fray?

You didn't pull the triangle of fabric out far enough and stitch in deep enough over it.

2. If my material is very loose and ravelly can I still make a buttonhole pocket?

Yes, but use a different fabric in a contrasting or matching color for the buttonhole strips. A closely woven wool flannel or suede cloth would be suitable and effective.

Welt Pockets

A welt pocket isn't too different from a buttonhole pocket, except that it has the decorative trim piece covering the opening. The trim piece may be shaped or straight. Like most sewing details, the secret of success in making a good welt pocket is accuracy in marking and stitching.

A welt is included here because it is likely to turn up in patterns that look simple. It's a nice detail, and one you can master quite easily. A flap pocket, on the other hand, takes time and you'll do better to make a fake flap pocket as shown on page 116.

A welt pocket is made from two pieces of material: a squarish one which will be folded to make the welt and a rectangular one which will be folded to make the pocket. The pocket might be cut in two pieces, but they are handled the same as a single piece.

Begin your welt pocket with accurate markings. These will be in the shape of a rectangle about one-half inch wide and three to four inches long. The markings should show both inside and outside. You may have to trace a line between the tailor tacks with chalk. Trans-

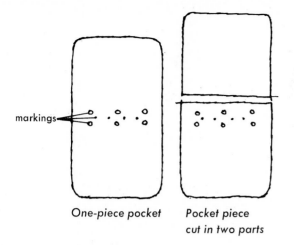

markings

One-piece pocket | Pocket piece cut in two parts

fer pattern markings for pocket to fabric.

If your fabric needs extra body to make a crisp welt, it's easy to give it a bit of help with interfacing. Fold the welt piece, right sides together, along the fold line. Cut interfacing the same size as the folded welt piece. Catch-stitch interfacing along one side of fold line of welt piece.

With welt folded, stitch ends together. Trim

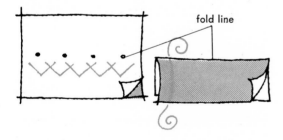

fold line

interfacing close to line of stitching. Trim end seam allowances. Turn welt right side out. Lay it with its seam line on lower stitching line marked on outside of garment. The folded edge will be down and the raw edge up. Stitch in place along seam line. At each end of the welt, backstitch as soon as the needle goes off the end. *Don't go one stitch short or one stitch beyond*, because this line becomes your guide on the wrong side. Trim welt seam to

¼″ and cut corners back on a slant as shown. Lay pocket piece right side down, over the

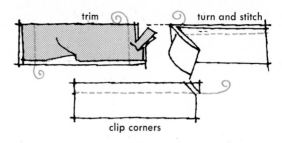

trim   turn and stitch

clip corners

welt on the right side of the garment. You will notice that the longer side of the pocket is above the welt. Pin pocket piece smoothly in place, aligning markings with stitching line. Turn garment section over. Now stitch along the rectangle you have marked. Stitch over the welt stitching line. Pivot precisely so you turn the corner exactly at the end of the stitching. Try to slant the stitching in just a tiny bit at the ends of the rectangle. In this situation you can turn the hand wheel, instead of using the foot pedal, for better control.

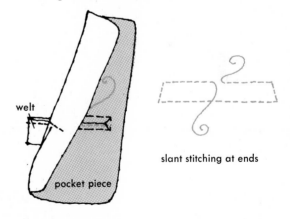

welt

pocket piece

slant stitching at ends

Now make a buttonhole cut on the garment and on the pocket piece between stitching lines. Turn the pocket through. As you smooth it down, the welt will fold upward by itself. Fold top of pocket piece down, pin pocket edges together. Starting at the top of the pocket

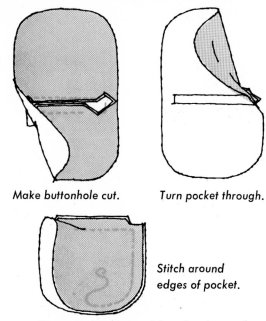

Make buttonhole cut.   Turn pocket through.

Stitch around
edges of pocket.

seam allowance and catching in the end triangle of the cut, stitch.

QUESTIONS OFTEN ASKED ABOUT
WELT POCKETS

1. Is there any easy way to be sure that I can
make the welt cover the opening?

Double check the stitching at the corners
before you clip! If you stitch, even one
stitch, beyond the end of the welt when
installing the pocket pieces, you then
clip too far and leave too big an opening.

2. Do the edges of the seams *inside* the pocket
have to match exactly?

It doesn't really matter whether the edges
come together, provided the pocket lies
flat under the opening.

Easy Pockets

There are a number of pockets which are
constructed right into the seams of clothes.
Inseam pockets and patch pockets are the
easiest for a beginner to make. Inseam pockets,

constructed right into the seam of a garment,
are purely utilitarian. Patch pockets, applied
to the outside of a garment, can be very
decorative.

INSEAM POCKETS

An inseam pocket is made by sewing the
pocket pieces to extensions of the skirt seam
allowances. A thin lining fabric can be used
for the deep inside pieces. The pocket opening
has a smoothly folded edge and is practically
invisible. (If you want to leave the whole
pocket out, just continue the skirt seam in a
line from upper to lower pocket marking,
where the pocket opening would be. Trim
off the extension.)

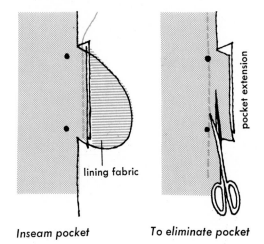

lining fabric

pocket extension

Inseam pocket   To eliminate pocket

PATCH POCKETS

Patch pockets may be hemmed, lined, or
hemmed and lined. In any case, the trick is
in making the edges smooth and even and the
hem as neat as possible. On a simple patch
pocket, hemmed at the edge and rounded at the
lower corners, follow these directions. Turn
under ¼" at the hem edge and stitch close to
the turned edge. Turn the hem back on its
fold line so that the right sides are together.
Stitch a ⅝" seam down the ends of the hem

and continue the stitching all around the pocket to make it easier to notch out the curves and press the edges under. Turn the hem right side out until the corners are sharp. Hem by hand or machine. Stitch the pocket in place, using top-stitching about ⅛″ from the edge. Backstitch at the upper corners, or reinforce with one of the designs below. In wools and silks the pocket sometimes is put on by hand, using a blindstitch or slipstitch.

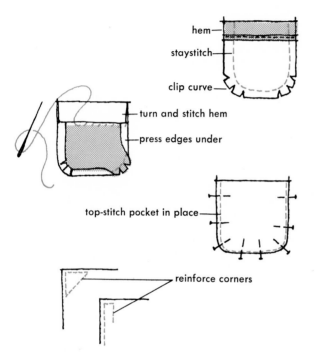

hem
staystitch
clip curve
turn and stitch hem
press edges under
top-stitch pocket in place
reinforce corners

HANDLING A LINING

If a pocket is lined to the edges, pin the pocket and the lining right sides together, being sure that the lining is pulled very tight. You may even push the upper layer away from the edges a little as you pin, so that it will naturally roll over and conceal the lining when it is right side out. Leave about a 2″ opening along the straight part at the bottom when you stitch. Trim the seam in half and notch out the curves and clip the corners to avoid bulk.

Turn the pocket right side out, being sure to push the edges out smooth and even before pressing.

A hemmed and lined pocket is just like a lined one, except that the lining must be sewn right sides together with the edge of the hem, leaving the 2″ opening for turning in the center of that seam. Then proceed to pin and stitch around the edge, trim, clip, and turn as before.

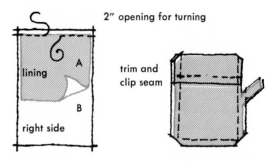

2″ opening for turning
lining
A
B
right side
trim and clip seam

Before stitching, join lower edges of lining (A) and pocket (B).

QUESTIONS OFTEN ASKED ABOUT PATCH POCKETS

1. Why are the curved edges uneven and lumpy?

Your notches should have been narrower, deeper, and closer together than you made them.

2. In a stretchy fabric such as a knit, how can I keep the upper edge of the pocket from stretching?

Lay a strip of tape in the top fold of the hem and tack invisibly in place.

Pleats for Plenty of Room

Pleats produce the greatest amount of fullness with the least bulk that a skirt can have. There are three kinds of pleats—knife, inverted, and box. The first two are most often used.

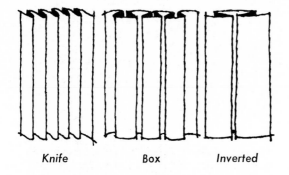

Knife   Box   Inverted

Many skirts have one to four pleats which allow an otherwise slim line to swing and move gracefully with the wearer. Skirts with up to four pleats are easiest because the fit of

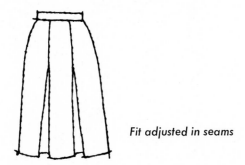

Fit adjusted in seams

the skirt is still controlled in the seams. In a skirt with more pleats, the pleating itself must be adjusted for fit.

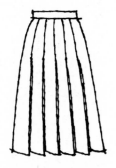

Fit adjusted in pleats

In a design with many pleats, the pleats are usually created by folding the piece of fabric on a given line. When only a few pleats are used, there is often a seam at the inner edge.

In the case of the inverted box pleat, there is even a separate piece seamed in behind the pleat.

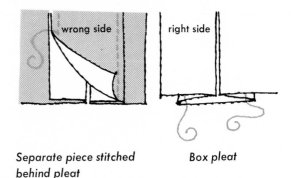

Separate piece stitched behind pleat   *Box pleat*

COLOR-KEY YOUR MARKINGS

When you tailor tack for your pleats, remember to use different colors of thread for different kinds of markings or lines. The line that says "Pleat" should be one color and the line that says "Meet" should be another, so that you know exactly where to press the pleats in. It will be helpful to put an extra row of tailor tacks up in the hip area where the fitting is so important, and one down at the hemline, to guide you in folding below the stitching. The ironing board is the best place to work because you can fold two or three pleats, pin them to the board, then press,

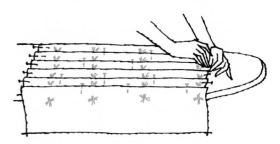

removing the pins as you go. Press to within 6" of the bottom, so that further pressing can be done after the hem is turned. Baste along the edge of each pleat at least as far down as

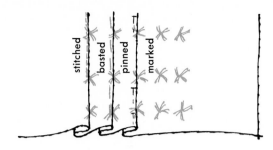

7″ below the waist so that the skirt may be tried on. *Remember that even ⅛″ slip on each line of pleats changes the fit of the skirt.*

Edge-stitch the pleats as far down as desired or as the pattern calls for.

Most pleats are stitched down in the hip area, either inside like a seam, or outside, sometimes quite decoratively. The length of the area stitched depends more on your height and figure than on the pattern, so pin or baste and try on before stitching. Be careful not to let the bottom of the stitching fall across the widest part of your hips.

HANDLING HEMS

Straight or flared pleats, seamed on the inside edges, are very easy to handle, provided you are careful at the hem. After the hem is measured and turned up, clip the seam just above the hem, so that it can be pressed together as it should, while the seam inside the hem can be pressed open flat for less bulk.

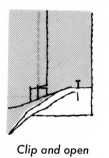

Clip and open seam in hem.

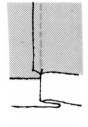

Fold in pleat.

For pleats in heavy fabrics, mark hem, then stitch toward seam line on an angle, and trim excess bulk, clipping off corner as shown. Turn up hem.

For heavy fabrics, remove excess bulk before turning up hem.

QUESTIONS OFTEN ASKED ABOUT PLEATS

1. I basted all the pleats and the skirt is too tight. Now what?

   Divide the extra ease you need by the number of pleats and add that amount to each pleat (⅛″ each on 24 pleats would give you a total of 3″).

2. If my fabric will not take a sharp crease for a pleat, what can I do?

   You can sew in a permanent pleat by edge-stitching the entire pleat along the fold. Follow directions for decorative top-stitching (page 68).

Tucks—Decorative and Useful

Tucks make you think of the last century, and ladies at lawn parties in dresses of sprigged muslin! The funny thing is that the top designers seem to rediscover tucks every few years and make marvelous use of them. There are two kinds of tucks, those that are stitched down all the way and those that are released at one or both ends. The latter serve a real purpose other than decoration; they create a tight fitting band and then release fullness like shirring or smocking. For these tucks, the folds are on the inside of the garment and only the seam shows on the outside. Here are examples of tucks used in fashion.

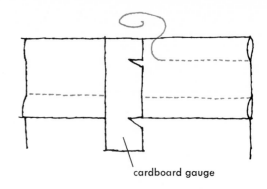

cardboard gauge

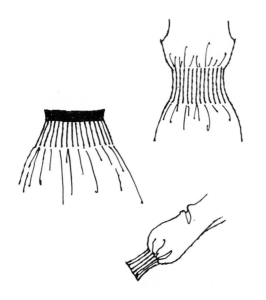

Be sure to use a fabric that will crease easily for tucks. Cotton shirtings, some medium-weight cottons, wool challis, crisp silk, and worsted knits are all appropriate. Permanent-press fabrics and soft fabrics such as tricot are not suitable for tucks. Test a sample first by pressing a fold with the wrong sides together, straight down the grain line. Stitch parallel to the fold, using the edge of the presser foot or the marked faceplate as a guide.

You must be sure of your grain line when you lay out a pattern for a garment with tucks, because it is almost impossible to get a crisp tuck if it is not folded right along the grain. Mark the fold lines with tailor tacks and crease each tuck line with the iron. Double check by measuring between the folds with a small ruler or cardboard gauge to indicate the

distance between the stitching lines of one tuck and the fold line of the next. Be sure that you stitch each tuck the exact depth called for in the pattern or you will change the size of the tucked area.

It is possible to tuck a piece of fabric all over and then cut a garment piece from it. Wide tucks spaced a bit apart are very attractive in

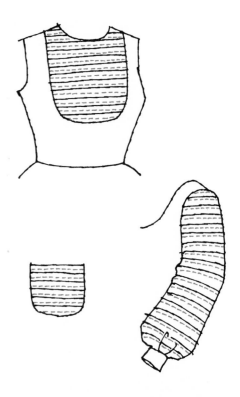

Dress sections cut from pre-tucked fabric

a sheer fabric. Some possible places for using this kind of done-ahead-of-time tucking are shown on the opposite page.

Tucking can also be done with the fancy pattern stitches on the new zigzag machines. Use a shade darker thread for a really great effect.

Make adjustments in the fit of a tucked garment the same way as in a pleated garment, by making the tucks larger or smaller.

QUESTIONS OFTEN ASKED ABOUT TUCKS

1. The edges of my tucks are uneven, and they won't press so that they all look alike.

Check your grain line! Try a striped dimity or voile, or ribbed piqué for your first sample; the lines are built in!

2. What is the best way to fasten the stitching at the end of an open tuck?

You can either backstitch, tie off or turn and stitch across the open end of the tuck.

ASSEMBLING THE PIECES

Your show-off details are completed, your fitting session has shown you where adjustments should be made, your markings are in place. Now you can work with darts to shape your garment, and then with seams to join the pieces.

Stitching Basic Darts and Seams

There are a few rules that apply to both darts and seams. Almost all darts and seams are stitched with the right sides of the fabric placed together, so that the outside of the garment shows only the line, and the excess fabric is hidden inside. For a variation on this basic arrangement, see page 142.

Both darts and seams may be pin-basted. To do this, use fine pins without plastic heads. Pin from the outer edge in, pinning right across the stitching line. This holds the fabric firmly, and your hinged presser foot will skip right over the pins without danger of breaking the needle.

CAUTION: If your machine is not equipped with a hinged presser foot, *do not sew over pins.* (To be sure, check the instruction manual that came with your machine.) Baste by hand instead of pin basting.

Accuracy, both in seams and darts, is all-important. If you make too deep a dart on the side of the bodice, the front will be shorter than the back. If the shoulder seams are a bit less than ⅝″ on the dress and a touch more than ⅝″ on the facing, the two won't fit together.

Darts Come First

Darts are used for shaping and fitting all around the curves of the body. (In more complicated couturier patterns shaping is done with multiple seaming, but simpler clothes use darts.) Darts are usually found around the bust line, the shoulders, and the hip line.

To join shoulder seams accurately, pin ends together across seam line, and pin down dart. (Note hinged presser foot. If your machine is not equipped with this type of foot, do not stitch over pins.)

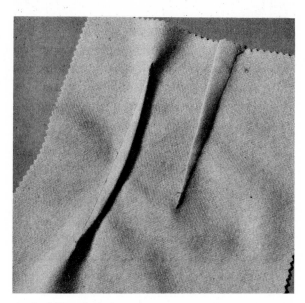

A double-ended dart shapes a waistline in a one-piece dress; a standard straight dart appears at back neck or shoulder and from waist to shoulder blade in bodice back.

There are two kinds: the ones that start at a seam and run to a point, and the ones used in princess and shift dresses which are double-ended to make the waist fit into the body.

The standard straight dart appears in the back neck or shoulder, in the elbow of the sleeve, and from waist to shoulder blade in the bodice back.

The darts in the bodice front are sometimes straight, but more often curved slightly to hug the rib cage around the bust. This is a convex curve, outward from the fold line.

The hip darts are the opposite, curving as the hip seam curves, or inward toward the fold line. The curvier your hips are, the curvier your darts will be.

Pin-baste the dart, following the line of the tailor's tacks or markings. (Check your manual to be sure your machine has the hinged presser foot that will sew over pins safely.)

A skirt dart curves slightly toward the fold line to conform to the curve of the hip.

MARK CAREFULLY

Careful marking will, of course, make it easier to stitch the dart lines properly. Cross-pin at each marking as you match markings, right sides together. Start stitching at the wide end of the dart, and follow the line, always remembering which way the shape

should curve or the straight line should point. The point of the dart should be very sharp and fine, with the last three or four stitches running close to the fold. Beware a lumpy-ended dart! To fasten off, backstitch for a few stitches straight up the fold, or tie the two thread ends together.

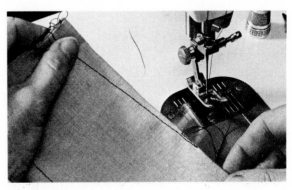

Backstitch straight up the fold of the dart to fasten off.

AN EASY TRICK FOR DOUBLE-ENDED DARTS

Are you wondering how to start stitching at the fine pointed end of a double-ended dart?

Here's a simple way out of that: just treat it like two darts. Start at the middle and stitch in one direction to the point. Then start a few stitches back on that stitching line, again at the middle, so the two rows are tightly joined. Continue again as for a single dart.

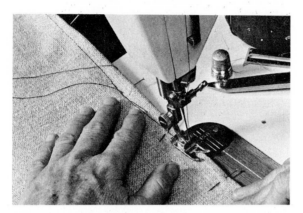

An easy trick for double-ended darts is to start in the middle and stitch to one end, then start again in the middle and stitch to the other end. Overlap stitching in the middle and backstitch at dart points.

A PRESSING REMINDER

Always press darts right after stitching them, and before a seam is sewed across them. See page 67 for pressing instructions. This is a top secret of fine dressmaking!

Sew a Fine Seam

Now, it's time to start joining all those separate pieces to make a garment. Generally, it's easy to decide which seams to stitch first, but your pattern guide sheet will give you instructions if you are doubtful. Did you know that the notches are numbered in order of assembly? Look on the pieces for Notch 1 and work from there.

Sometimes there are alternate ways of assembly that work well if you think through

to the final result. For instance, it is usually easier to set in a raglan sleeve before the underarm seams are sewed together. This makes pressing easier, too. Sew the front and back

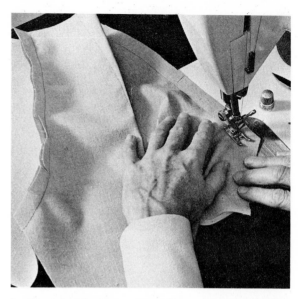

In the assembly of a raglan sleeve, note the dart at the shoulder top and the careful joining of clips at the front and back bodice sections.

sleeve seams to bodice; then the side seams all in one, and finally the shoulder darts and seams. The sleeve-to-bodice seams are almost never adjusted for fit, so they can be permanently stitched before final fitting.

FABRIC CONTROL

You may have heard of "directional stitching," but don't worry about it. Sewing is easiest and most accurate if the work is kept to the left of the needle, so the throatplate guidelines are visible.

To control the fabric while stitching so that it doesn't creep or stretch, pin-baste crosswise to the seam line (first being sure your presser foot can safely sew over pins); adjust machine to correct tension, pressure, and stitch length; and push the upper layer gently toward the foot. This offsets the slight drag that the action of foot and teeth creates. For ex-

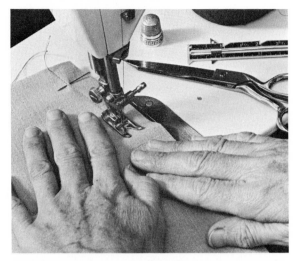

For fabric control, push the upper layer of fabric toward the presser foot to offset the drag of foot and teeth.

ceptionally slippery fabrics, you may have to use a special foot (in some machines a built-in device) to control shifting.

You can achieve a perfectly marvelous sense of accomplishment by pinning or basting all the seams you can find that do not conflict with each other such as skirt seams, sleeve seams, bodice seams, and facing seams. Then sit down at the machine and stitch them all up, one right after the other, in assembly-line method. You can press them all at once, and go on to the next steps.

A WORD ABOUT SEAM WIDTHS

Check seam widths carefully when cutting and marking. The majority of seams on the patterns you will buy are marked at ⅝", but there are a few exceptions. There are some-

times ¾" or ⅞" seams for decorative effect with top-stitching. Once in a while there is a ½" seam around a neck or facing area, and sometimes no seam allowance at all when the neck and armholes are to be bound instead of faced. There's nothing tricky about any of these except marking them carefully. New machines have throatplate markings to make it easy to keep track of seam widths.

You can make your own marks on an older machine with a ruler and nail polish or transparent tape.

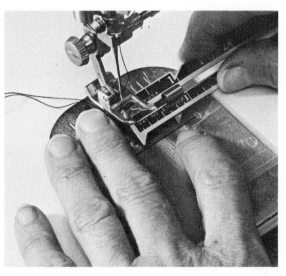

If your machine does not have throat plate markings for standard seam allowances, make your own with nail polish or transparent tape at the ⅝" line.

CURVING A SEAM

Sometimes even an easy dress presents an involved seam. A curved seam is a very attractive way to shape a bust line instead of darts. The two pieces that must be fitted together are opposite curves, and may fight back at you when you first try to pin them. Here is the easy way to do it.

Staystitch the concave curve just a fraction

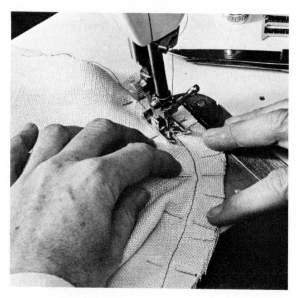

Before stitching a curved seam, staystitch the concave curve just short of seam line so that you can safely clip the seam allowance to a depth of about ⅜".

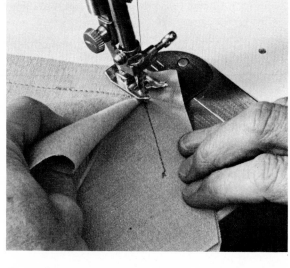

To stitch a corner, first staystitch and clip the corner piece. Then stitch the first side, pivot the fabric on the needle, and stitch the second side.

short of the seam line and clip slightly. Pin the markings together, each tailor tack and notch, pinning right on the seam line. Work the curve between markings over your fingertips, and keep the raw edges together.

CORNERING UP

Corners are a bit like curves, and must be very precise. Remember, back in the chapter on staystitching, that you stitched and clipped the corners. Now, pin the seams together with corners matching. With clipped piece uppermost, stitch toward corner, directly on seam line. Keep the staystitching inside seam, and hold toward you the fold of fabric at the corner. When the needle is exactly in the corner at the end of the clip, lift the presser foot, turn the fabric, pull the fold of fabric out of your way toward the back of the machine, and proceed along the next side. In other words, you never stitch around the corner.

You pivot it on the point of the needle. (See page 37 in chapter on staystitching.)

MORE EASE AND GATHERING

Ease and gathering were discussed on pages 38 ff., but they must now be dealt with as part of a seam. The ease thread, like the staystitch,

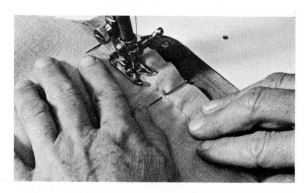

In stitching an eased seam, keep the ease thread inside the seam and stretch slightly across the stitching line to keep the ease smooth. (Note hinged presser foot for safety in stitching over pins.)

must be kept inside the seam while stitching the seam. If you stitch very close to the ease thread, and stretch the fabric slightly across the stitching line as the fabric passes under the presser foot, the ease should remain smooth.

In gathering (page 39), it is important to keep the two lines of thread spaced so the seam may be stitched between them. Pin the gathered section to the flat section carefully, moving and spacing the gathers as you go. If

Stitch between the lines of gathering and pull out the gathering line that shows after stitching. The pins across the seam line are hidden by the gathers.

the gathers are pinned evenly, and the pins are right across the seam line, you should have perfect gathers after you stitch the seam. Just pull out the thread that shows on the dress, and admire your handiwork.

TAMING TEMPERAMENTAL FABRICS

Some fabrics are easier to sew than others. If you come across a fabric that fights back with puckering or slipping, you'll have to adjust your sewing machine pressure, tension, and stitch length. Get out your machine man-

ual, and test on a double layer of fabric till you hit the right combination.

Here are a few helpful hints on the subject.

Velvet stitches better if the machine foot runs along in the direction of the nap.

Very fine fabrics, sheers, and thin knits respond better to a very fine machine needle, such as a size 11.

Knits are better stitched with a zigzag stitch. The newer machines have many kinds of stitches designed especially for knits. Try an ordinary zigzag stitch set at a medium length and narrow width to provide enough stretch to keep the stitches from breaking during wear. If you don't have a zigzag sewing machine, sew knits with a bit longer straight stitch and loose tension.

To prevent skipped stitches when sewing synthetic knits, use a ball-point needle on your machine.

One final hint: if your sewing machine needs oiling, adjustment, and a general overhaul, it will start misbehaving on delicate and temperamental fabrics first. So if the suggestions above don't work, try a good oiling and cleaning, as described on page 151.

For fine seam finishes, see page 98. For handling specialty fabrics, see page 109 ff.

QUESTIONS OFTEN ASKED ABOUT DARTS AND SEAMS

1. Why do my skirts seem tight just at the top of the hip and then almost puckery and full lower down at the end of the darts?

You didn't shape the skirt darts to the rounded line of the upper hip.

2. How can I avoid having extra length on one layer at the end of a long seam, especially in soft fabrics?

Match every marked spot first when pinning. Match ends, then match between. Reduce the pressure on the machine so the foot does not pull the upper layer so much.

3. What can I do to keep the seam on a bias skirt from puckering and the stitches from breaking?

If you have a zigzag machine, sew a bias seam with a zigzag stitch. Otherwise, hold the seam taut with both hands as you stitch with a measured length of tissue paper on top as a guide.

Pressing Toward Perfection

There is no way to overemphasize the need for pressing as you sew. This means that pressing equipment must be handy to the sewing area. For convenience, you may use a small fold-up traveling board and a travel steam iron. You will also need a press mitt and a transparent press cloth.

The first rule of pressing is *press every dart and seam before sewing another seam across it!* This prevents an ugly little fold from being stitched into the end of the seam or dart.

Here are some other rules that are to be followed almost without exception. When a pattern definitely requires changing one of these, there will be very explicit directions in the guide sheet.

1. Side seams, shoulder seams, and most other main seams should be pressed open flat.

Do not trim these seams to less than ⅝″ as they become more difficult to handle when they are narrow.

2. Concave seams must be *clipped before pressing* so that they lie flat. Several clips are better than one as they let the curve open more gently. Double-ended darts are treated like concave curves.

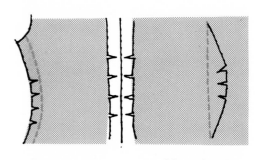

Concave seam   Double-ended dart

3. Convex curves may be notched out if they cause bulk. If the curve is not too deep and the fabric is soft, the fullness will sometimes blend out with steaming.

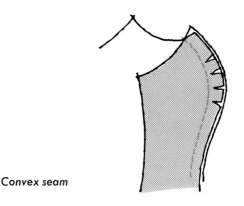

Convex seam

4. If a seam has gathers or ease along one side, such as a dirndl skirt joined to a bodice, or a set-in sleeve seam, *the seam is not pressed open flat.* It is pressed away from the ease or gathers, the direction in which it goes most naturally.

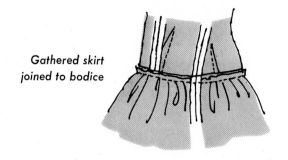

Gathered skirt joined to bodice

5. Horizontal darts are pressed down and vertical darts toward the center. The patterns are cut so that the edges fall in smoothly at the wide end of a dart when this rule is followed. The position of the vertical dart is supposed to give a slimmer effect than if the dart were pressed outward, so you will be glad to remember that part of the rule!

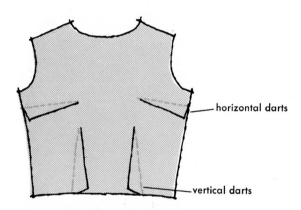

— horizontal darts

— vertical darts

6. In a heavy fabric, provided it is underlined or does not ravel too easily, darts may be split to within an inch of the end and pressed open to avoid bulk at the seam.

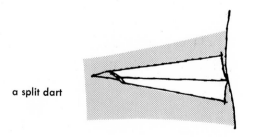

a split dart

SUCCESS TIPS FOR PRESSING

There are techniques in pressing as well as rules. Remember that you're not ironing a starched shirt. You are molding a garment into shape. Use the steam of your iron more than the weight. Tease a seam open gently, before pressing down hard. The seam is easier to handle if you press it flat first, exactly as it was stitched, pulling the length a little to blend fabric and stitching.

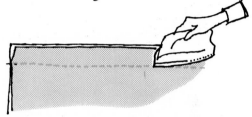

Use your hands to mold the shape of the garment over a mitt or ham. The round line of the bust, shaped by either darts or curved seams, can be worked smoothly by running steam through the garment as it lies over the mitt, then shaping with the hand, then pressing a bit harder. The curves of hips and shoulders should be treated in this manner rather than flat on the board.

Shape darts.

Curve a seam.

Here's how to press set-in sleeves for a smooth, professional look. After the seam is completely stitched and trimmed around the armhole, lay the sleeve on the board in the exact position that it was on the machine when you stitched. Put just the tip of the iron into the cap of the sleeve and steam the last bit of fullness out. Move around the top of the sleeve and press a little at a time. *Do not press outside.*

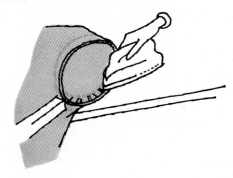

Special fabrics require special treatment in pressing. If you have any doubt about pressing certain fabrics, test a piece. Some delicate fabrics, such as peau de soie, *cannot be pressed with steam.* A needle board is helpful for pressing corduroy, velvet, and velveteen. If you do not have one, try placing a leftover scrap of your fabric face up on the ironing board and lay the garment right side down on top of it. Then steam the seam open gently. For rough textured wools, use a terry towel in the same way to keep the texture from being flattened.

If you are working on such delicate fabrics as peau de soie or an impressionable fabric such as wool doeskin, the edge of a pressed seam may show on the underside. To avoid this insert a strip of brown paper between seam and garment while pressing and, as in all pressing, do not bear down heavily on the iron.

After all the press-as-you-go pressing is done, you will still want to shape the entire garment from outside. It is usually wise to use a transparent press cloth, a piece of fabric, or a terry towel over the outside to prevent slick marks. If you don't trust yourself, take the dress to a good cleaner for a professional pressing.

QUESTIONS OFTEN ASKED ABOUT PRESSING

1. If I pressed a seam too hard, how can I correct it without making worse lines or more shine?

When you pressed it too hard the first time you slicked the fabric. Keep steaming it without any weight, then brush gently.

2. Why does my steam iron spit and drip on the fabric?

You are not giving it enough time to heat, or you are not careful about the settings, or the iron needs cleaning, or the thermostat needs resetting by a repair service.

Tips on Top-Stitching

Top-stitching is a decorative finish for casual clothes. It must be done carefully to be effective.

There are two kinds of top-stitching: the kind along interior seams which must be done at a certain point in the construction, and edge-stitching which is done after everything else is finished. The edge-stitching is easier because you can use the seam guide on the machine to keep it even.

Some threads make especially attractive top-stitching. One of the best on wools, linens, and heavy silks is Buttonhole Twist. Here are tips to make the thread easy to handle.

Make a seam of scraps of the fabric you are

using, and practice stitching. Adjust tension as necessary. Use a size 16 machine needle, eight stitches to the inch, Buttonhole Twist on top and your regular thread in the bobbin. Go slowly and carefully.

You may also use the twin needle, which is standard equipment on some of the newer machines. Then use a standard thread, not Buttonhole Twist.

Top-stitching as trim

TOP-STITCHING ON INTERIOR SEAMS

To top-stitch on interior seams, first check your guide sheet for the order in which these seams must be top-stitched, and in which direction the seam must be pressed. The entire seam is often pressed in one direction to make a thick pad under the top-stitching. This is one place where you may have been given a seam allowance wider than ⅜". Press the seams so they are very smooth before starting to top-stitch.

A TRICK FOR ACCURATE STITCHING

Check the guide sheet for the width of one row of top-stitching, that is, the distance from the seam. Cut a piece of typewriter paper six inches long, and exactly as wide as the top-stitching. As you start stitching, lay this paper against the seam and stitch at the other edge of it. The paper is firm enough to be maneuverable, yet thin enough so that the presser foot

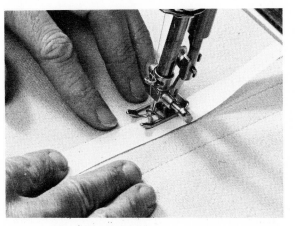

For accurate top-stitching, cut a strip of medium-weight paper to serve as a gauge and allow it to run under the presser foot.

can run over it easily. There is a double benefit in that the paper not only makes a gauge, but also keeps the presser foot from pushing the fabric too fast and causing it to ripple. Every now and then lift the presser foot, being sure that the needle is firmly in the fabric, and slide the paper along. For additional rows, lay the paper against. the previous row as a guide.

Edge-stitching is easier because you can use the marks on the faceplate of your machine as a guide. See page 98 to learn how the facing or seam edges should be trimmed and treated, as this must be done before the edge-stitching.

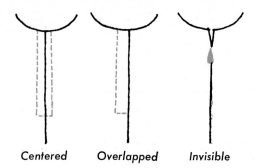

Centered   Overlapped   Invisible

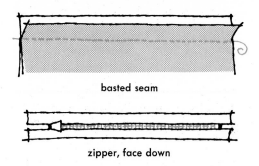

basted seam

zipper, face down

Zippers—Three Easy Insertions

There are three basic zipper insertions: the centered, the overlapped, and the invisible. Here are tips that apply to all three kinds, with special suggestions for each.

A zipper is usually inserted before the waistband or neck facing which will later cover it. Always make sure that the two sides of the zipper opening are of even length.

Always start zipper teeth a full inch below the top opening to allow ample room for waistband or neckline facing seam. Be sure to press flat any cross seam, waistline, or yoke in zipper area to avoid bulk. If the seam presses one way, clip one layer of it 1¼″ from the end as illustrated.

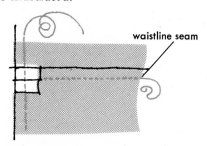

waistline seam

CENTERED ZIPPER

Step 1. Baste zipper opening together exactly on seamline with longest machine stitch. Work from the bottom up, and be sure that all seams across zipper, such as waistband or yoke, meet exactly. Press the basted seam open flat.

If you are using a zipper adhesive, follow directions on back of package. No basting or pinning of the zipper tape will be necessary. If you do not use it, follow Step 2.

Step 2. To position the zipper for stitching

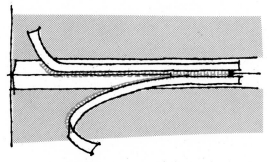

Zipper in position for stitching

without using zipper adhesive, open the zipper and lay the teeth of one side along the basted seam, just touching the seam. Remember that teeth should start 1″ below the raw edge at the top. With the zipper foot on the machine, stitch one side of the zipper tape to one layer of the seam, from the bottom up. Do not stitch through to outside of garment. This line of stitching is only to insure correct placement of the zipper. Always be sure that the zipper foot is correctly set, so that the needle just clears it and so that the foot is away from the zipper teeth.

Step 3. Close the zipper and work from the right side of the dress. No further basting is needed; the zipper will stay in place for stitching. Stitch across the bottom to about ¼″

from the seam and then upward in a straight line, widening out slightly at the top to allow room for the slider. Move the foot to the other side of the needle, stitch across the bottom again, for reinforcement, and up the other side of the zipper, again ¼" from the seam.

Machine stitching

On delicate fabrics you may wish to hand-stitch the zipper. Use a small backstitch, (see p. 101) barely showing on top and running about ¼" underneath. Work about ¼" from the seam on both sides as with the machine.

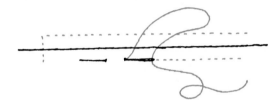

Hand stitching

Now pull out the basting. Steam gently with the press cloth on the outside. Pull the zipper tight and then steam again until it lies very flat.

QUESTIONS OFTEN ASKED ABOUT THE CENTERED ZIPPER

1. When I position the zipper, does it matter which side of the zipper tape I stitch to the seam allowance?

It makes no difference which side.

2. Can I use a centered zipper in any seam?

Yes, a centered zipper can be used in the front, the back, or the side of a garment.

OVERLAPPED ZIPPER

An overlapped zipper can be used in almost any place that a centered one can, but it tends to look more casual. If you cannot find a fairly good color match or blend, you may prefer to use this one, as it is covered. In fabrics with long loops that can catch in the zipper, the overlap piece should be faced with a lining fabric.

An overlapped zipper is most often used in a hip-line seam of pants or skirts, with a ⅝" seam.

Step 1. On the underlap side (skirt back) run a row of machine staystitching ½" from the raw edge of the zipper opening. On the overlap side (skirt front) run a row of machine staystitching exactly on the seam line.

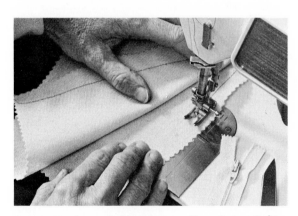

For an overlapped zipper, run a line of staystitching along the underlap, ½" from the edge, and along the overlap, ⅝" from the edge.

For a variation to prevent snagging, face overlap edge by laying 1½" bias strip of lining fabric right sides together with garment along seam edge. Stitch seam at almost ⅝", that is, between ½" and ⅝".

Step 2. Press the edges under along the stay-stitch lines. In the case of the variation, the overlap will still be pressed at the ⅝" line.

This will turn the facing just inside so that it will not show. On the underlap piece there will be a tiny fold at the bottom of the opening. The purpose of this indentation is to position the zipper under the overlap.

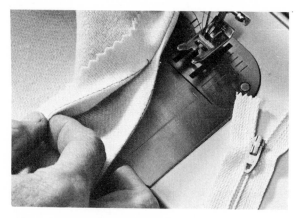

Edges are pressed under, along staystitch lines, preparatory to placing zipper.

Step 3. Working from the bottom up, with the zipper foot away from the teeth of the zipper, stitch the underlap very close to the zipper teeth. Work on the right side of the fabric, stitching about ⅟₁₆″ from the folded underlap edge.

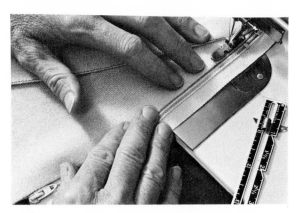

Working from the bottom up, stitch underlap close to zipper teeth. Note the use of the adjustable zipper foot.

Step 4. Bring the overlap side just over the stitching, covering totally about ⅛″ of the underlap side. If it will help keep it even to pin or baste or mark with chalk, do so. Stitch across the bottom to about ⅜″ from the seam, and then at that distance up along the zipper, widening slightly at the top to make room for the slider. Feed the fabric evenly into the machine with your hand so there is no ripple.

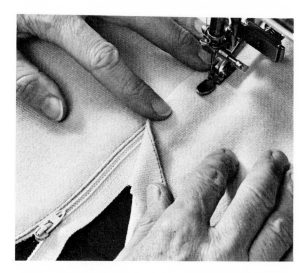

With the overlap folded over the stitching on the underlap, stitch overlap ⅜″ from folded edge. Note that the zipper foot is now on the opposite side of the needle.

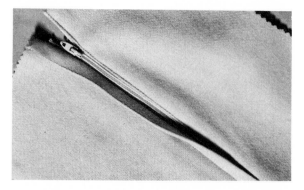

Here is how the overlapped zipper should look after installation.

QUESTIONS OFTEN ASKED ABOUT THE OVERLAPPED ZIPPER

1. Can I do the overlapped zipper by hand, as it seems so much easier to keep it from pulling?

Better yet, you can do the concealed, easier underlap by machine, and the overlap by hand. In a heavy fabric, use Buttonhole Twist for a decorative effect.

2. When should I substitute a centered zipper for an overlapped zipper?

When you are working with heavy fabric, an overlapped zipper may give a lumpy effect. A centered zipper is smoother.

THE INVISIBLE ZIPPER

One of the best things to happen to zippers is to make them disappear, leaving only a nice neat seam.

The instructions that come with the invisible zippers are very clear and easy to follow. Be sure you buy the special foot this zipper requires.

Make your first trial run on a piece of medium-weight, flexible flannel or linen, or similar fabric. Use a large machine stitch so that you can rip the zipper out and put it back again several times for practice.

The directions that come with the zipper suggest that you leave the entire seam open during insertion, stitching together the lower part after the zipper is in. This works fine on firm fabrics. On soft stretchy fabrics, it will be easier to match the lower seam edges if you sew the seam below the zipper first. Leave the opening exactly the same length as the teeth on the zipper. You will still set the zipper down 1″ from the raw edge as with any other zipper, but there will be a 1″ extra tail hanging down inside at the bottom.

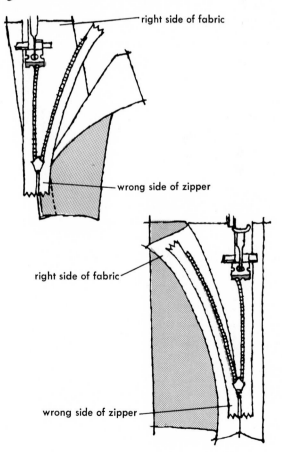

right side of fabric

wrong side of zipper

right side of fabric

wrong side of zipper

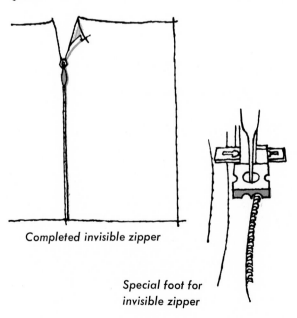

Completed invisible zipper

Special foot for invisible zipper

Lay the zipper tape and the seam allowance *right sides together*. Put on the special foot, grooved so that the teeth of the zipper move along in the groove, while the needle goes in very close to the teeth for perfect stitching. Stitch one side of the zipper to one side of the seam, along the ⅝″ stitching line. Working from the top down, with the zipper open, stitch the other side in exactly the same way.

You may do any pinning or basting that helps you, but you cannot sew over pins with this foot. Proper placement of the second side of the zipper may require pinning when you have a cross seam or a plaid which must be matched. The easiest way to do this is to close the zipper and pin or tape the second side with zipper adhesive tape, or mark it with chalk or pencil, then open the zipper and stitch. *Remember to remove pins as you stitch.* Tack the loose tail of the zipper to the seam allowance by hand or machine.

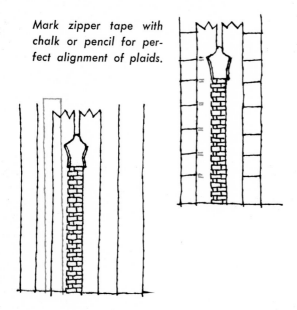

Mark zipper tape with chalk or pencil for perfect alignment of plaids.

Tape zipper in place for extra accuracy.

QUESTIONS OFTEN ASKED ABOUT THE INVISIBLE ZIPPER

1. Can I use the invisible zipper in almost any fabric?

You will probably still prefer the hand-stitched centered zipper for delicate sheers, but the invisible is perfect for even dressy fabrics like brocade.

2. Must I pre-shrink the zippers made on polyester tape?

No—the polyester keeps the tape from shrinking. Be sure to use polyester tapes with synthetic garments.

Necklines, Armholes, and Collars

A facing is a piece of fabric shaped like the neckline (or armhole or opening) it is to be stitched to, and serving the purpose of a hem. When you made doll clothes, remember how you tried to hem around a neckline, and it wasn't satisfactory because a hem won't turn very well on such a deep curve? So, if you cut a piece of fabric, 2″ to 3″ wide, as a hem is, but shaped to fit the edge that you want to finish, you will come out a lot better than you did with those doll clothes.

An alternative way to face a curve is by using a piece of bias fabric, which will curve around when handled properly, and have very little bulk. This is used most often on children's clothes where the areas to be faced are tiny. It is also used around the armholes of sleeveless blouses.

BASIC RULE FOR FACINGS

There is one basic rule which will apply anywhere a shaped facing is used. If you enlarge or take in a seam to be faced, you must

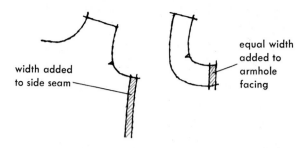

width added to side seam

equal width added to armhole facing

make the same adjustment in the corresponding seam on the facing. If you don't do this, the two pieces will not fit together.

THE SIMPLEST FACING—A ROUND NECKLINE

The most basic, and most frequently encountered neckline facing is the one used to finish the round or jewel neck. You have already installed the zipper in the back of the dress, and joined the shoulder seams on the dress and those on the facing.

Finish the facing outer edge according to one of the systems on page 98. Pin the center front of the facing right sides together with the center front of the dress. Pin the notches together and pin shoulder seams together. At the back, fold under the ⅝" at each end of the facing and pin the folded edge to the folded edge of the dress above the zipper. Actually, it won't hurt to fold a tiny fraction more than ⅝" on the facing, so it just barely comes to the folded edge of the dress. Now, pin several more times in between, being especially

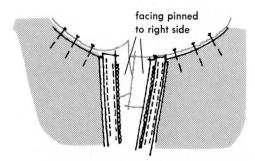

facing pinned to right side

Applying facing to neckline after inserting zipper

careful to pin down the seams at shoulders so that when you stitch across them they won't fold up into lumps. Mark ⅝" from neck edge all around with ruler and chalk, to help you stitch an even circle.

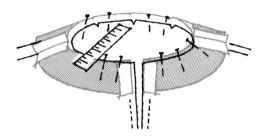

Stitch all the way around, checking to make sure that you started and ended exactly the same distance above the zipper teeth at each end of the facing. It is easier to backstitch at start and finish than to tie off.

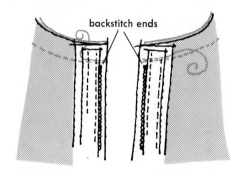

backstitch ends

GRADING FOR A SMOOTH SEAM

If the fabric is light to medium weight, trim the seam allowance approximately in half. If

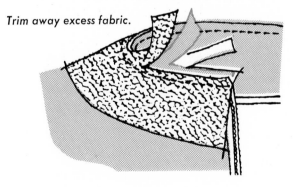

Trim away excess fabric.

both dress and facing are of fairly heavy fabric, grade the seam. This means to trim it in unequal layers. If there is an interfacing, trim it almost to the stitching. Trim the next layer to a scant ¼″ and the last to ⅜″.

Clip all layers, almost to the stitching, at intervals of about ½″ around the neck. This enables the curve to turn over smoothly. It is almost impossible to clip too much, *but beware of trimming too deeply!* If there is too much bulk at the seam intersection and the top of the zipper, trim out the useless squares of fabric at the corners.

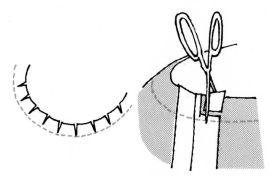

Clip for a smooth curve.   Trim excess at corners.

UNDERSTITCHING AND TACKING FOR FLATTER FACINGS

The last important step to a perfectly finished facing is the understitching. This is just what it sounds like: stitching which is underneath, not on the outside, of the garment. It holds the seam and facing smoothly together, and almost eliminates the need for pressing. Here's how it is done. Lay the facing over on the seam away from the garment and hold it tight and smooth. Put it on the machine with the right side of the facing uppermost. Stitch about ⅛″ from the seam all around the facing, through facing and seam allowance only, holding it very flat (A). Sometimes on delicate fabrics and in places that are hard to reach,

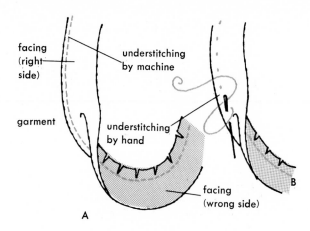

you may want to understitch with a small backstitch by hand (B).

Tack the outer edge of the facing in place only at seams, darts, and along the zipper where it won't show on the right side.

FACINGS FOR OTHER NECKLINES

On a *low, round neck,* if you put in an ease thread as suggested on page 38, pin the facing in place with right sides together and all markings matching, as usual. Run an ease thread in the facing, corresponding to the ease thread in the garment. The facing will then ease in the

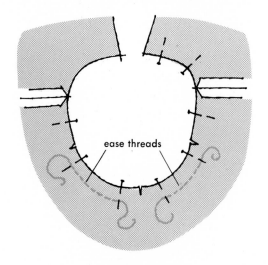

Low round neckline

same spot as the neckline. Square necks pose no problem except for reinforcement of the corners. The easiest way is to go back and restitch each corner on the same lines that you first stitched them. Trim or grade the seam as for the round neck, and clip the corners and any rounded area toward the back.

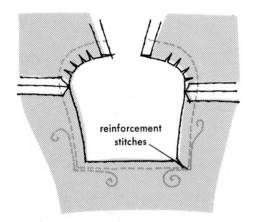

Square neckline

A *plain V-neck* is easy to face. Use the rule that applies to staystitching narrow slashes (page 38). Make one stitch across at the point when joining the facing to the neckline. Restitch the point of the V for added reinforcement. Clip deeply.

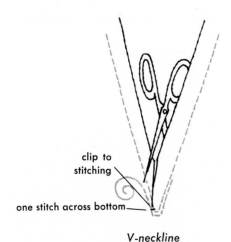

V-neckline

A *V-neck with a seam* in the dress and facing, coming up to the point of the V, requires a bit more skill and accuracy. There will be four markings at the intersection of the center front seam and the neckline seam. Stitch the center front seam only to this point on both dress and facing, and backstitch to hold. Pin these exact points together when pinning the right sides of the facing together with the neckline. Hold the center front seams back out of the way, and stitch from the tack around the neckline to center back. Do the same on the other side, at no time including the center front seam. For added security backstitch the neckline seam at this point instead of tying off. If you're careful, all the seams will meet exactly at the intersection.

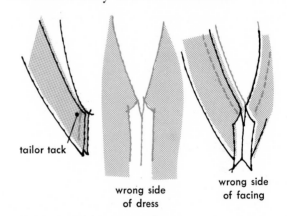

tailor tack

wrong side of dress

wrong side of facing

BIAS FACINGS MADE EASY

Bias facing is cut as described on page 104. It should be cut about 2″ wide. Turn back one end (wrong sides together) and lay it down at

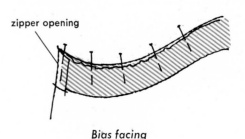

zipper opening

Bias facing

the zipper opening, right sides together with the neckline. Keep pushing the bias together so that it is full at the seam, but lying almost flat to the fabric at the outer edge. Pin crosswise along the seam about every inch. Turn other end back and cut off the excess material.

Trim, clip, and understitch the bias-faced neckline exactly as you did the other. Turn under the raw edge, and top-stitch or hand-stitch it in place. If you use a bias facing on an armhole, it should be done in exactly the same way, and the turned-under ends should meet at the underarm.

FITTED ARMHOLE FACINGS

Fitted armhole facings are not very different from fitted neckline facings. Most of them are made with only one seam, and that seam is usually at the underarm. Finish the outer edge of the facing before you pin it in place. See pages 98–100. Match the seams, match the notches, match the top tailor tack to the shoulder seam, and pin the facing right sides together with the armhole.

When the facing is stitched on, trim, clip, and understitch in that order, according to directions for facing the round neck.

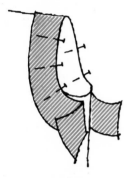

Facing armhole with bias strip

Ends folded to meet at underarm

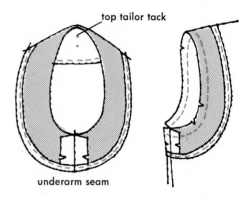

Fitted facing. At right: stitched in place around arm-hole

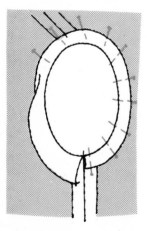
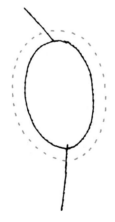

Bias armhole facing turned inside and pinned in place

Bias armhole facing after stitching

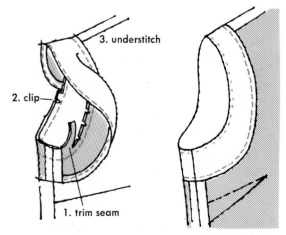

At right: Fitted facing turned to wrong side of garment and tacked in place

BASIC KINDS OF COLLARS

Collars for dresses fall into two categories: the shaped collar set in between the dress and the facing and the bias roll collar set on a garment without a facing. A shaped collar is made of three pieces—the top collar, the interfacing, and the undercollar which is sometimes called the collar facing.

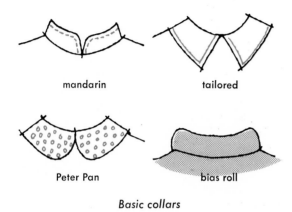

mandarin

tailored

Peter Pan

bias roll

Basic collars

The purpose of the interfacing is to hold the collar's shape and give it body. The stand-up kind and some of the other very stiff ones work very well with non-woven interfacings. The bias collars and those that·have to roll into the proper shape should have woven interfacings. On dresses and blouses all interfacings should be very lightweight. (See page 20.)

The interfacing is applied to the wrong side of the undercollar of any shaped collar such as a Peter Pan. Baste on the interfacing around the edge. Lay the top collar right sides together with the undercollar, pin the pieces together so that the undercollar is pulled very tight and the top collar is a little bit full. You may even see a bit of the undercollar edge sticking out from the top collar edge. This is done so that when the collar is turned, the top collar has a built-in tendency to roll over and completely conceal the undercollar.

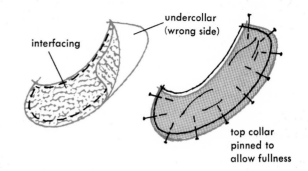

After stitching all collar pieces together trim or grade the collar edge, and notch out the convex curve to get rid of all bulk. Turn the collar right side out. You can get your fingers inside and hold the seam toward the undercollar so that you can understitch by hand. (See page 76.)

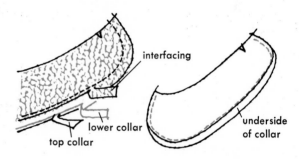

Understitching holds roll of top collar.

The Peter Pan or Pointed Collar

If the collar is separated at the front like a Peter Pan, tack it together at the center front mark, being sure that the ends match. Lay the collar underside down on the right side of the garment, matching all neckline markings, center front, center back, shoulders, notches, etc. Pin the collar in place along the seam line. Make the upper collar roll up and over by pushing the upper collar seam edge away from the neck slightly. Stitch around neck edge of collar and garment just inside the $\frac{5}{8}''$ allowance with a long machine stitch.

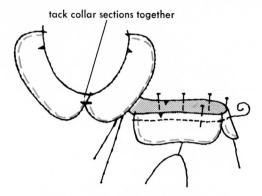

tack collar sections together

At right: *Collar in position for stitching*

Lay neckline facing right side down over collar, matching all marks again. Follow all the previous rules for facings. Stitch from the wrong side of the dress following the row of large stitches that hold the collar in place.

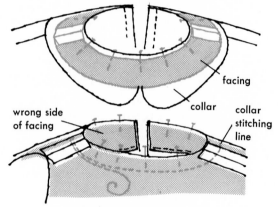

facing

collar   collar stitching line

wrong side of facing

Stitch from wrong side.

Trim all the layers of the collar out to ¼" in the neck seam. Trim the dress and facing seams to ⅜" or ½". Clip every half inch al-

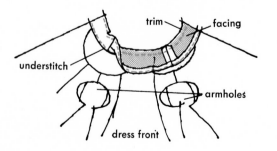

trim   facing

understitch

armholes

dress front

most to stitching, and clip out any seam corners that cause bulk. Turn and understitch. Tack the facing down at seams and anywhere that won't show through on the right side.

The Mandarin Collar

The same process is used for the mandarin or stand-up collar, except that it does not roll over. The object in putting it together is to get the outside piece to round over the inside piece that is next to your neck.

A mandarin or stand-up collar has an inside collar piece and an outside collar piece instead of a top collar and undercollar. Place the interfacing on the inside collar piece, and be sure to hold that piece tighter than the outside collar in assembling them. This collar is placed with the outside collar piece against the right side of the dress, stitched in place, and then the facing placed right side down over it. The final clipping and trimming are the same as in the shaped collar.

The Turtleneck Collar

Bias roll collars, or turtlenecks, require a woven interfacing. If a very thin interfacing is used, it is cut exactly like the collar and put in across the entire wrong side. If a medium to firm interfacing is used, cut it ⅝" deeper than half the width of the collar. In either case, baste it on to the wrong side of the collar

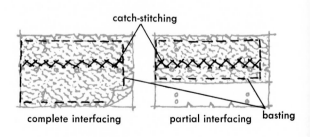

catch-stitching

complete interfacing   partial interfacing   basting

Bias roll collar

around the edges, then catch-stitch next to the fold line as shown.

With the collar still open flat, pin the collar edge nearest the row of catch-stitching right sides together with the garment neckline, matching all markings. Leave ⅝″ of collar beyond the zipper at each end. Stitch all around, being sure to start and finish exactly the same distance above the zipper teeth at each end, and then backstitch at each end. Trim and clip the seam.

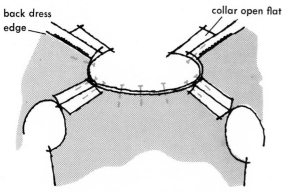

Bias roll collar in position for stitching

Fold the collar back on itself along the fold line, with right sides together. Pin the end seams along the ⅝″ line. Stitch from the fold to the end of the neckline seam, backstitch at each end. Trim or grade the seam, cut off and clip out any excess corner fabric.

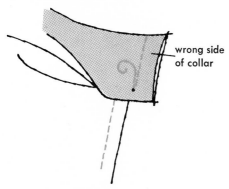

Trim after stitching.

Turn the collar right side out. Fold under ⅝″ along the raw edge inside the garment, and match center and shoulder markings. Pin to neckline seam. Blindstitch by hand.

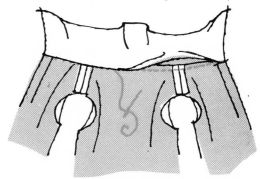

Blindstitch collar in place.

As you read the other sections of this book, you will find that the trick for roll collars works on skirt bands and band cuffs too. The trick is—*don't sew the seams at the ends first!*

For further suggestions on making collars, facings, necklines, and armholes thinner and more flexible when you are working in heavy fabrics, see "Success Tips" on page 113.

QUESTIONS OFTEN ASKED ABOUT FACINGS AND COLLARS

1. Why does my facing still roll out a little after I've understitched?

    You either did not clip first or did not clip deeply enough. Remember that the order in which you finish a facing is *trim, clip, understitch*. Be sure that you have clipped often enough and deeply enough.

2. How can I keep my undercollar from showing beyond the upper collar?

    Be sure that you put the upper collar onto the undercollar with a little extra fullness, so that the upper collar wants to roll over. And, understitch the collar edge seam by hand.

3. When I am pinning the facing onto the neck edge, I have a hard time matching all the markings because the facing seems to be too small and there is never a full ⅝″ left over at the zipper seam in the back. Did I cut the facing pieces wrong?

You probably stretched the neck a little in working on the dress. Make it ease back into the size of the facing. The pieces were cut to match, and part of the job of the facing is to hold the neckline to size.

Cuffs and Casings

There are two kinds of cuffs that are identical to collars, so we don't need to do more than identify them. One is the shaped cuff,

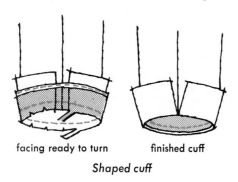

facing ready to turn   finished cuff

Shaped cuff

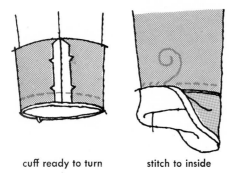

cuff ready to turn   stitch to inside

Bias roll cuff

which is put on the bottom of a sleeve with a facing, in exactly the way that a shaped collar is joined to a neckline. The other is a bias roll cuff, which is usually put on without a facing in the same manner as a bias roll collar. (See pages 80–81.)

SHIRT-TYPE CUFFS—THE EASY WAY

There are two kinds of cuffs used on long full sleeves (shirt or bishop sleeves) that appear to be the same. They are different only in that one is made in one part and folded, such as a plain buttoned cuff or a French cuff.

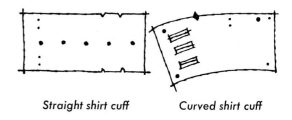

Straight shirt cuff   Curved shirt cuff

The other is made in two parts. If the cuff is more than 2″ high, it is shaped to fit the arm.

Either of these cuffs requires an opening in the sleeve just above the cuff, so that the hand will go through easily. There are several types of bindings and facings shown in guide sheets, but the simplest opening is a small hemmed space, inconspicuous and neat. This can be used above any cuff on a full sleeve, no matter what the pattern shows.

Run a staystitch along a 2″ space, on the ⅝″ seam line at the point marked for an opening (on a line with the elbow). Clip to the

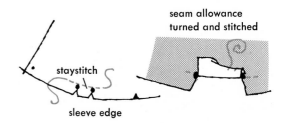

seam allowance turned and stitched

staystitch

sleeve edge

staystitch in two places about 1¼″ apart. Turn the seam allowance to the wrong side and turn under the edge to form a ¼″ hem. Hem with small whipping stitches, being sure to catch any loose threads at the raw ends. You are now ready to apply the cuff. Wasn't that a time-saver?

APPLYING A BUTTONED CUFF

Stitch the underarm sleeve seam and press it open flat. Gather the lower edge of the sleeve from one side of the opening to the other. Lay the cuff edge right sides together with the sleeve edge and pin all the marked points together. You will notice that the underlap extension of the cuff, or button end, is always at the end of the opening nearest the underarm seam.

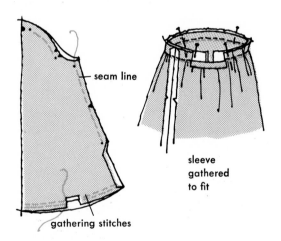

seam line

sleeve gathered to fit

gathering stitches

With the cuff still open flat, stitch the cuff to the sleeve, right sides together. Fold the cuff back at the fold line with its right sides together and stitch the ends. If you look back at the instructions for a bias roll collar on page 81, you will see that the folded cuff is attached in the same way. At the underlap end, stitch around the corner to the end of the opening, forming the underlap extension.

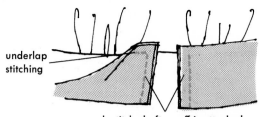

underlap stitching

ends stitched after cuff is attached

If the cuff is in two parts, sew the outer cuff, right sides together with the sleeve, matching markings. Then pin the inner cuff, right sides together with the outer cuff, and stitch around the three remaining sides.

Trim the seams and clip off the corners. Turn the cuff right side out. Turn the raw edge under ⅝″ over the gathering. Match all the markings and pin the free edge in place. Stitch down by hand, using a blindstitch.

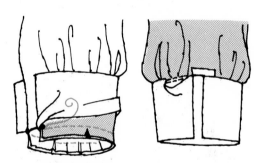

Turn cuff to right side.   Stitch edge in place.

CASING AND ELASTIC

A simple casing and elastic is often used instead of a cuff on both short puffed sleeves and long full ones. This is a quicker and more casual finish than the cuffs just described.

Usually this casing is no more than a ½″ wide hem, stitched in by machine around the bottom of the sleeve. Turn under ¼″ on the raw edge first, then turn the ½″ hem. Stitch very close to the upper edge of the hem, so that maximum space is left inside for the elastic to be drawn through. Leave an opening

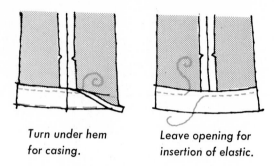

Turn under hem
for casing.

Leave opening for
insertion of elastic.

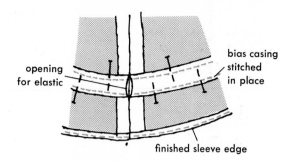

bias casing
stitched
in place

opening
for elastic

finished sleeve edge

of about ½″ between the beginning and the end of the row of stitching. Backstitch for security at each end.

Now cut ¼″ elastic 1″ longer than the arm measurement. Run it through the casing with a bodkin, bobby pin, or safety pin. Overlap the ends ½″ and tack them together by hand.

A RUFFLED EFFECT

There is another type of casing which creates the effect of a ruffle at the bottom of the sleeve.

The edge of the sleeve is hemmed narrowly by hand or machine. If there are not already tailor tack markings for the casing, make chalk marks on the wrong side of the sleeve, 1″ or however far you wish above the finished edge. Cut a bias strip of lining fabric, 1¾″ wide. Use a ¾″ wide strip of shirt cardboard as a pressing guide. Fold the edges of the bias over the guide and press.

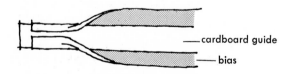

cardboard guide

bias

Pin the bias along the marking *wrong sides together with the sleeve.* Pin in place along both edges. Turn each end under ½″, cutting off any excess bias. Machine-stitch around

very close to each edge, crossing over the turned under ends to hold them securely. Run the elastic through from the opening at these ends. This is a standard casing used in waistlines of full dresses, sometimes wider than described here, but done in the same way.

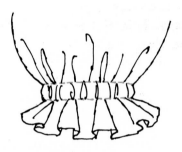

Ruffled effect created by elastic above sleeve edge.

QUESTIONS OFTEN ASKED ABOUT CUFFS AND CASINGS

1. My pattern shows a rather long and elaborate sleeve opening above the cuff. Will the one described here allow me enough room to get my hand in?

The 1¼″ clipped and hemmed opening will allow adequate hand room above a cuff which has been fitted comfortably to the wrist.

2. My pattern shows a bias facing at the edge of a sleeve that has an elastic. Can I make the hemmed casing?

Use the hemmed casing if you are working in any light to medium dress-weight fabric. On a very heavy fabric a bias facing of lining fabric (page 20), might be better. It will also work better around a neck curve for a drawstring neck.

Painless Set-in Sleeves

Set-in sleeves fall into two categories, one slightly easier than the other. The ones used most frequently on adult clothes are those that are smoothly rounded on top. They require more care because there is some fullness in the cap that should not show in the finished garment. This fullness has to be eased with great skill. The puffed or gathered type used on children's clothes and on blouses and some dressy adult clothes are a little easier to set into the armhole since the fullness is meant to show.

Here is an easy system for setting in sleeves plus a few tricks to outwit the problems.

MARKINGS COME FIRST

First of all, be sure that you put in the shoulder marking and both sets of notches on the sleeve itself. Actually, the other markings

around the seam line are not necessary, because the ease or gather will fall in place naturally between the shoulder marking and the notches.

If a pattern has both a sleeved and a sleeveless version, there will probably be extra sets of markings at the underarm of bodice front and back. These are the seam-line markings for the set-in sleeve so that the armhole is a bit lower than in the sleeveless version. Measure and draw a cutting line ⅝" above the markings. Then trim away excess fabric.

EASE IN FULLNESS

For the smooth rounded set-in sleeve, run an ease thread around the cap of the sleeve, from notch to notch, on the ⅝" line, or as indicated. See page 38 for detailed information on ease. Notice that the grain of the fabric is straight for about 1" across the top of the sleeve, but bias along the sides between that point and the notches. Some patterns suggest breaking off the ease thread in the straight area. However, this makes too many loose ends to cope with. Just be careful not

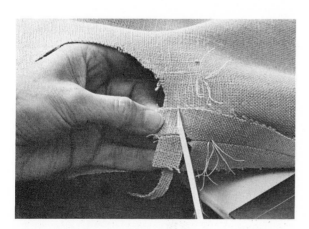

A set-in sleeve requires a lower armhole than a sleeveless garment. Remember to trim away excess fabric before basting.

Run an ease thread around the cap of the sleeve along the seam line, from notch to notch.

to pull up ease in the straight area. If the easing is done primarily in the bias area, there will be less chance of wrinkles forming.

THE FOUR-POINT SECRET OF SLEEVE PINNING

Sew the shoulder and underarm seams of the bodice and the underarm seam of the sleeve and press them all open flat. Hold the sleeve right side out and turn the bodice over it so that the right sides are together. Pin the sleeve to the bodice at the *four important points, shoulder, underarm, and both sets of notches.* Turn the sleeve out over your fingertips between the shoulder and one set of notches. Pull the ease thread gently till the sleeve feels tight over the bodice armhole. *Do not ease too much!* Put in a few more pins across the ease line, distributing fullness evenly. Repeat between the shoulder and the other notches. Add a few more pins at the underarm.

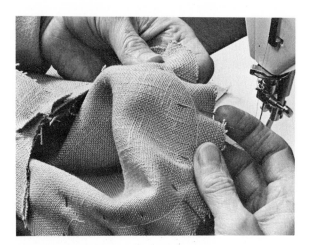

Turn the sleeve over your fingertips to pin it smoothly to the bodice.

STITCHING TIME

Starting at the underarm, and working inside the sleeve, stitch around carefully, maintaining a ⅝″ seam all the way. Be sure the needle is down in the fabric every time you readjust the position of the seam as you will have to do around such a pronounced curve. The stitching outside the ease thread will conceal the ease thread in the seam. If ease thread does show on the outside of the sleeve, it can be removed when you have finished the stitching. As you stitch, keep the fabric pulled tight from side to side across the row of stitching to prevent little puckers forming ahead of the needle.

CHECK FOR FIT

Set in both sleeves and try on the garment for a final check on fitting. Stitch around again ⅛″ inside of the first row of stitching (½″ from raw edge). Trim off not more than ¼″ of seam all the way around, *evenly.* No further trimming or clipping will be necessary.

PRESS FROM INSIDE ONLY

Steam-press with the point of the iron, continuing to work from inside the sleeve as you did while stitching. *Do not press outside!* (See page 68.)

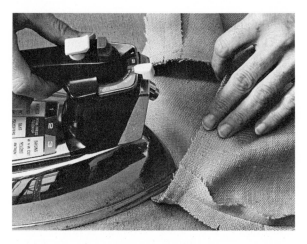

Steam-press sleeve seam, working with the point of the iron and pressing from the inside only.

GATHERED OR PUFFED SLEEVES

Gathered or puffed sleeves are pinned and stitched in exactly the same way that smooth ones are. The only difference is that there are two rows of stitching for gathers instead of one for ease. You should have no trouble at all in distributing the gathers to fit the armhole area. There will be no problem with the straight grain space at the top. You just gather right through it. As a matter of fact, gathered sleeves are so easy that you may have a whole wardrobe full of them!

Run a double row of gathering stitches for a puffed sleeve and stitch between the gathering stitches.

QUESTIONS OFTEN ASKED ABOUT SET-IN SLEEVES

1. If my dress has a panel side and no true underarm seam, what is the matching point at the underarm?

In a panel side, there is no underarm seam on the dress, but there are very clear markings which you may have missed. There are some other variations like this, notably yoked shoulders.

2. Why does the armhole on a knit dress with set-in sleeves sometimes feel tight and look bunchy?

Knit eases better than any other fabric! It eases so well that you probably pulled too much, and then actually eased the armhole to fit the sleeves, making them both too tight! It might be better to work without any ease thread on very soft fabrics.

Kimono Sleeves and Gussets

A kimono sleeve is cut all in one with the dress. It has a high underarm curve, which pulls and wears easily, and therefore should be reinforced. If no gusset is used, a piece of stay-tape, as described on page 118, placed along the underarm curve when you stitch, gives the seam the strength it needs. Clip the curve of the seam several times, but do not clip the tape.

A gusset makes moving easier and fit more trim and precise. Try to avoid choosing a pattern with a gusset because it takes practice and patience to learn how to insert one properly. If you find that you are faced with this problem, however, read carefully through the following instructions before you begin.

There are many kinds of gussets but basically the construction is the same. Slashes are made in the underarm area and a piece of fabric, cut to shape, is set in. A slash creates not only a weak point in the fabric, but also a precise point in stitching. *Reinforcement becomes a necessity.* The trick here is knowing how to turn a corner in a seam. (See page 64.)

There are usually four slashes, marked on the pattern with staystitch and slash lines. Staystitching alone is not enough, so it is wise to use some thin firm lining material. Cut a bias

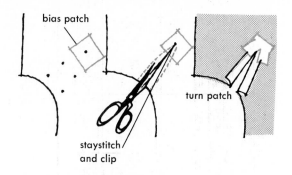

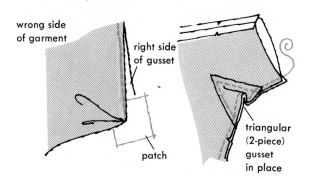

strip of the lining, about 2″ x 8″, then cut it up into four squares. On the right side of fabric, lay one square at the end of each slash mark, so that at least ½″ of the square is beyond the point. Pin squares in place *on the right side of the dress*. Staystitch on the marked lines, taking one stitch across at the point, to make room to slash between the lines of stitching. Slash with sharp scissors, *all the way to the point*. Fold the lining square to the inside and press gently. Be sure you've pulled the lining back far enough so that a tiny edge of the fabric begins to show. Now, you are ready for any kind of gusset!

TWO-PIECE GUSSET

The two-piece gusset is the easiest of all, and therefore most apt to be used in a simple dress. One triangular gusset piece is set in the front of the dress and one in the back, before the side seams are joined. Remember in turning the corner that the *needle must be down in the fabric when you lift the foot*. Stitch very close to the staystitching, but be sure that the staystitching will be hidden in the seam. At the point you will not need to take a stitch across; you will be able to pivot around it. Hold the edge of the lining patch firmly in your right hand so that you can be sure it won't fold back. It acts as a sort of seam allow-

ance at the narrow end of the slash. All you have to do to complete this gusset is to stitch the side seams.

ONE-PIECE GUSSET

The diamond or one-piece gusset is much like the two-piece one except that you will be working in a far more confined area. The side seams and underarm sleeve seams will have been stitched, *exactly to the designated marks*. It is very important to tie off or backstitch the ends of the seams. Now, if you made your tailor tacks in several colors to show the different corners (see page 34), it will be easy to drop the diamond-shaped gusset right into place. Don't even try to get the whole gusset pinned in place at once; work along one slash at a time. Start at the backstitched end of the side seam or underarm seam and complete the stitching of half the diamond along the two

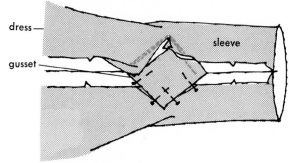

Diamond shape gusset pinned and partially stitched

sides of the slash, ending at the other back-stitching. It is wise to backstitch or tie off both ends of the seam you have just made also.

Now stitch the other half of the diamond into the other slash. The trick is never to try to cross any seams, underarm or side, as you stitch in the diamond; stop and start again, skipping over the seams.

QUESTIONS OFTEN ASKED ABOUT GUSSETS

1. Why don't my seam edges in the gusset come out even?

Work with the slash side uppermost on the machine! Pin together the seam lines, don't worry about the edges meeting. The seam on the gusset is a true ⅝", but the one on the slash decreases in size as you stitch toward the point.

2. On a soft material, how can I further reinforce the gusset?

The seam is pressed toward the garment, away from the gusset. You may top-stitch through all thickness, about ⅛" from the seam.

Smoothly Fitted Skirts and Bands

It has been said that the difference between a cheap and an expensive skirt (aside from the fabric) is in the shaping of the darts and the waistband. Who could know better how to shape a skirt to your needs than you? Go back to page 61 and see how hip darts are curved. Keep working till you can shape darts exactly to your figure. A little measuring, a little basting will do it.

TO LINE OR NOT TO LINE

To hold the shape of a skirt a full or partial underlining may be used. A partial lining ex-

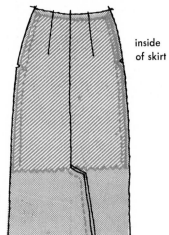

inside
of skirt

Partial lining
for skirt back

tends, just across the seat area, about ¾ of the way down the back. Or you may use a loose lining, hung in just before the band goes on. You can choose which is best by considering the shape of the skirt and the weight and texture of the fabric.

A gathered skirt probably will not need a lining. An all-around pleated skirt should be made of the kind of hard crisp fabric that will not require a lining. A narrow skirt, especially one made of a soft fabric, should always be underlined, at least in the seat. Skirts made of knit fabrics rarely need lining. They spring back to shape after each wearing.

A LOOSE LINING

A loose lining is cut exactly like the skirt, but a couple of inches shorter. Make alterations exactly as you made them in the skirt. Remember that the lining is worn with the right side toward the body. Leave an opening for the zipper in the lining to correspond to the placement of the zipper in the skirt.

After the zipper is in the skirt, hang the lining wrong sides together with the skirt, just

*Full lining
for skirt*

folding in the edges of the zipper opening in the lining. They can be hand tacked along the zipper later. Pin the skirt and lining together around the top edge. Now you can stitch in a gather or ease thread as needed before you attach the band.

FOR PERFECT FIT

Put the skirt on now for its most important fitting with proper shoes and undergarment. At this point it should hang easily on the hips so that the raw edge at the top rests a little above the waist. Stand in front of a mirror, tie a string or narrow tape around your waist over the skirt. Adjust the skirt so that it hangs well, side seams are straight, there is no sag under the seat. You may find that your waist dips down slightly in the back, a common cause of baggy-looking skirts. Pull the back of the skirt up a

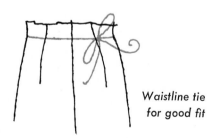

*Waistline tie
for good fit*

bit under the tape. One hip may be a fraction higher than the other. Pull the skirt up on the side with the lower hip. When you have adjusted the skirt all around, mark along the tape with chalk or pins. (Yes, you can do it without being double-jointed.)

Run an ease thread around the skirt on this marked line. Trim the seam above the line to an even ⅝″. This is now your very own marked waistline which insures straight side seams, a no-sag seat, and an even hemline.

FOLDED WAISTBAND

This is the band most often used both in skirt patterns and in the skirts you buy. It is made of one piece of fabric folded over a stiff interfacing, preferably belting, before it is attached to the skirt. It is most suitable for light- to medium-weight fabrics.

Try cutting the band by measurement following the fabric grain rather than by pattern. You will find it easier to adjust to your exact waist size.

The easiest interfacing to use is a ribbon belting, or grosgrain ribbon which you have pre-shrunk. Cut it 2″ longer than your waist measurement. Cut the fabric twice as wide as the belting, plus two seam allowances, and 3″ longer than your waist measurement. The band may be either cross or length grain, depending on which way the fabric will look better.

Draw a long chalk line on the wrong side of the fabric band, directly along the fold line or center of the strip. Lay the ribbon belting on the wrong side of the fabric, one edge touching the chalk line, ½″ of fabric extending at each end. Machine-stitch along the selvage edges of the belting. This is now the stiffened side of the belt.

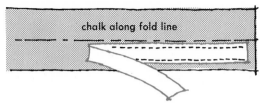

Ribbon belting used as stiffening

Press the band wrong sides together along the fold line. The two rows of stitching that show on the fabric will be toward your body when the band is on the skirt. Mark a seam line with chalk on the wrong side of the unstiffened half of the belt. This can be done most accurately by folding back the seam line of the stiffened side and marking along the edge of the belting on the unstiffened side.

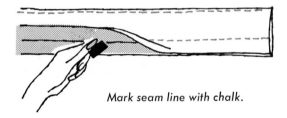

Mark seam line with chalk.

Put the band around your waist over a slip, or blouse if you intend to wear one tucked into the skirt. The end of the band that will eventually line up with the zipper opening is called the overlap end. Mark the point at which the ½″ seam allowance at this end touches the band when it is comfortably adjusted around your waist. The portion of the band beyond that point is called the underlap extension. Make a chalk line where it meets overlap mark.

Lay the band right sides together along the upper edge of the skirt with the underlap marking at one side of the zipper and the overlap marking at the other. Pin all around, joining the chalk line on the unstiffened side of the band to the marked seam line on the skirt,

pulling up the ease thread to adjust the top of the skirt to the band if necessary. Remember, *fit the band to you and fit the skirt to the band!*

Stitch along the marked seam line, backstitching at each end. Be sure that the band is exactly the same distance above the zipper at each side. Since the top of the skirt is curved, clip the skirt seam all around. Trim the seam allowance of the band in half, turn the band up from the skirt and press the seam upward. At the ends fold the band right sides together on the fold line and stitch the seams, straight down the overlap end and around the corner of the underlap end, exactly as you did on the long sleeve cuff. Clip off the corner, trim the seams, and turn the ends right side out. Turn under the free edge of the band and blindstitch it to the seam just above the stitching.

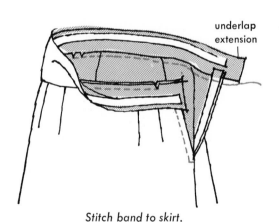

Stitch band to skirt.

underlap extension

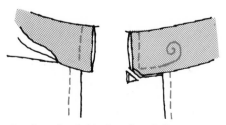

Stitch ends of skirt band and clip corner.

THE GREAT NO-BAND FINISH

Even though the pattern may call for a waistband, you don't have to put one on. Instead, you may try the smoother, sleeker no-band waistline. This is easier and often fits better.

Cut a bias piece of lining fabric, 3″ wide and 3″ or 4″ longer than your waist measurement.

Piece it if necessary. (See page 104.) Fold the strip in half lengthwise, wrong sides together. Turn in one end about ¼″ and press. Trim the skirt at the top to a ⅜″ seam instead of ⅝″ above your marked waistline. At one side of the zipper opening pin the folded end of the bias on the right side of the skirt, with the raw edges together. Continue to pin around the waist, easing the bias a little all the way. In this way you can keep the bias lying flat along the curve of the skirt, not curling up or pulling at the lower edge. You will probably use up most of the extra 3″ or 4″ length of bias that you started with. Turn in another ¼″ at the other zipper edge.

Cut a piece of narrow twill tape or linen tailor's tape to your exact waist size. Lay it over the bias along the ⅜″ seam line. The skirt and bias will ease to fit the tape. Stitch the seam through tape, bias, and skirt for a firm,

non-stretch seam at the waist.

Clip the seam slightly as you would any curved seam. Press the bias upward to cover the seam. Understitch ⅛″ from the seam line, through the bias and the seam, not through the outside. Turn the bias strip down inside the skirt and tack the folded edge at seams and darts.

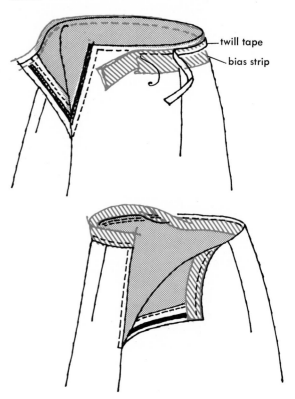

— twill tape

— bias strip

Turn bias to inside and tack in place.

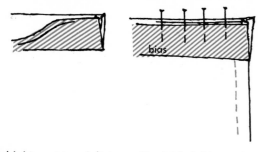

Fold bias strip of lining fabric.   *Pin folded bias strip to right side of skirt.*

QUESTIONS OFTEN ASKED ABOUT SKIRTS AND BANDS

1. Why do my skirts seem to stretch out of shape no matter how carefully I underline them?

The problem occurs if the skirt is not pulled up sufficiently at the waist in the back when band is being fitted to skirt.

2. I like folded bands on skirts because I wear

tuck-in shirts; is there any way to make them thinner?

Look in the "Sew a Little Lighter" section (page 113) and you will find a thinner version of the folded band.

3. Are the band and no-band finishes any different on a skirt with a back opening than on a skirt with a side opening?

The no-band finish is identical for both openings. The band overlaps from front to back on a side opening and from right to left on a back opening.

FINISHING DETAILS

Now take a moment to admire your work! It is assembled, collared, sleeved, zippered, and pressed. Now you have only the final details to complete—the worked buttonholes, the hems, trims, and hand stitching. Allow plenty of time for these final steps—this is where careful workmanship really shows, making the difference between a homemade look and a custom look. Extra care at this last stage will pay off in extra satisfaction every time you wear your new creation.

Worked Buttonholes by Hand and by Machine

A worked buttonhole differs from a bound buttonhole in that it is edged all around with fine, tight stitching instead of fabric. The stitching may be done either by hand or by machine. Worked buttonholes are more common and lots easier than bound ones, and are used on skirts, blouses, sportswear, and children's clothes.

While a bound buttonhole is done very early in the construction of the garment, a worked one cannot be done until the collar and facing or the skirt waistband are in place, and the garment nearly finished.

YOUR TALENTED SEWING MACHINE

If you're the lucky girl who owns a new sewing machine with the automatic built-in buttonholer, then run—don't walk—to get out your instruction book and learn how to work it. With these new machines, it takes no time at all to became a buttonhole expert.

Of course, any zigzag machine will make worked buttonholes, but you must do a bit more of the planning and guiding than with a built-in buttonholer. A buttonhole attachment for a straight-stitch machine works very well, too.

MARK AND MEASURE

Go back to page 45 and read again the instructions about lining up buttonholes. Remember that accuracy is just as important for worked buttonholes as for bound ones. The safest markings are still with chalk or basting threads. The grain line is important in any buttonhole, and a well-matched thread color makes for a more professional look. On some very fine fabrics, a silk thread makes a prettier buttonhole. Buttonhole Twist, in spite of its name, is unsuitable for machine-worked buttonholes.

MAKE A SAMPLE

As always, the best test is to try out different techniques on a sample piece. Use the same number of layers of fabric that you will be using in the actual garment. Try the stitches at different settings for width and length, and with different shades of thread, or with silk thread. Try going around twice if you think the wear and tear on the buttonhole will be great. The machine instructions suggest a way of cording the buttonholes by letting a piece of very fine cord run through under the foot, so that the stitching goes back and forth over it. This is very attractive; try it, using Buttonhole Twist as the cord.

A HAND-WORKED BUTTONHOLE

To make a hand-worked buttonhole, you need only the instructions for the buttonhole stitch on page 102, some patience, and some practice. It also helps to stitch a small rectangle

94

around the buttonhole area. Use small machine stitches, about fifteen to the inch. Split down

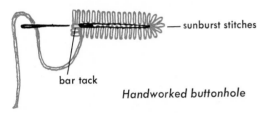

Stitch around buttonhole.

the middle of the rectangle with very sharp scissors.

Using a sample of your fabric, test several threads—cotton, silk, or synthetic, single or double, or Buttonhole Twist single. Using the buttonhole stitch (page 102), start at the end of the buttonhole nearest the edge of the garment. Make a sunburst of stitches at the other end, and finish with a strong bar tack (several

— sunburst stitches

bar tack

Handworked buttonhole

buttonhole stitches in a row) across the end where you started. The stitches must be deep enough to cover the row of machine stitches. Work evenly and keep the thread pulled up firmly. If you're a girl of the machine age, you may go back to perfecting your machine technique with buttonholes.

QUESTIONS OFTEN ASKED ABOUT WORKED BUTTONHOLES

1. When I work by hand, my stitches never look as close as machine-worked buttonholes.
    They're not meant to! The aim is to get them even rather than close.
2. When making a machine-worked buttonhole on a knit or stretchy fabric, how can I prevent the buttonhole from looking ripply and uneven?

A firm interfacing, no matter how thin, is necessary inside any knit or soft fabric.

A Pretty Hemline

You have sewed all the seams, and pressed carefully as you've gone along, and now it's time to put in your hem. Most hems require three steps: marking for length, finishing at the edge, and hemming, usually by hand.

There are really two basic kinds of hems, straight and curved. The straight are easier at every step! Besides very slim "straight" skirts the straight hem skirts include dirndls and pleated-all-around ones. All leave an almost straight grain line around the bottom.

MAKE YOUR MARK

Marking may be almost unnecessary on straight skirts, especially if you have adjusted the pattern and fitted the dress so that it hangs well on you. You may be able to turn up an even number of inches all around and not call on your neighbor to come running with the pins.

Flared skirts, half-circle skirts, and circle skirts all have a definite curve at the bottom, and must be marked hanging on you. A marker which blows chalk is fine, provided you turn the hem up before the chalk rubs off. You can use this type with reasonable success on yourself. A yardstick and pins may be used, but the pin markers are the very best. The skirt is held tightly in a clamp while the pin is inserted, so there is less margin for error. This is especially important if the dress is underlined. Only when pinning is done in this way can you be absolutely sure that the lining and the dress are hanging evenly and not pull-

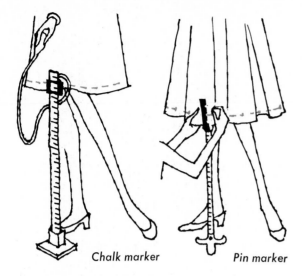

Chalk marker   Pin marker

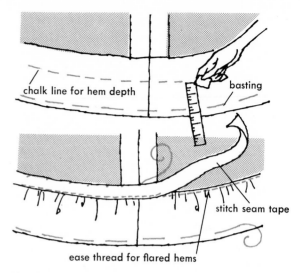

chalk line for hem depth   basting

stitch seam tape

ease thread for flared hems

ing against each other. Be sure you are wearing the right shoes and undergarments when the marking is done.

TURN AND BASTE

After the skirt is marked, turn it up and baste it about ½″ above the folded edge. This leaves the rest of the hem free so that you can finish the edge.

Decide now how deep a hem you want. Straight skirts can be turned up to almost any depth but it is unwise to make the hem more than 3″ if you are using a heavy fabric. Sheers are often turned as much as 6″. A slightly flared skirt can have about 2½″ of hem. The more flared the skirt, the narrower the hem should be. A circle skirt can have little more than a 1″ hem.

With a ruler and chalk mark the hem depth all around. If the skirt is flared, run a machine ease thread (see page 38) around just below the chalk line. It is wise not to try to ease the whole skirt on one thread, so stop and start over again at intervals of slightly less than a yard. Lay the hem against the skirt and pull the thread gradually until the hem edge fits

the part of the skirt it is lying against. *Never get it too tight!* You may trim the fabric off ¼″ above the ease thread, or you may apply the finish first and then trim off the excess fabric.

CHOICE OF FINISHES

There are a number of ways to finish the raw edge of a hem, but they break down into two basic categories: the stitched finish, in which some form of stitching alone keeps the raw edge neat; and the fabric finish, in which the raw edge is covered by some kind of ribbon or fabric. The hem finish is usually applied after the hem is turned and basted.

The following list will help you decide which finish to select. (For detailed instructions see "Hem, Seam, and Facing Finishes," page 98.)

Pinking alone is a satisfactory finish for most polyester knits, sturdy non-ravelly cottons, felt, vinyl, bondeds, some heavy coatings.

A stitched and pinked finish is used on closely woven fabrics, and on knits with little tendency to fray. Zigzag stitching is also good for knits.

Stitching and overcasting provides a good

finish for coarse, ravelly weaves. Overcasting may be done by hand or machine.

The turned and stitched finish is used on lightweight and sheer fabrics.

Seam binding is flat ribbon tape used to secure the raw edges of fabrics that are loosely woven, or that tend to ravel. This finish is most successful for straight hems. For eased or circular hems, use bias seam binding or seam lace.

Seam lace may be substituted for seam binding as a finish for fabrics that ravel. It is decorative as well as useful.

Bound finish is used on fabrics with a pronounced tendency to ravel. This can be done with either a ready-made bias binding or with a bias strip made of the dress fabric or lining.

STITCHING TECHNIQUES FOR HEMS

After you have applied the most appropriate finish to your hem, you may then secure it with a slipstitch or whipping stitch (page 101) being sure to keep the stitches about ½″ apart, and catching only a thread or two of the outer fabric with each stitch. Never pull too tightly and be sure that the effect is even.

If you want to make a very strong hem for a child's skirt, throw the thread so that the needle comes up through a loop at each stitch. This is almost a blanket stitch, and locks each time you pull up the thread. On heavy fabrics and knits, you can make a French or tailor's hem. The edge can have the bias finish or be zigzagged or staystitched and pinked. (See page 98.) Then fold the edge of the hem back ¼″ and slipstitch loosely to the garment. The edge is not held down hard to the fabric, and does not create as much ridge on the outside as it would if a very heavy fabric were hemmed by one of the other methods.

The French or tailor's hem is also good for heavy knits, especially with the edge pinked or zigzagged. It is better to finish the edge without tape because the knit needs to be allowed freedom to stretch. Knits can be hemmed with a catch-stitch also for more "give."

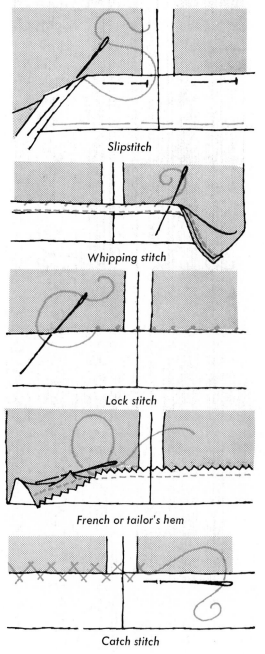

Slipstitch

Whipping stitch

Lock stitch

French or tailor's hem

Catch stitch

Hem, Seam, and Facing Finishes

The nice finishes you see inside of clothes are a matter of choice. It is not necessary to slave over every seam in a cotton dress for a three-year-old, but the brocade that you're wearing to a very formal party might feel better to you if you knew that the inside was beautifully trimmed and finished. There are other garments, too, such as unlined vests and jackets, that must be properly finished along every raw edge.

The same finishes are applicable for seams, hems, and facings. Certain ones are better for certain fabrics, and some work better along curved edges. So, again, you must sort out the possibilities and make up your own mind.

STAYSTITCHING AND PINKING

Staystitching is the simplest of all finishes. It can be used in combination with pinking or overcasting by hand. Very fine fabrics and some knits look finished and neat if they are staystitched and pinked, or, in some cases, just pinked. Pinking alone is a finish which is used more for seams and facings than for hems. For knits, pinking alone is preferable even on hems. Staystitch with overcast is used on coarse weaves like linen which ravel easily.

OVERCASTING

Modern machines have done away with the necessity for hand overcasting almost entirely. Zigzag stitching, set at its widest, will keep even the coarsest fabric from fraying. If you plan to use this finish, it is wise to cut a $\frac{1}{8}''$ extra allowance on all seams to be zigzagged. This makes it possible to stitch a fraction from the raw edge and then trim off the excess fabric, leaving the smoothest possible edge. Some machines even have very fancy decorative stitches which are suggested for finishing edges, and some have a factory-type overlock stitch for knits.

TURNED AND STITCHED

The finish most often called for in pattern guide sheets, especially for facing edges, is the turned and stitched edge. It is a very good finish for both facings and seams, but not on heavy fabrics. It is apt to cause a ridge which will press through to the outside. It is especially good on the fairly straight side seams and long sleeve seams of blouses, but will not work around the deep curve of an armhole. It is fine on facings in the lighter fabrics.

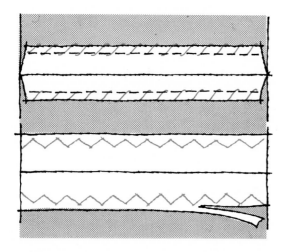

Top. *Staystitch with overcast*   Bottom. *Zigzag stitching*

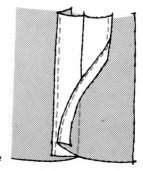

Turned and stitched edge

If the turned and stitched edge is to be used on seams, the seam should be stitched first, trimmed to an even width if necessary, and pressed open flat. Turn the seam edge under about ¼″ toward the garment, and stitch as close to the turned edge as possible. The edge must not turn deeply enough to prevent the seam from pressing flat. If you have trouble making the fabric turn under around the curve of a facing, *do not* resort to pinning, pressing, or basting. Run a row of machine staystitching around first at the edge of the fold, about ¼″ from the edge. The fabric can then be folded with the fingers on the staystitch line as you stitch.

Turned and stitched on a curve

FLAT-FINISHED EDGES

Straight seam binding (which is ·really a rayon hem tape) works best as a finish for hems. It is made like ribbon with two selvages, and is rather stiff and unyielding if you try to fold it over an edge. On hems it is simply applied flat. Lay it over the raw edge of the fabric at a depth of at least ¼″ and stitch it

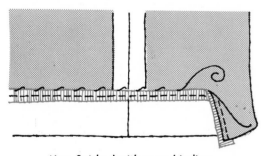

Hem finished with seam binding

very close to its selvage. Be sure never to pull it while stitching, as it may get too tight for the skirt and cause puckering around the outside.

Seam lace is an attractive alternative to seam binding. It comes in many colors, is only a little more expensive than binding, and gives a professional appearance. It is handled exactly like the binding, just laid flat over the edge and stitched, but it is much easier to work with. It is more flexible than seam binding and therefore can even be used on seams and around facings. On curved facings it must be eased on, which takes a little practice.

Straight and curved edges finished with seam lace

BOUND FINISHES

The pièce de resistance of all inside finishes is the Hong Kong or designer's edge—a bound edge made with lining fabric cut on the bias. You need only to be skilled enough to stitch fairly straight to make this type of binding look like the most expensive custom touch. It is the perfect seam and facing finish on a jacket, where your work is apt to be on public display. It works well on hems that are to be handled in the French or tailor's method described on page 97.

Bias binding makes a neat finish for skirt seams and hems when you are working with a fabric which tends to ravel, like brocade. One great feature of this type of binding is that it can be cut from the same fabric used to line the garment, so that everything matches perfectly.

Here's how to do it. Cut thin lining fabric into bias strips at least 1¼" wide and piece together as much as you need (see page 104). Lay a strip right sides together along the edge of the seam which has been stitched and pressed open, and trimmed if necessary. Stitch a scant ¼" seam, joining bias strip to seam allowance. Fold the strip firmly over the edge of the seam allowance so that the raw edge of the bias is now under the seam allowance. It may help to press it gently at this point.

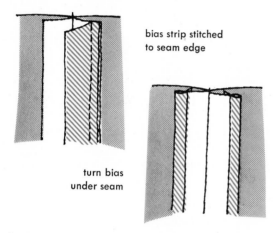

bias strip stitched
to seam edge

turn bias
under seam

This kind of bias binding made out of lining fabric is used in the Hong Kong or designer's finish.

Pin before stitching. Then stitch through the seam allowance and the under layer of bias close to the seamed edge of the binding. This method of stitching is called the "stitch-in-the-ditch" method. No stitching will show on the surface side of the binding, but there will be a line of stitches next to it in the fabric of the seam allowance giving a smoothly finished appearance. The under, raw edge, can be trimmed to within ⅛" of the stitching line without fear of fraying because bias fabric does not

ravel. The side of the binding next to the dress lies very flat and smooth.

If you want to save time, you can buy ready-made bias seam tape. Simply fold it over the raw edge of the seam and stitch down both folded edges of the tape at once.

This group of finishes should cover any needs that you may ever have. The only trick from here on is to decide by the weight and weave of your fabric, and perhaps a test sample, which one to use.

QUESTIONS OFTEN ASKED ABOUT SEAM AND FACING FINISHES

1. When I zigzagged the seam edges why did they stretch and look messy?

You should have cut extra width on all seams so that you could work in a fraction from the raw edge. Perhaps the line was bias, which really requires no finish, and which certainly does stretch when zigzagged!

2. Why does the lace around my facing edge pull and make the facing curl up?

The lace should have been eased on more along the edge that was stitched to the facing. Many laces have a built-in ease or gathering thread in the straight edge.

A Variety of Hand Stitches

There are a number of useful hand stitches, most of which can serve several purposes. Don't worry about which one is correct—just use the stitch that does the job and looks nice. Here are the most basic ones.

The running stitch is an in-and-out, in-and-out stitch used to join seams. Make it very small for permanent use or very large for basting.

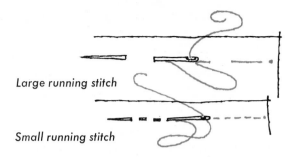

Large running stitch

Small running stitch

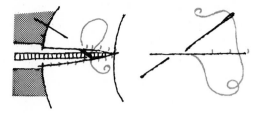

Blindstitch on a facing

Blindstitch on an outside finished edge

The slipstitch is a running stitch worked between two folds of fabric, picking up only a little fabric on each piece. It is sometimes used in hemming and basting.

Slipstitch

The backstitch is as sturdy as machine stitching. Bring the needle up through the fabric, take a stitch backward, then run under the fabric for the length of two stitches, up again, back one stitch to the last stitch, under for the length of two stitches, up and back, etc. If you wish to use this stitch decoratively, as for setting in a zipper by hand, bring the needle back only a very short distance on top, then under for about ¼″, up and back a short distance, so that the effect on top is just a tiny "picking" in the fabric.

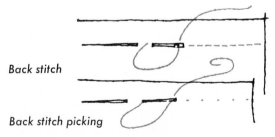

Back stitch

Back stitch picking

The blindstitch is also strong, and almost invisible on the top side. It must be worked in places where the underside will not be seen,

and where it holds a finished edge down to another layer. Use it to hold trims and pockets onto the outside of garments when you don't want to use top-stitching, or to hold down the edges of linings, or facings along zippers. Bring the needle up through the edge, just over, and in again directly above where it came up. Run under the fabric about ¼″, up and over again.

The whipping stitch is for hemming, and a variation of it is used for overcasting raw edges. It is especially desirable on garments that are given hard wear such as children's clothing or sportswear. The motion with the needle is in, up, and over. For a hem catch only the tiniest bit of the outer fabric, up through the

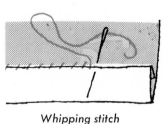

Whipping stitch used on hem

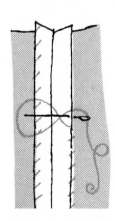

Whipping stitch used on seam edge

hem, over, and carry the thread for about ¼″ to ½″, then in, up through, and over. The only trick is to keep the spacing even.

The catch-stitch is flexible, therefore perfect in bias areas and on knits. It can be used for hems and for many other things, especially in tailoring. Take a stitch to the left, move the needle up and over to the right, take another stitch to the left, move the needle down and over to the right, etc., forming a crisscross effect.

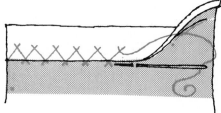

Catch stitch

The buttonhole stitch is done over an edge, and must be even, close, and precise. Put the needle in vertically to the edge, with the thread thrown all the way around the needle. This forms a tightly knotted stitch, called a purl, on the exact edge. For uses see section on worked buttonholes, pages 94–95.

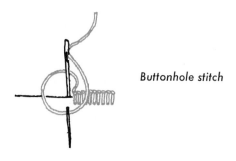

Buttonhole stitch

The blanket stitch is very much like the buttonhole stitch, except that the thread only passes once under the needle. Work vertically to the edge and hold the thread with the left

thumb, so that the needle comes out over it. For use in dressmaking see section on fastenings, page 107.

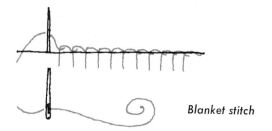

Blanket stitch

Belts for Everyone

The belt that you need to make most often is a slightly stiffened one with a buckle fastening.

THE BACKED BELT

To make one easy belt, use ribbed belting or grosgrain ribbon if you cannot find belting of the correct color and width. To make sure it is pre-shrunk before using it, actually dip it in water. Cut the belting 6″ or 8″ longer than your waist. Cut a point at one end. Cut a strip of fabric on the straight grain, two ⅝″ seam allowances longer than the belting, and twice as wide as the belting plus two ⅝″ seam allowances. Overlap the belting one seam allowance on the wrong side of the fabric. Stitch very close to the edge of the belting. Fold belting down on wrong side of fabric.

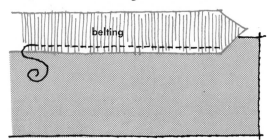

belting

Fold the fabric back, right sides together, so that fold of fabric and edge of belting meet. Pin belting to double layer of fabric at pointed end and at straight end. Stitch fabric close to point of belting (as shown) and close to edge of straight end of belting. Trim seams and clip out points of fabric to avoid bulk.

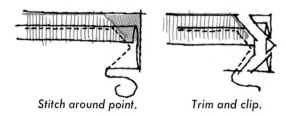

Stitch around point.   *Trim and clip.*

Turn the fabric right side out so that it wraps around the belting; press so that edges are sharp. Turn the remaining raw edge under so that it comes almost to the folded edge and press, or baste and press.

Slipstitch or blindstitch the loose edges in place. You may top-stitch the finished belt for effect or leave it soft.

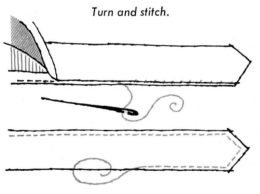

Turn and stitch.

Top-stitch for tailored effect.

Use a slide buckle and a hook and eye or a buckle with a tongue and eyelets. You may purchase an eyelet kit, which has a punch and an assortment of colored metal eyelets. Some machines work a very good eyelet with the automatic buttonholer, or you can work one by hand. You should have at least three eyelets, for normal, thin, and fat days.

A very attractive fastening is made with two large buttons and buttonholes when you cannot find a satisfactory buckle.

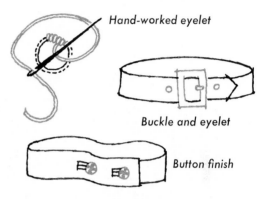

Hand-worked eyelet

Buckle and eyelet

Button finish

VARIATION

If the fabric is heavy, buy two lengths of ribbon or belting and cut the fabric only as wide as the belting plus two seam allowances. Proceed as before, but cover the back with the extra length of belting instead of wrapping fabric all around. Pin and hand-stitch it into place.

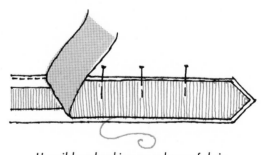

Use ribbon backing on a heavy fabric.

Try a layer of embroidered ribbon stitched to a layer of firm grosgrain for a decorative belt. Two layers of grosgrain work beautifully and there's such a wide color range. Wide upholstery braid, 1½″ to 3″, with two rings to pull the free end through, makes a handsome sports belt. Spaghetti cord, as described on page 49, made over ¼″ to ½″ cord and knotted at the ends is a great self-belt.

Check the trimming counter for cording, rickrack, and other trims which can be braided or stitched together for imaginative new effects in belts.

QUESTIONS OFTEN ASKED ABOUT BELTS

1. My fabric is very slippery and stretchy. How can I make it fold and handle correctly when stitching it to the belting?

Use one of the fusibles to anchor it to the backing instead of just the row of stitching.

2. In making a buttoned belt, can I make a machine buttonhole through the fabric and belting?

Yes, but make several test buttonholes first through identical fabric layers to test the machine settings.

Trim with Bias Strips of Fabric

Bias strips of fabric, identical to a garment or in contrast, can make an interesting trim.

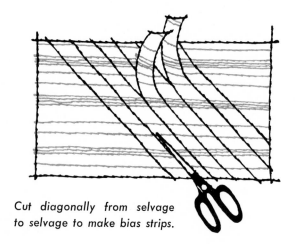

Cut diagonally from selvage to selvage to make bias strips.

It is also easier to find the color you want and get the width you need if you cut your own trim from fabric.

CUT YOUR OWN BIAS TRIM

Cut the bias strips. (See page 26.) Leave the ends on the straight grain, preferably along the selvage. Lay these ends right sides together so that the bias strips are at right angles to each other. Stitch seams about ¼″, being sure to work from V-point to V-point where the strips cross.

Open the seams and press them flat. Cut off the triangular pieces that extend beyond the edge. Now you have a strip of trimming ready for many uses.

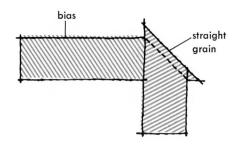

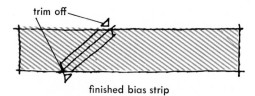

finished bias strip

CORDED PIPING

Corded piping is a good trim for necks, armholes, and many other edges. Fold the bias strip wrong sides together around cable cord of the desired size. Using the cording and zipper foot, stitch against the cord with a long stitch. Don't stretch the bias or let the upper layer pull and twist. To apply it to an edge, lay the stitching line of the bias along the seam

Bias strip folded right side out over cording

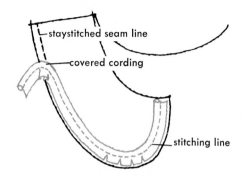

staystitched seam line

covered cording

stitching line

line of the garment, on the right side, as shown. Stitch again over the same line.

Leave ends loose about ½″ so that they can be tucked into the seam when facing is joined. Pin facing to garment, right sides together, over the cording. Turn over to wrong side of garment itself and stitch, following the line of stitching that can be seen. If the piping is very thick, the cord can be pulled out and cut off from the ½″ that tucks into the seam.

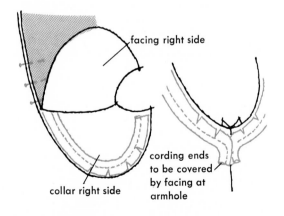

facing right side

cording ends to be covered by facing at armhole

collar right side

BOUND EDGES

Bound edges are popular as a trim finish for simple clothes. Some patterns plan for them

and give no seam allowance on those edges. In other cases you should trim off the seam allowance. *Do not bind over a seamed edge.* Cut the bias four times the width of desired trim finish. With right sides together, seam it along edge of garment, using not quite one-fourth of the total width for the seam. *On a concave edge, stretch the bias a bit. On a convex edge, ease it a bit.*

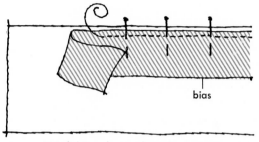

bias

Stitch bias along edge of garment.

Press the bias up and over the edge, turn the raw edge under, and slipstitch it by hand just inside the seam. If you want machine stitching to show on the binding, reverse the whole procedure. Seam the bias right side to the wrong side of the garment. Press over and turn under the raw edge, top-stitch down on the right side of the garment.

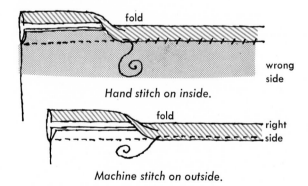

fold

wrong side

Hand stitch on inside.

fold

right side

Machine stitch on outside.

DOUBLE BIAS

An alternative system to be used with very sheer fabrics is the double bias. Cut the strips

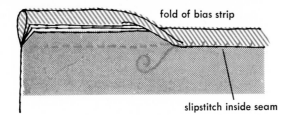

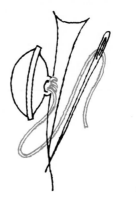

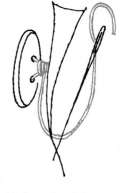

fold of bias strip

slipstitch inside seam

Double bias

Button with its own shank   *Make a shank for a button with holes.*

six times the desired finished width. Fold wrong sides together down center. Stitch the double raw edge to the garment, taking up not quite one-third of the folded width. The far edge is already finished and does not have to be turned under. Otherwise it is handled exactly as the single bias binding.

Fasten Everything Down!

Finally the end has come. You're almost ready to wear your creation, but you need a few buttons, snaps, and hooks to hold it all together, and keep your closings beautifully smooth.

BUTTONED UP

Mark all placements for buttons with pins through the finished buttonholes. Stretching the dress flat on an ironing board makes it easier to get the two fronts to come out even. Check and recheck to see that all buttons are the same distance from the edge, and evenly spaced.

How often you've heard the expression, "She can't even sew on a button!" Well, you're way past that stage now, so let's sew them on. Buttons either have shanks or holes. The shanked ones are easy, because you don't have to do much about them but sew several times through the shank and through the fabric and fasten off tightly. Buttons with holes need

to be sewed loosely so that a slight shank is formed with thread.

How to Make a Shank

Only on quite thin fabrics can you sew a button with holes absolutely flat, giving it no shank at all. One easy way to create a thread shank is to put a small object like a toothpick between the button and the fabric and sew back and forth through the holes in the button and through the fabric, while the toothpick holds them at a slight distance apart. Slip the

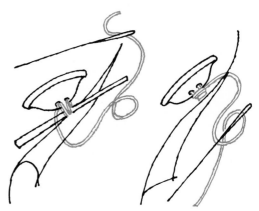

Build a shank with a toothpick.   *Wrap thread around to secure shank.*

toothpick out, wrap the thread shank several times, then pass the needle back and forth through the shank and fasten off. Little plastic shanks in various sizes are available at notion counters and are very useful.

What Kind of Thread?

Whatever thread you used for sewing the dress is suitable in most cases for sewing on buttons. You can put two threads double through the eye of an embroidery needle, to speed up the job! Heavy-duty thread, double or quadruple (if you can get it through the needle), is good for buttons on children's clothes and other things that have to withstand wear. A very heavy treated thread called carpet warp is useful on heavy overcoats and fabrics that can't be damaged by the pull of the thread itself.

IT'S A SNAP!

Snaps are sewn flat to two meeting pieces of fabric, two or three times over the edge from each hole. The ball part of the snap should be sewn on top, the hole part on the bottom. The hole in the center of the bottom part also makes placement marking with a pin very easy. Use snaps at upper corners above the top button and between buttons if there is a tendency for the dress to pull open. Place them back far enough from the edge and sew carefully so that the stitching doesn't show on the outside.

HOOKS, EYES, AND THREAD LOOPS

You will rarely find reason to use the long loop eye that comes with the hook and eye set. It is preferable in most places to use a thread loop, which lies very flat on the fabric. Here's how to do it. Make a small loop of double thread by fastening the thread in the fabric edge, then again ¼″ away. Insert the needle in the edge again, so that there are four threads in all. Pull the threads until the loop is flat, then work a blanket stitch over them. Sew the hook flat to the fabric, being sure to go under the head as well as through the rings. This is useful on a back-neck closing.

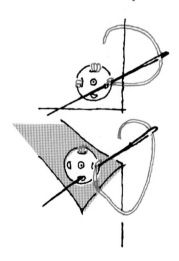

Snaps in position on right and wrong sides

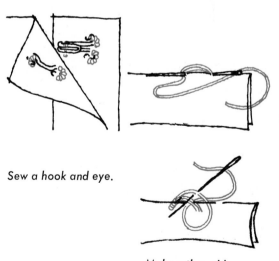

Sew a hook and eye.

Make a thread loop.

NOW YOU CAN TRY...

Slacks are an important part of everyone's fashion wardrobe, for dressy as well as casual occasions. Slacks are easy enough to sew.

Secrets for Slacks

The time-consuming part of making slacks is getting them to hang gracefully and feel comfortable. The best way to do this is to use a basic pattern to make a muslin for fitting. This can be transferred later to heavy brown paper which you can then use as a master pattern.

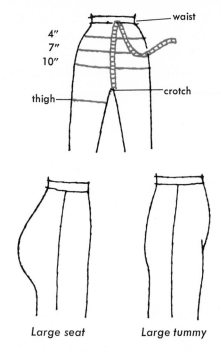

Large seat   Large tummy

PICK A PATTERN

Buy a standard simple pattern with no pockets, no extra details or yokes. The legs should be quite straight. If you have a small waist but lots of hip curve, choose a basic pattern with eight darts at the top. If your waist-hip area is straight, pick a four-dart pattern. With or without a waistband, the waist should be at your natural waistline.

Buy your pattern by hip size. If your measurement falls between two sizes, the smaller one may prove to be more flattering.

TAKE A MEASUREMENT

Make a complete pants measurement chart, measuring over normal undergarments. These are the measurements you will need:

waist
hip at 4", 7", 10" below waist
full part of thigh
waist-to-ankle length
crotch, from waist front to waist back, comfortably

Now compare your silhouette with the two silhouettes shown here. Some figures are flat in front and curved in the back; others carry their extra curves in the tummy area and have a fairly flat bottom. A rounded derriere calls for extra length in back; a rounded tummy needs the extra in front.

ALTER THE PATTERN

The hip can be enlarged in the same way you do a skirt, by adding to the side seam. Allow two inches of ease over your close hip measurement, and two or more inches in the thigh. The waist can be made larger or smaller by controlling the darts. The leg length can be altered on the line marked for this purpose across the pattern leg.

The crotch itself must fit well, so take your time in thinking out this alteration. Measure the total curve, front and back, on the pattern, and compare with your own measurement. For instance, if you need to add 2", you can add an inch in front and one in back for the first muslin fitting.

If you find you need extra length in back,

try putting 1½″ in the back and ½″ in front. Be sure, though, that you taper to an equal amount on the side seam—in this case, 1″. Reverse the process for more front length and less back.

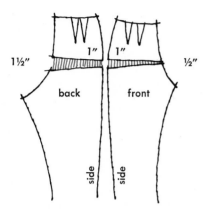

Adding length to front or back

If you need more room vertically in the seat, split the pattern as shown and add extra tissue paper.

If there is too much fullness, fold in the same places, maybe even taking out one dart entirely.

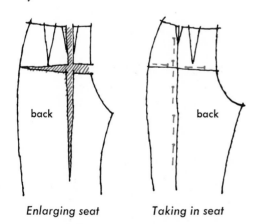

Enlarging seat *Taking in seat*

Cut your pattern in muslin and stitch together with large stitches. Make any further changes to get your pattern just right. Trans-

fer corrected pattern to brown paper, and use that as a pattern for basic slacks, and as a comparison pattern for other styles. Make each leg separately, sewing inseams and side seams. Press seams open flat. Put one leg inside the other, right sides together, and stitch crotch seam. This procedure is recommended in most patterns. Handle waistband, zipper, hems, and pressing as you would for any other garment.

Once you learn how to handle slacks, you'll find you can whip them up in a couple of hours. It's a wonderful way to expand your wardrobe.

Sewing with Specialty Fabrics

After you've done some sewing with nice, firm cottons and woolens, you may want to work on specialty fabrics. Among these are knit, stretch, and novelty materials.

DOUBLE KNITS

Double knits are quite easy to sew, and many of the pattern catalogs have special sections for knits. Choose your pattern from these groups. Staystitch all curved or bias edges; see page 37. Use polyester/cotton thread for wool and polyester knits. Mercerized thread is also satisfactory. In straight stitching, stretch seams slightly. Zigzag stitching is preferred if you have a zigzag machine. The newest machines have a stretch stitch specifically for knits.

NYLON TRICOT

This fabric demands special sewing techniques and practice for good results. Use polyester/cotton or nylon thread and a ball-point sewing machine needle. This is a needle which has been designed just for knits, since the rounded end goes between the tough synthetic fibers instead of piercing them. If you can't find a ball-point needle, use a fine, sharp, new size 9 or size 11 needle. A zigzag stitch is preferred for this material. Use a basic zigzag or multi-zigzag stitch, at fifteen to eighteen stitches to the inch. Test the stitch to determine tension and pressure settings. You will probably find that the pressure should be a bit heavier, and the tension at normal or slightly lighter. If your machine only does straight stitching, set machine for long stitches (ten to the inch), light pressure, and stretch the fabric along the seam line as you stitch.

PERMANENT-PRESS AND WASH-AND-WEAR FABRICS

Most summer and casual outfits, as well as children's garments, should be made of permanent-press materials, to cut down on ironing. These fabrics are usually made of cotton and synthetic blends, processed for crease resistance and offered in a cheery range of colors, solids, prints, plaids, borders, and special designs.

Check the grain line before buying a permanent-press fabric to be sure it is on grain. The same finish that makes the fabric crease resistant also locks the grain so that it is difficult, if not impossible, to straighten. If a fold has been pressed down the center of the fabric, wet it and press it. If it still won't come out, you may have to cut around it.

To make garments of these fabrics carefree throughout, choose wash-and-wear seam binding, decorative trims, lining and contrast materials, and zipper tapes. Use polyester-blend thread if the fabric has a synthetic content.

These fabrics have a tendency to pucker,

so test the stitch to find the best tension, pressure, and stitch length. Use your most careful stitching techniques; press carefully to avoid setting in creases. If your seams are smooth, they will stay smooth and flat through many launderings, for the life of the garment.

STRETCH FABRICS

Fabrics with crosswise stretch are available for home sewing and may be used in garments which require extra give across the back and hips. Slacks should have lengthwise stretch, and pattern pieces should be placed crosswise on the fabric. Sew stretch fabrics with polyester/cotton thread and a medium straight stitch, zigzag stitch, or stretch stitch, stretching fabric slightly as you sew. In areas where no stretch is desired, as in the shoulder seam, lay tape over seam line to sew. (See page 117.) A fabric with lengthwise stretch (used for ski wear) is also available, as is swimwear fabric that stretches in all directions.

BONDED FABRICS

Bonded fabrics consist of a face-fabric bonded to a backing. They have become popular because the backing gives the fabric more body, but bonded clothes will hold their shape better if they are lined. If the fabric has been finished off-grain, there's no way to straighten it. Fine dressmaking details are impossible with bonded fabrics. Before buying a bonded fabric, try pulling it. If it is solid, it will be satisfactory. If it stretches under pressure, forget it, as pressure during wearing will stretch it further.

LAMINATED FABRICS

A laminated fabric differs from a bonded

fabric in that the face-fabric is joined to a backing of foam which gives the material warmth without weight. Garments made of laminated fabric should be lined to protect the foam backing. The main difficulty in stitching a laminated fabric is the tendency of the foam to cling to the presser foot or the feed. To prevent this, you can use tissue paper between the foam and the metal, stitch through the paper, and then tear it away after stitching. Select simple styles with few darts and seam details. Both bonded and laminated fabrics may be stitched with a size 14 needle, medium stitch length, and medium tension.

VINYL FABRICS

Vinyls are surprisingly easy to stitch, and offer many fashion possibilities. Choose a design with simple lines and few seams, such as a cape or wrap skirt. Make pattern alterations carefully. Pin *inside seam allowance only*, or hold pattern pieces on with transparent tape. Pin marks remain in vinyl, so don't pin where the marks will show. Baste with paper clips or tape. To sew, use a size 14 needle and long stitch. Except for decorative zigzag effects, straight stitching is used. When working on the right side, your vinyl may seem gummy because of heat or humidity. Then sew through strips of tissue paper. Go slowly when crossing one seam with another or when working with more than two layers. Top-stitch seams instead of pressing.

FAKE FUR

Follow layout and directions for napped fabrics, to insure that the pile of the fabric all runs the same way. Do not try to cut notches, but mark on wrong side with chalk. Cut and

sew from wrong side. If you are working with a long-haired fur, you must control the pile to avoid getting the hairs caught in the stitching. Use a fine comb or a big needle to pull pile out from seam after stitching. Slash darts to eliminate bulk and shear away extra pile from seam allowances and darts after stitching. Since pressing may mat the pile, smooth out seams with thumbnail.

Lingerie—Lacy and Lovely

Do you dream of a drawer full of lovely, lacy lingerie in luxurious fabrics and melting colors? Your dream can come true. Lingerie stitching is easy and satisfying, and you'll find you can make such items as a lace-trimmed half-slip and matching panties quite quickly.

CHOOSE AN EASY FABRIC

Sewing lingerie does not necessarily mean sewing with nylon tricot. Very sheer Dacron® cotton batiste is also lovely, is far easier to handle, and is just as easy to launder. It's cooler on muggy midsummer days, and it won't creep up along your panty hose the way a synthetic knit does. You can use fine batiste for such garments as half-slips, full slips, petti-pants, gowns, and peignoirs. Polyester crepe is also easy to stitch and works nicely for lingerie.

If you really want to sew with nylon tricot, see the specific instructions for this fabric on page 109. But try your pattern in sheer batiste first.

You will find all the ingredients for lingerie stitching in well-stocked fabric shops. There are color-matched shoulder straps and elastic in ⅜″ and ¼″ widths for waist and leg bands;

stretch lace in glamorous colors is available for trim.

LINGERIE PATTERNS

Patterns are available for full and half-slips, panties, nightgowns, and peignoirs. In addition, large department stores may stock special lingerie patterns which include bras and panty girdles. Slips and nightwear are well within a beginner's range. Bras and girdles, however, present special fitting problems. The exceptions are the playsuit or swimsuit bra for a budding teen-age figure and little flat bras for little girls. These present no fitting challenges and are fun to sew according to pattern instructions.

Buy and alter a lingerie pattern as you would any other pattern. Both half-slips and chemise-type slips are very simple to make. A slip with a waistline seam (usually in larger sizes) or a full slip with a bra top should be fitted over your normal undergarments. If you are making a bra or panties, the easiest way to figure out the fit is to cut apart an old garment and compare it with the pattern pieces. Gowns and peignoirs offer few fitting problems and are rewarding to sew.

WAISTBAND FINISHES

Waistbands of panties and half-slips may be finished with a casing (see page 83), or by stitching special lingerie elastic directly to the raw edge. To do this, mark off the waist section of the garment in equal sections. Mark off elastic strip in corresponding equal sections. Match markings and pin in place on wrong side of fabric. The decorative edge of the elastic should extend just past the raw edge of the fabric. Straight-stitch or zigzag-stitch fabric and elastic together, stretching elastic from marking to marking and working along straight edge of elastic. Fold elastic to right side along stitching line and secure with a second row of stitching close to decorative edge.

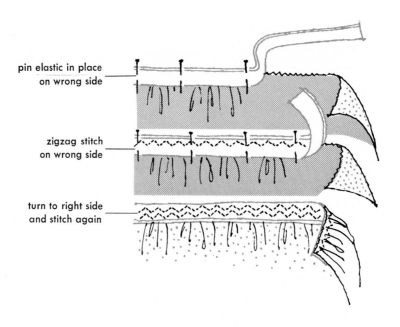

pin elastic in place
on wrong side

zigzag stitch
on wrong side

turn to right side
and stitch again

PROFESSIONAL SUCCESS TIPS
AND DESIGNER FINISHES

Sew a Little Lighter

Some things are better left undone in sewing, or done with fewer layers or fewer stitches. You can "sew it to death" if you're not careful and a little bit independent in your thinking. When the pattern shows two layers of fabric and one layer of interfacing for a dress collar and then says to underline all pieces, you might ask yourself, "But, do they know what fabric I am using?"

LIGHTEN A NINE-LAYER NECKLINE

Let's say that you're using a tweed. The dress collar is the kind that goes in between the neck of the dress and the facing. The pattern has also shown the facing cut of the fabric, and it is assumed that you will want to underline that too. In that one neck seam you would have two layers of tweed collar, plus two layers of underlining and one of interfacing, and the dress and facing in tweed plus two more layers of underlining. All of this will be sandwiched into that one spot! How can we get around this problem of extra bulk and still have a collar?

First we can dispense with the wool facing and its underlining. A facing cut of taffeta or firm lining material will be more comfortable against your skin than tweed, and ever so much thinner. Does that collar really need five layers? If the shape of the collar doesn't require much stiffening, perhaps you could leave the underlining in and take the interfacing out. Perhaps you'd rather work with the interfacing because it's a stand-up collar; then leave out the underlining or at least one layer of it.

If leaving out the underlining makes the fabric in the collar look paler than the rest of the dress, don't leave it out.

Thick velvets, velveteens, corduroys, as well as wools, can have undercollars made of taffeta or a fine flannel to lessen bulk. This is a great idea, provided that you've mastered your collar technique so well that the undercollar never shows from under the edge seam. Just be sure to give the upper collar a little fullness when pinning it, and then to understitch properly by hand around the edge. (See page 76.)

OTHER DETAILS

The same sort of treatment applies to pocket flaps, turned-back cuffs, decorative tabs, belts, and skirt bands. It is a matter of choosing a thinner fabric with equal qualities of washability or dry-cleanability and a good color match for the under-piece. The same system is used as for a collar, always being sure that the under layer is pulled tight and will not show at the edge. Understitching is also helpful on most of these pieces.

THIN SKIRT BAND

There is a way of making a skirt band with one layer of fabric and one layer of ribbon belting that is like the skirt band described on page 90, but thinner.

Cut a piece of belting 3" longer than your waist measure. Cut fabric strip 1" (two seam allowances of ½" each) wider than the belting and 3" longer than your waist measure. Lay the belting on the right side of the fabric, overlapping one seam allowance. Stitch very close to the selvage of the belting.

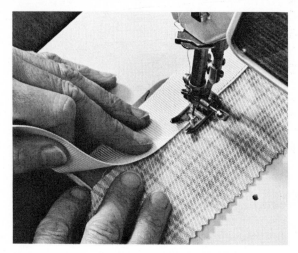

Stitch belting to right side of waistband strip, working very close to belting selvage.

Fold the band along the edge of the belting so that just a tiny bit of the fabric shows above the edge of the belting. With chalk, mark the fabric along the other edge of the belting. This is the seam line to be sewn to the skirt. Mark a cross line ¾" back on the overlap end of the band. Put the band around your waist and mark the spot that this mark meets. (See page 91.)

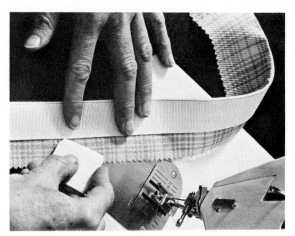

Fold belting down against wrong side of waistband strip and mark seam line with chalk on fabric.

Open band flat again and lay the fabric right sides together with the top of the skirt, one chalk mark at one side of the zipper and the other one at the opposite side of the zipper. Pin ends in place. Ease the skirt in between the ends. (See page 91.) Pin crosswise along seam line and stitch, being sure that you start and finish the same distance above the zipper ends.

With right sides together, pin skirt and band along chalked stitching line.

If there is too much bulk, trim the waistband seams to about ¼" and cut out any seam corners. If there is a lot of curve at the top of the skirt, clip the skirt seam but do not trim it as there is a great deal of weight and pull on it.

Turn the band over so that the belting covers the seam, just to the stitching line. Cut away the belting ¾" at the overlap end and turn the remaining loose piece of fabric back

Trim seam of waistband, but do not trim skirt seam. Clip skirt seam to control curve.

Turn belting over and blindstitch to wrong side of skirt. Note that belting has been trimmed ¾" at overlap end of zipper. Fabric is turned over belting and will be overcast to finish.

over the end. Pin it in place; pin the belting along the stitching line. Sew the belting down by hand with a blindstitch, and sew the end down tightly with overcasting. Finish the underlap end by machine-stitching back and forth to keep it as flat as possible. You may topstitch the band after it has been attached for a more tailored effect. Sew on hooks and eyes.

Sew-Quick Secrets

If it's good and easy sewing tricks you want, this is your special chapter. Here's where you'll learn how to get around some of the time-consuming dressmaker details, by leaving them out or by faking them.

Believe it or not, you don't have to have every last detail suggested in the pattern. You can leave out pockets much more easily than you can put them in, you can sew snaps under a button more easily than you can make a buttonhole.

You can also learn to fake a pocket or a buttoned closing. Don't feel you're cheating;

Fakes are better than bulges.

even high-priced ready-to-wear clothes are likely to have a decorative pocket flap with no pocket underneath!

FAKE A FLAP POCKET

Flap pockets are simple to simulate. Don't make the flap too stiff; a minimum of interfacing or underlining is best. If the fabric is heavy you might even use a layer of lining for the underside. Lay the flap right sides together with the garment, upward from the pocket markings, and pin in place. Pull the under layer down tight, so that the flap wants to turn over. Machine-stitch along the seam line of the flap, backstitching at each end. Cut off the raw corners of the flap seam. Turn the flap over its seam and top-stitch to conceal seam completely. If seam is too wide, it can be trimmed to the desired width. If you do not want outside stitching, tack the flap down from underneath with a slipstitch.

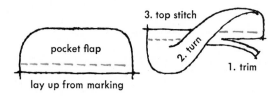

WAYS WITH WELTS

Welts can be faked in exactly the same way as flaps. Though a welt used in a pocket should be fairly stiff, a faked welt should be as thin as possible for easy handling. After it is stitched on and folded up, hand-tack or machine-stitch

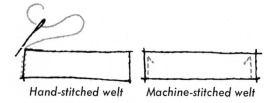

Hand-stitched welt   Machine-stitched welt

the ends in place, exactly as you would do on the real welt pockets.

THE BUTTONHOLE POCKET

Buttonhole pockets can be beautifully faked, with no loss to the style of the garment. In simulating a buttonhole pocket, make the buttonhole part, but no pocket behind it. Use a rectangle of the dress fabric to blind stitch all around the lip seams of the buttonhole "pocket." This is an especially good idea when you have several pockets that are strictly for decoration.

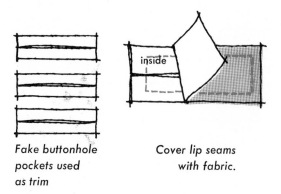

Fake buttonhole pockets used as trim   Cover lip seams with fabric.

BUTTONHOLES CAN BE FAKED

Buttonholes can be made on the front of the garment but never worked through the facing. The button is sewn on top at one end of the hole. The advantages to this are that in a thick loose-woven fabric, you will have less bulk and less chance of raveling if you don't have to work through the facing, and if the button is not constantly pushed through the buttonhole.

BUTTONS WITHOUT HOLES

Another alternative is to sew the button on without even a semblance of a buttonhole. This is exactly what is done on the cuffs of men's suits, and can perfectly well be done in

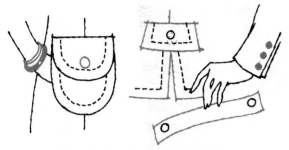

These buttons have no buttonholes.

similar places where buttons serve no function except decoration.

There are buttons that are so decorative that they were never really meant to be buttoned. They are usually elaborately jeweled, or carved of wood or heavily embossed metal. If you want to put them on a real opening that must be usable, just sew them to the upper layer and sew heavy snaps on behind them. You can even get fabric-covered snaps in colors for the purpose.

A great way to decorate with buttons and make the dress look like it opens is to sew button loops (see page 49) in a seam and sew buttons through them. Zip the dress in the back.

A simulated front closing

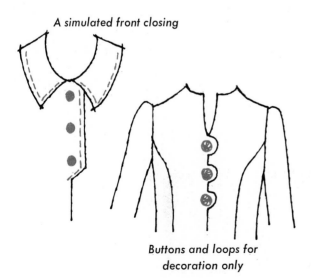

*Buttons and loops for
decoration only*

Holding Actions

Have you ever noticed how a particular pair of pants have ripped in the seat seam, or a sleeve has pulled out just at the back of the arm? These things happen because the fabric is soft and on the bias, and the strain at that point makes the seam stretch until the stitches break.

Sometimes you may notice that a pattern has directions for using a narrow tape along a seam to hold it and keep it from stretching or breaking stitches.

Sometimes you must use your own judgment on taping.

TAPES FOR HOLDING ACTION

There are three kinds of tape that are good for this holding action. The most available, usually right out of your sewing box, is straight seam binding folded in half, so that it is twice as thick and half as wide (¼″ now) as usual. There is also a cotton twill tape available in ¼″ width, and if you're very lucky, you may find thin, fine linen tailor's tape. It is the best and most durable. Both the twill and the linen tape come only in black or white.

WHEN TO TAPE?

There are many places where taping is desirable and some where it is not. For instance, don't tape a long skirt seam on a knit or a bias fabric, because it is supposed to have some "give" and flexibility. Seams of that kind should be stitched with zagzag or the newer stretch-knit stitches, or stretched as they are stitched with a straight stitch.

Sometimes a seam should actually be eased and then the tape applied to keep the ease stitch from breaking. One such place would be the scooped neckline as shown on page 38. Whenever two gathered lines are sewn together, like the waistline of a blouson dress with a gathered skirt, the stitching will surely break if it is not taped.

The prime places in which you might need tape, and you will undoubtedly recognize most of them as frequent candidates for the mending basket, are shown below:

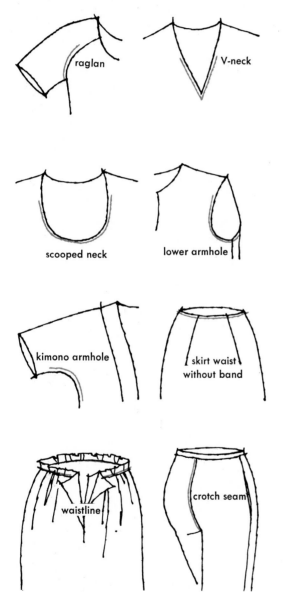

HOW TO TAPE

To install stay-tape properly, pin or baste the seam first, without including the tape. As you stitch, lay the tape along the seam and stitch as nearly through the center of it as possible. If it is a curved seam that has to be clipped after stitching, don't clip the tape. Try to let the tape run easily; don't pull it tight as you stitch.

If corded piping is used in a seam for decoration (see page 104), it acts as stay-tape, so that there is no need to use both.

There is a way of staying a waistline, which also makes a very pretty inside finish. Use a piece of ½" grosgrain ribbon to match the dress. Fit it around your waist, and cut it about 2" longer than feels comfortable. Fold back ¾" at each end and tack it. Sew hooks and eyes on the double thicknesses (you will have ½" overlap). Tack it by hand over the waistline seam, with the opening at the zipper

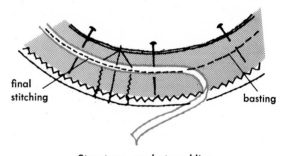

Stay-tape used at neckline

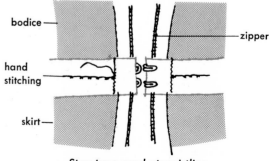

Stay-tape used at waistline

opening. Leave the last inch on each end un-attached, so that you can hook the band together before zipping the dress.

Flip Linings and Facings

Can you believe that you can line and face a dress in one easy step and improve the dress in the process? The secret is called a flip lining, and it's just what it sounds like—a lining that is stitched outside the dress and flipped through to the inside. It makes a perfect finish for the inside, as finished as the outside, and covers all the raw seams.

Besides being a finish, the flip lining has several other advantages. It supports the outer fabric without changing the character of it, so a soft dress can still be soft, without being clingy and saggy. The flip lining can replace the slip and protect sensitive skin completely from scratchy fabrics. It also makes a firmer and thinner finish for the neck and armholes than separate facings which are sometimes hard to keep tucked inside.

Flip linings are perfect for overblouses, tunics, dresses without waistlines, and the bodices of many dresses with waistlines.

THE BASIC FLIP LINING

Here's how to do the simple basic lining that can be used in a sleeveless dress or blouse with side seams and a center back seam.

Do not use the facing pattern pieces. Cut all the main body pieces from your dress fabric. Mark them and remove the pattern pieces. Cut the lining fabric from the same pieces and mark them. You're really making a dress to go inside your dress!

Sew all the darts and the shoulder seams in the dress and press. Do the same in the lining pieces. *Do not sew the center back seam or the side seams.*

Right Sides Together

Lay the lining right sides together with the garment. Match the shoulder seams and all notches and markings around the neck and armholes in the same way that you would lay facings in place for stitching, page 75. Pin all around, pulling the lining tight as you go so lining won't show in the finished garment.

With right sides together, pin dress and lining in place around the neck and armhole.

Stitch the neck and armhole seams as though you were installing facings. If you end the stitching and backstitch about ¾" from the fabric edge at each end of the neckline, it will make the zipper installation easier.

Trim and Clip

Trim and clip neckline and armhole seams

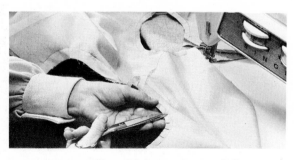

After stitching, trim raw edges and clip.

as you would do on facings. Now, you're ready to turn it all right side out.

Flip lining has been stitched in place around neck and armholes. The seams have been trimmed and clipped. Side and back seams have been left unstitched.

Reach inside the shoulder between dress and lining from the front and pull each half of the back through its own shoulder. Now dress and lining will be wrong sides together.

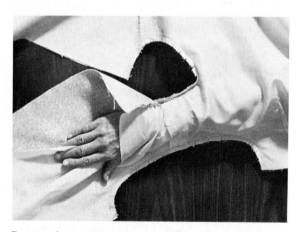

To turn lining in so it hangs inside dress, reach up from the front with your hand between the lining and the fabric. Grasp lining at back and work gently to turn it through the shoulder. Repeat for the other side.

Understitch

It is possible to understitch the edges by machine, but it will take a little more time than with ordinary facings because it must be

done in sections. Understitching by hand is very easy and just as effective. Whichever way you do it, the important thing to remember is that you must do the understitching at this point in the construction.

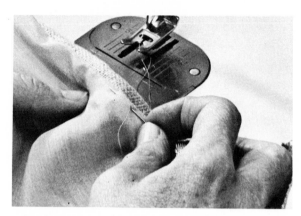

After lining has been turned, understitch by hand or machine. Understitching by hand is smooth and effective.

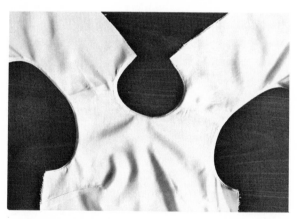

Neck and armhole seams of this lining have been understitched by machine.

Then Stitch

Stitch the center back seam of the dress, leaving an opening ½″ longer than the zipper. Stitch the center back seam of the lining in the same way. Keep the lining folded back out of the way and install the zipper in the

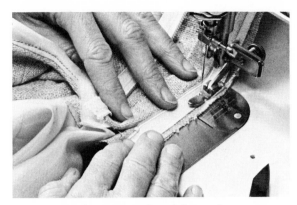

Stitch zipper to dress fabric only.

garment. The top of the zipper should be about ⅜" below the seam at the neck.

Place the side seams of the garment right sides together, then place the side seams of the lining right sides together. In each case be sure to match side seam notches and the ends of the armhole seams. At this point the dress and lining are joined only at the neck and armhole seams. Pin crosswise all along the seams (keeping dress and lining separate), and stitch the side seams from the lower edge of the lining to the lower edge of the the garment in one operation. Clip along curves; press

Stitch from bottom of side seam of lining up across the bustline dart and armhole seam, then continue stitching down side seam of dress.

seams open flat. When you hold the dress up, right side out, the lining will fall in place inside. Press around the armhole and neck.

Turn the lining under along the zipper, pin in place, and tack. Hem the dress. Put it on and have someone mark the lining at the finished edge of the dress. Then hem the lining about an inch above the mark. Instead of hemming the lining, you can zigzag a piece of lace on the bottom, so it will be even more like a slip.

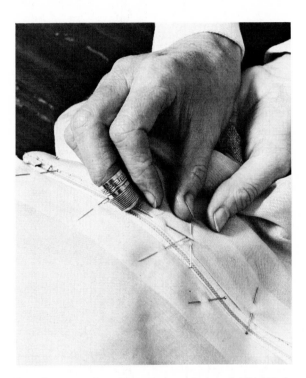

Turn lining under along zipper edge and blindstitch by hand.

You can use this lining on a simple wool jumper or an elegant velvet overblouse. Any fabric will pull through a shoulder which is 2½" wide or more. Some thin fabrics will pull through an even narrower shoulder, but don't press your luck.

Patterns sometimes have all-in-one facings for neck and armholes which can be handled like the flip lining, provided the shoulder is wide enough. There *must* be two side seams and a center back or front seam that can be left open or the trick won't work on a sleeveless garment.

OTHER TRICKS WITH FLIP LINING

Now, you ask, how many more ways are there to use a flip lining? Will it work on a dress with a collar, or sleeves?

A Dress with a Collar

It may seem unbelievable, but a collar doesn't change anything! It's as easy as sewing a collar on with any other facing; look back at page 79 and see how that works. Place the collar on the dress, matching markings, pin all around, and machine-baste it in place. Then proceed with the flip lining as though the collar weren't there.

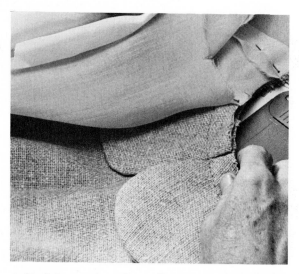

A flip lining works with a collar too. Just baste collar in position and continue with lining as though the collar were not there.

It Is Simpler with Sleeves

Sleeves make the whole flip lining even easier! The side seams and center back seam don't need to be left open. As a matter of fact, it doesn't even matter whether you have these seams if you have sleeves. Sew the garment together, all darts and side seams, shoulder seams, etc. Sew the lining separately, exactly the same as the outside. Use the lining as a facing for the neck only. When the neck seam is finished, trimmed, and clipped, understitch and turn it inside. Baste the lining armhole inside the dress armhole so that all markings match. Set in the sleeve as shown on page 85, catching both the dress and lining in the seam. It is also possible to line a short sleeve from the lower edge and include its lining in the armhole seam. This makes it possible to have a clean finish on a very short sleeve without the bulk of a hem.

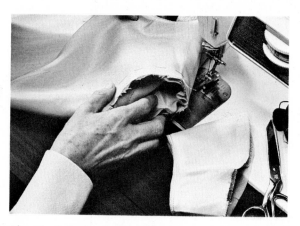

The flip lining is easier with sleeves. Just catch both dress and lining when setting sleeves in. A short sleeve, such as the one shown, may be given a complete lining also.

Lining a Bodice

A bodice can be flip-lined and the lining used as a finish over the waistline seam. Line the bodice in the way you would line a dress, depending on whether it has sleeves and collar. A gathered skirt usually does not require a lining, so you will only be joining the one layer of skirt to the dress bodice. *Leave the bodice lining free.*

After the waistline seam is stitched and the zipper is in, smooth the lining down. Turn the edge of the lining under along the zipper and along the waistline seam; pin it at darts and

The flip lining of a bodice may be used as a finish over the waistline seam of a gathered skirt. Pin in place before blindstitching.

seams. Blindstitch the lining in place along the waistline by hand. This is especially good on fabrics that ravel easily because only the skirt seams are left to be finished with stitching or binding. All other seams are covered by the lining.

Lining a Skirt

Plain skirts, without pleats or gathers, can be flip-lined from the waist if you don't want a band. When the skirt and lining are both completed except for the upper edge, lay them with right sides together. Pin around the waist edge, matching notches and seams. Cut a piece

of stay-tape the exact size of your waist and lay it along the waistline seam, easing the skirt if necessary. Stitch through the tape, trim, clip, and understitch. Finish the skirt and lining as you would any flip-lined dress.

Lining a Vest, Bolero, or Sleeveless Jacket

A vest or bolero or sleeveless jacket can be flip-lined in such a way that all edges, including the bottom, are finished in the one operation. Pin the jacket and lining right sides together around all raw edges except the open side seams. Stitch and do all necessary trimming and clipping. Reach in the side seam opening on the back and pull the front through. When the whole garment is right side out, understitched, and pressed, sew the side seams of the garment, then turn the lining side seams under and slipstitch together by hand. Isn't that a quick trick?

To flip-line a bolero, pin fabric and lining together around all raw edges except side seams. Turn through side seams after stitching, trimming, and clipping.

QUESTIONS OFTEN ASKED ABOUT FLIP LININGS

1. How can I make my dress and lining fit together closely without wrinkles?

   If they are cut from the same pattern, careful stitching of seams and darts will keep them the same size.

2. What would happen if I put the zipper in the back seam first?

   You could never pull each side of the back through its shoulder. The dress would just pull round and round until you had a large ball of fabric!

3. Why does my lining show at the shoulders? Pull the lining very tight under the garment when you pin around the neck and armhole. It won't hurt to let the garment fabric puff up a bit. That will insure the lining staying underneath when it is all right side out.

BRAINSTORMING THE BUDGET

No question about it—the sewing machine is the biggest aid to the average household budget since the piggy bank. Manufacturers of ready-to-wear figure that the cost of a dress is divided forty percent for labor, thirty percent for design, and thirty percent for materials. All that you really have to consider is the cost of materials—you get your design inexpensively by spending from one to five dollars for a pattern, and your own time and labor are not reckoned in cash terms.

Remember, though, that labor is still the most expensive ingredient in a dress. Your time and skill are worth more than the fabric. Use them wisely, and don't waste time on poor-quality fabrics for the sake of the budget alone. The trick is to use your time not only to help the budget but to provide clothes that will wear well and look attractive for the whole family.

Things to Sew for Yourself and Your Family

Don't try to sew every single stitch your family wears. Some garments are so well made and reasonably priced that it isn't worth the time and effort even for an expert seamstress to try to duplicate them at home. Blue jeans and similar types of work clothes, uniforms, baby's stretch pajamas and plastic-lined pants would fall in this group. Nor, as a beginner, are you yet equipped to tackle tailored items such as coats or suits.

There is, however, a long list of things to sew which are well within your abilities, will save you money, and give you a creative thrill besides.

THINGS TO SEW

For Yourself:
  simple summer dresses
  simple evening dresses
  one-piece wool dresses
  skirts and blouses
  slacks, shorts, play clothes
  unlined bathrobes
  nightgowns and pajamas
  half-slips
  maternity clothes

For Your Daughter:
  practically everything
  except jeans, suits, coats, and
    rain and snow wear

For Your Son:
  shorts and slacks (small sizes)
  sport shirts
  beachwear
  pajamas
  unlined bathrobes

For the Baby:
  christening outfit
  buntings
  sunsuits
  play clothes

For Your Husband:
  sport shirts and vests
  unlined bathrobes
  pajamas
  beachwear
  scarves
  ties

The more you sew, the easier it will seem and the more you will enjoy it. You will find that you are working more quickly and accurately, and the results will be more satisfying. You will be prouder than ever to say, "I made it myself!"

Other Budget Tips

There are plenty of other ways to save money with your sewing machine besides sewing new things. There's a whole world of mending and make over which is part of the normal process of caring for a family wardrobe. Our grandmothers were experts at this game; there was a revival of it during the early 40's, and spiraling prices now cause us to seek new ways of sewing-to-save.

WHAT IS MENDING?

Mending can cover a broad area of clothing repair, including darning, patching, stitching ripped seams, sewing tears, and generally stretching the life span of a garment. It may be done by hand, by machine, or by iron-on products. Mending is an inescapable part of running a family and a home. While recommended mending techniques exist for most situations, it is a highly individual job.

A MENDING QUIZ

What is your approach to the mending question? Does it fit into any of these categories?

The major-project mender. This type saves all the mending for a rainy weekend and attacks it with determination, energy, and some fierceness.

The don't-let-it-get-ahead-of-you mender. She keeps a mending basket by the washer or by the ironing board, and catches up tiny rips and missing buttons as they appear.

The on-the-run mender. She keeps a handy needle and thread in the hall closet, and is adept at getting the button back on the snowsuit while the squirming child inside struggles to get away.

The living room mender. She's akin to our hardworking grandmothers, and has the mending basket to keep her company when she relaxes with guests, stereo, or TV. She enjoys fine handwork.

The never-say-die mender. This type just won't let anything wear out. She will mend and remend and even put patches on patches.

The mender who would rather not. This lady won't even bother with iron-on patches, she simply cuts off the blue jeans above the knee.

No matter how you approach it, there are a few basic mending tips and techniques to keep in mind. A well-equipped sewing center will have needles and thread, thimble and scissors, iron-on mending muslin, denim patches, buttons, pins, and fabric scraps. But, wherever the main equipment center may be, do keep a small supply of thread and a needle on your dressing table for morning emergencies, and another small supply in the kitchen or front hall. It's easier to take a quick stitch with any color thread than to run upstairs while the car pool honks outside.

Mending by Machine

Most small mending jobs are more conveniently done by hand. However, an automatic zigzag machine has a marvelous stitch called multistitch zigzag or mending zigzag.

It may be used for almost all flat mending, such as joining the edges of a three-corner tear, or pulling together the edges of a simple rip. It is also used for stitching elastic.

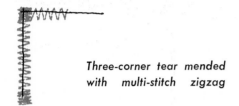

Three-corner tear mended with multi-stitch zigzag

Before starting to sew, press the edges of the rip so they lie flat. If the fabric is strong, the mending stitch alone will hold the rip. If you suspect the fabric is worn, back the rip with iron-on mending muslin.

Darning by Hand

A darning egg is a worthwhile addition to your sewing basket. Sock darning is not the big job it used to be thanks to long-wearing synthetics, but there is still darning to be done on mittens, tights, and knits.

To darn a small hole, work on the right side. Run a row of small stitches alongside the hole, just beyond the edge of the worn area. Make a parallel row of stitches, close to the first row, and go back and forth till the hole is filled with vertical threads. Then turn your work and stitch crosswise, going over and under the vertical threads to reweave.

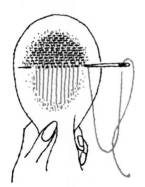

Hand darning with darning egg

Don't make knots when darning socks; knots cause blisters. Match thread to fabric; yarn for wool, cotton darning thread for cottons, nylon thread for nylon and other synthetics. For blends, use thread that matches the dominant fiber.

Darning by Machine

If you have a lot of darning to do on household linens, it's worthwhile to set up the machine. Check your instruction book for specific directions for your machine. The material is moved back and forth under the needle so the hole is filled with tiny, even stitches. An embroidery hoop is sometimes used to keep the fabric taut. Machine darning is smooth, flat, long-lasting, and well-suited to flat items.

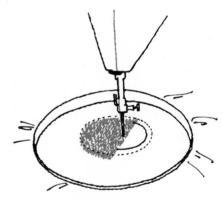

Darning by machine

What About Iron-Ons?

Iron-on tapes and patches have earned their place in the mending box. While they lack the craftsmanship of a perfect darn, they do save time and are perfectly acceptable in many situations. Be sure to read directions carefully and follow them exactly. If the iron-on product is correctly applied, it will survive countless trips through washer and dryer without peeling off. While there are many different kinds of iron-ons, the most useful are mending muslin and denim patches for jeans. Soft cotton knit patches are also available for mending children's and men's underwear and T-shirts. The muslin is useful for backing a tear which will be covered by stitching or another fabric. A strip of muslin will stretch the life of a worn sheet when the first rip appears.

Patching

If a hole is too big to darn, and the item is otherwise worthwhile, you can patch it. There's a lot to be said for a neat, inconspicuous patch, and even more to be said for a decorative one. To make a more-or-less invisible patch, use a piece of matching fabric cut so grain and design match the torn area. Cut out torn part in a neat square. Clip corners diagonally and press under raw edges ¼". Cut patch 1" larger all around the hole and pin or baste in place underneath, matching grain and design. Blindstitch turned-under edge of opening to patch. Turn patch and catch-stitch down raw edge on other side. If you apply a

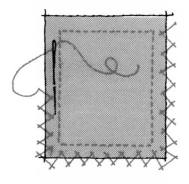

Catch-stitch raw edges on wrong side.

patch by machine, top-stitch around turned-under edge of opening. The raw edge of the patch may be secured with a straight or zig-zag stitch.

Patches on knees of small pants can be a trial unless you have a free-arm machine or prefer to put patches in by hand. There is, however, a different kind of tailored patch which does not require getting the worn part under the needle. Begin as for patch described above, cutting out worn part, clipping corners to allow you to fold under raw edge ½", and cutting patch 1" larger than hole. Pin patch in

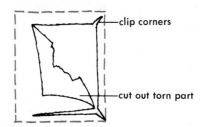

Mark pressing line with chalk.

clip corners

cut out torn part

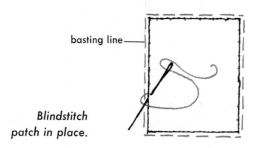

basting line

Blindstitch patch in place.

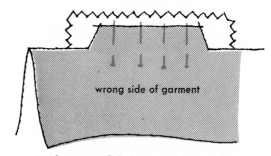

wrong side of garment

Pin-baste patch before machine-stitching.

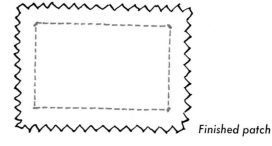

Finished patch

position, using folded section as seam allowance. Stitch along fold line, taking one diagonal stitch at each corner.

Decorative Patches

You can let your imagination run wild with decorative patches for children's wear. Though the exact size, shape, and design of a patch depend on the size of the hole or stain and the kind of garment, the patch possibilities are limited only by your own creative sense. Decorative patches offer a grand opportunity for using the decorative stitches on your zigzag machine. See page 142.

Alterations You Can Make

It's a rare person who can always find ready-to-wear clothes that fit perfectly, or whose figure remains the same, season after season. Most of us find ourselves involved in alterations on ready-made garments because our figures have changed, the fashions have changed, or because a new garment is just right except that it needs a little refitting.

Obviously, it's more creative and fun to make a new dress from a crisp length of new material. But it's very rewarding, in a different way, to use your alteration know-how to get another year's wear from a dress you are fond of, or to be able to take advantage of a bargain.

There are plenty of things you can do quite easily to improve the fit of your clothes. You can:

shorten or lengthen a hemline
adjust a hip line
raise a waistline
shorten or lengthen sleeves

Alterations to avoid:
lowering a too-high waistline
changing a set-in sleeve
changing a neckline
letting out when there is too little seam allowance

SHORTEN A HEMLINE

Mark correct hemline with chalk marker or pins. Rip out old hemline. In a manufactured garment, the hem will be secured with a chain stitch. If you pull the right thread, it will unravel easily. Plan to use the same type of hem

To unravel a chain stitch

finish as was used originally. Turn up hem along marked line and baste in position near fold. A straight hem should be 3″ deep; a flared hem should be 2″ deep. Trim away excess fabric and finish raw edge. See page 98. If there is extra fullness, run a row of machine basting ¼″ inside cut edge and pull up bobbin thread till the hem fits. Shrink out fullness with a steam iron. Pin and stitch hem in place and give it a final pressing.

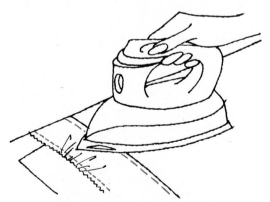

To shrink out excess hem fullness

The Back Pleat Problem

If shortening a skirt involves removing too much of a back pleat, trim away the excess material, then either stitch the pleat closed, or make a back slit by hemming down the seam allowance on each side and finishing with a close zigzag bar tack.

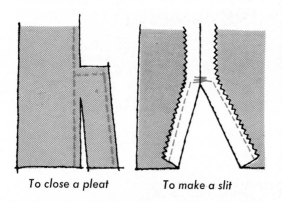

To close a pleat   To make a slit

SHORTEN A COAT HEM

With pins or chalk, mark desired length. Open facing at lower edge. Take out original hem. Open lining up to point about 6″ above marking. Run basting stitch all around inside of coat at this distance from the marking to hold coat and lining together. Cut coat material 3″ below marked line. Cut lining 2″ shorter than coat. Using hem gauge for accuracy, turn coat up 3″ and lining up 2″. Pin, baste at fold, and press. If necessary, cut out

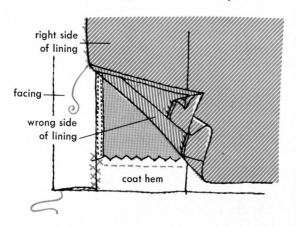

right side of lining

facing

wrong side of lining

coat hem

excess hem fabric under facing to eliminate bulk. You can decide whether this step is necessary by looking to see whether the fabric was cut out on the original hem. Press under raw edge of lining ¼″ and machine-stitch lining hem. Finish raw edge of coat with line of straight stitching and trim with pinking shears. Hem coat by hand. Fold facing back into position and stitch it to coat hem. Slipstitch lower edges together. Stitch lining to facing. If coat had thread chains joining lining to coat, replace chains in original positions. Remove basting stitches.

LENGTHEN A HEMLINE

Whether or not a garment can be lengthened depends entirely on the amount of material in the hem, and in the case of a coat, on whether the excess fabric under the facing has been trimmed from the corners.

To lengthen a dress or skirt hem, first take out old hem. Then wash or dry-clean the garment to remove the crease. (If the old hemline still shows use trim to cover it.) See whether there is enough fabric. If you can let the garment down, simply mark, turn and press the hem, and stitch it in place, keeping the original hem finish.

If there is just a bare 2″ hem in the dress, you can still lengthen it by facing the hem and using almost the entire 2″ for extra length. Skirt facings must be bias. You can buy bias facings in taffeta or cotton, 2″ wide with edges folded under. If you have extra dress material, you can make your own bias facing by cutting bias strips 2½″ wide and joining the strips till you have a piece about 2″ longer than the unfinished hem edge. Lay skirt over ironing board, right side up. With right side of facing against right side of skirt, pin facing in place.

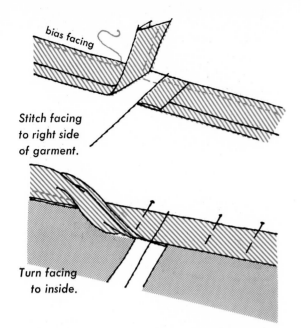

bias facing

*Stitch facing
to right side
of garment.*

*Turn facing
to inside.*

Stitch facing to skirt edge, with ¼″ seam allowance. Turn under raw edges at ends of facing. Turn facing to inside, then pin, baste, and press. Press under raw upper edge of facing. Stitch facing to garment.

It's possible to face a coat and lining in the same way, but remember about the interfacing which gives body to the front edges. It will have to be extended also, to keep the corners crisp. If fabric has been cut from the corners, you might consider another lengthening approach.

OTHER LENGTHENING TECHNIQUES

You can also lengthen a garment by adding matching or contrasting fabric as a trim to achieve the right length. For example:

A too-short coat can take a band of fur at the hem.

Decorative trim can be inserted above the hem of an unpleated skirt. Try a band of leather-look vinyl for winter.

A band of eyelet for summer.

A flounce, a ruffle, or a band of trim can be added to the hem.

Add fur.   *Insert vinyl.*

Insert eyelet.   *Add a ruffle.*

TAKE IN A HIP LINE IN A SKIRT

Of all possible alterations, the happiest one is taking in the hip line of a skirt. To do this, first open hem for a few inches at side seams. Put on your too-roomy skirt and pin in the side seams so the skirt hangs comfortably. Leave 2″ for ease. Remove skirt and transfer markings to wrong side. Do this by chalking along pinned seam line on wrong side. Remove pins and repin seam along chalk lines. Remove zipper. Open waistband at side seam and on either side of zipper opening. If waistband is also too big, take it off entirely. Press seam allowances together. Baste new seam line along pins. Try skirt on. Adjust seams if necessary. Stitch new seams. Take out old stitching, trim seams, finish seam edge, and press open. Replace zipper and finish hem. Replace waistband, adjusting to fit new skirt measurements.

LET OUT A HIP LINE

Is this the job you've been postponing against the day when you shed five pounds? Don't put it off any longer. You will feel and look slimmer if you can move around inside your skirt a bit. Hopefully, there's enough fabric in the seams to give you the ease you need. If you can stitch just ¼″ closer to the edge on each of four seams, you'll come out with a full half inch extra on each seam for a grand total of two inches. That's worthwhile!

A Word of Warning

Before you start ripping the skirt, use your tape measure to determine whether you can get enough ease. Measure your hips 7″ below the waist and add 2″. Measure the skirt at the same place. If you can add enough width, take off the zipper and open the hem. Remove old stitching and press edges together. Baste new seams and try skirt on. Stitch along basting lines. Replace zipper and waistband section, then restitch hem.

Letting Out a Gored Skirt

Sometimes it's better to raise a gored skirt from the waist to gain extra room in the hips, especially if you can let down the hem to get

Raise a gored skirt to enlarge hipline.

the right length. Take off waistband and put on skirt. Raise it till it fits easily at the hips. Then tie a string around your waist and adjust the skirt. Mark new waistline with pins or chalk. Remove zipper. Trim away top of skirt ⅝″ above new waistline and replace zipper. If waistband is too snug, add new material to the end, or replace it with a firm grosgrain ribbon.

RAISE A WAISTLINE

If there is too much material at the top of your garment, it's an easy job to raise the waistline and slick up the bodice fit. Try on the dress, and tie a string around your natural waistline, pulling bodice fabric down for smooth fit. Mark new waist with pins or chalk. Remove zipper. Rip out waistline stitching and baste in new seam along marked line. Try on. Stitch new seamline and trim away excess fabric. If necessary, adjust darts for fit.

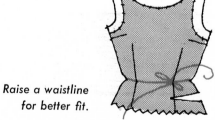

Raise a waistline for better fit.

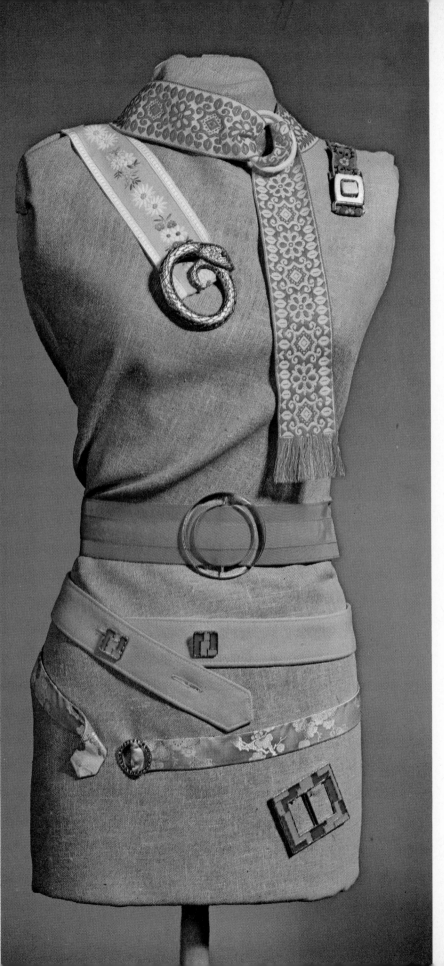

Belts are easy
to make! Easiest
or all is a fringed
strip of braid,
to pull through
a pair of white
plastic rings.
Try a tailored
buckle on a narrow
strip of flowered
braid, or the
whimsical contrast of
a silvery snake
buckle against a
dainty ribbon.
A double layer of
grosgrain shows
its colors through
a clear buckle.
The button fastening
with machine-worked
buttonholes is
effective. And for
a dressy belt, satin
damask stiffened with
belting takes a
rhinestone buckle.

Trimming tricks to try. *Sew row upon row of pretty lace edging to plain fabric, and cut out to make a bib effect; edge a pocket with scallop trim; use jumbo rickrack to make a peekaboo insertion across a bodice; stitch handsome ribbon across a patch-pocket section before stitching.*

Little touches of glamour. *A single row of glitter is the only decoration you'll need, at the neck of a simple velvet gown. A double row of pleated nylon edging is stitched back-to-back for a jabot effect. A strip of ribbon takes a band of seam lace for an old-fashioned sleeve trim. And a pair of ruffles-with-headings, trimmed in narrow braid, make much of a simple gathered sleeve.*

Lingerie like this is a joy to make! *Try a simple rose-sprigged nightie with elasticized neck and sleeves; a lace-trimmed batiste with scalloped hem done on a zigzag sewing machine; a tailored topper edged in eyelet, with cording forming a row of figure-eight buttonholes for double-buttoning down the side.*

Gifts to sew—his and hers: A single Mexican bedspread makes a tunic for her and a shirt for him, both with laced closing to show off the work of an eyelet punch. The necktie, made of solid material from a standard pattern, has a single stripe done with twin-needle stitching. A cheerful fish adds interest to the pocket of surfer shorts, with waves done by the scallop stitch of an automatic zigzag machine.

Ideas for gifts children love: *The flowered turtle, belonging on any child's bed, is made from a pattern. The kangaroo on the wall is appliquéd with satin stitching, and used on a zippered pajama bag. Directions for the delightful, colorful railroad grow-chart are on page 145. And the little girl's dress features tucking with contrasting rickrack inserted in the seams.*

Costumes for Halloween and other dress-up times. *Here are a few perennial favorites: the supersleuth wears an all-purpose cape of green corduroy; the woodland ballerina a petal-trimmed dancing costume; and the little lady of the covered-wagon era wears a dress made from a standard pattern cut to eighteenth-century length with a ruffled hem.*

A charming wardrobe for a lucky three-year-old. *Three variations on a single pattern: at the top: stylized butterflies are appliquéd with a simple satin stitch. Center: a flirtatious scalloped hem takes a contrast facing. At bottom: decorative machine stitching joins with pretty ribbon and braid to make an unusual and easy yoke treatment. Delightful braids and trims are made specially for children's wear; a few are mounted on the ladderback of the chair.*

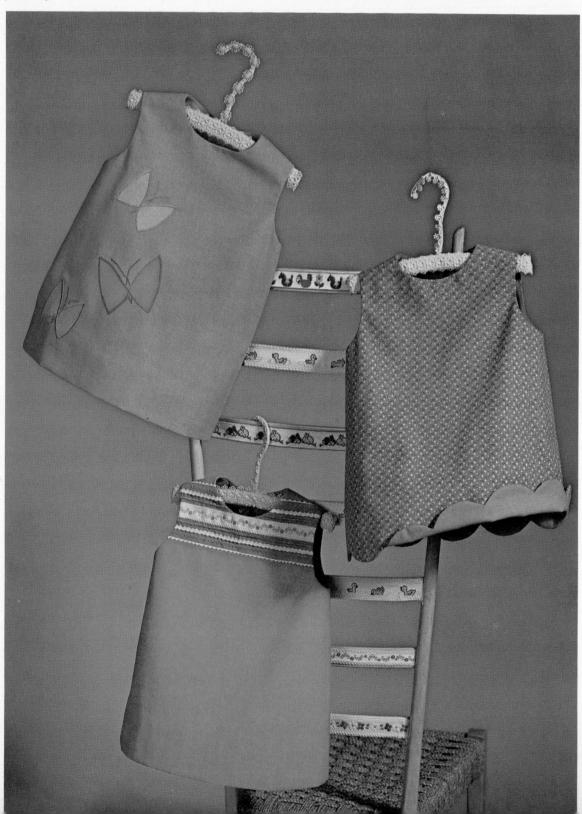

SHORTEN OR LENGTHEN SLEEVES

A sleeve hem can be handled in much the same way as a skirt hem. If it needs shortening, cut off excess fabric to give a hem of 1″ to 1¼″. If there is a cuff, remove the cuff, cut off excess sleeve length and restitch cuff in place. To shorten the sleeve of a boy's or a man's shirt, simply take a tuck in the upper arm.

If a sleeve needs lengthening, you may add fabric facing if necessary, just as you would for a skirt hem.

To lengthen a cuffed sleeve, insert a band of matching or constrasting material or a strip of decorative trim above the cuff.

Good fit is a very important element of good fashion. If the garment is in good condition, made in a becoming style, and is reasonably fashionable, it will be well worth your time to make it fit properly. A successful alteration can make a ready-to-wear dress look as though it were custom-made for you.

Make-over Magic—
Remodeling Tips and Suggestions

It's hard to lay down exact rules for making over and remodeling clothes. Only you can decide whether the remodeled garment will be worth the time and effort you must put into it.

One thing is sure: the material you are working with must be good and reasonably new. Fabrics age at different rates, and some, like people, age more gracefully than others.

Remember, too, that fabrics have changed in the last decade. Fibers and finishes are new and sophisticated, geared to easy sewing and easy care. It seems silly to put make-over time into a fabric that requires ironing, when you can stitch up a garment of new material that practically takes care of itself. Remember that your own time is the most expensive element of a garment. Spend it wisely.

There are some circumstances which justify remodeling. Here are a few:

A favorite dress has worn out in the armhole and elbow areas. You can remove the old sleeves and create a sleeveless dress or jumper. You can also put in contrasting or knitted sleeves.

An unfashionably short dress can be turned into a tunic by shortening it a bit more to wear over slacks or a matching skirt.

A big-sister dress can look new for little sister with pretty pockets, coverup pinafore, and a new collar.

An evening dress is likely to have a decent amount of usable, unworn fabric in the skirt, to turn into a blouse, tunic, or short skirt.

A full-length evening coat or bathrobe can be cut off to a shorter length.

Slacks can be turned to shorts.

Long sleeves may be cut short.

These remodeling techniques require little effort, and are designed mostly to extend the useful life of a garment. On the other side of the coin is complete make-over, when you make a totally different garment from an existing one. This takes more time than making a new garment from new fabric, and should be done only when the material is so good or so pretty that you can't let it go.

Be sure the garment is clean before you start to work on it. Rip out seams carefully. Press the pieces. Select a new pattern that will

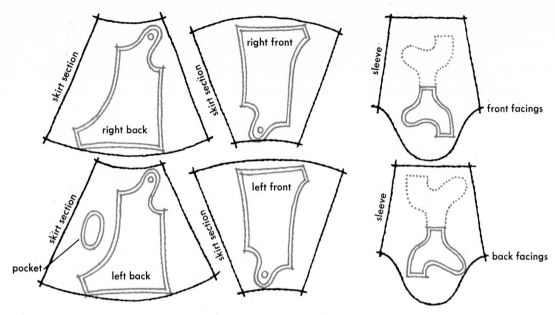

Child's sunsuit cut from adult dress

fit inside the old garment pieces, making allowance for the straight of grain and pattern matching. Once you have the new pieces cut out, proceed according to your pattern instructions. You will probably be able to get a child's dress, skirt, or sunsuit from a full-skirted adult dress.

Make Your Own Patchwork

Patchwork is an attractive way to use up fabric scraps and remnants, either from your own scrapbag or from the remnant sale table in the fabric store.

You can combine pieces of similar weight, texture, and fiber content in gay designs to make a patchwork skirt or apron without a pattern, or you can join your patches so you can lay out pattern pieces just as though you are working with regular fabric. Solid and small-pattern cottons are best for casual clothes and children's wear; silks, satins, and velvets

may be combined to make a terrific evening skirt. Smaller patches allow more flexibility. Larger squares are less work but require simpler designs.

To make your patchwork, begin with a pattern cut out of shirt cardboard. For finished 4″ squares cut pattern piece 5″ square, to give ½″ seam allowance all around. You can make all the patches the same size, or you can make your basic square of two triangular or rectangular pieces in constrasting fabric. To make basic units which will stitch up to perfect 4″ squares, cut your pattern pieces like this:

    5″ square
    triangle, 5¾″ on straight sides
    3″ x 5″ rectangle
    3″ x 3″ square

These may be put together in a variety of arrangements. Just be sure to cut accurately on exact lengthwise and crosswise grains of fabric, and to keep an exact ½″ seam allow-

Basic patchwork shapes can be arranged in many ways.

ance on all seams, and your patchwork will come out perfectly.

For straight strips of patchwork, lay out patches and join small sections to get basic squares. (Clip ends of seam allowance after joining triangles.) Stitch squares together to form strips. Press seams open. Pin together corners of patches before sewing strips so that joining will be even. Stitch strips together and press seams open.

To keep seam edges from raveling and to give a flat, finished look to the patchwork, top-stitch on the right side $\frac{1}{8}$″ on each side of seams, using neutral or harmonizing thread. Underlining is almost essential for a garment made of patchwork, and the underlining may be basted in place at this point and stitched in with your top-stitching. This will give a quilted effect to the underside. Use any good woven lining material in a harmonizing shade.

If you are making a garment from patches, try arranging the patches on the paper pattern before joining them, to be sure that the patches fall into a balanced composition. When laying out a pattern on patchwork fabric, pay attention to matching blocks at seam lines, just as though you were working with a plaid fabric.

HOW TO MAKE A PATCHWORK EVENING SKIRT

It's easy and fun to make an evening skirt from patchwork. Choose your colors and fabrics carefully, because this will be a skirt you'll love for years. It will never go out of style. The width of the skirt should be about two and one-half times your waist for light-weight fabrics. For lasting fashion, make the

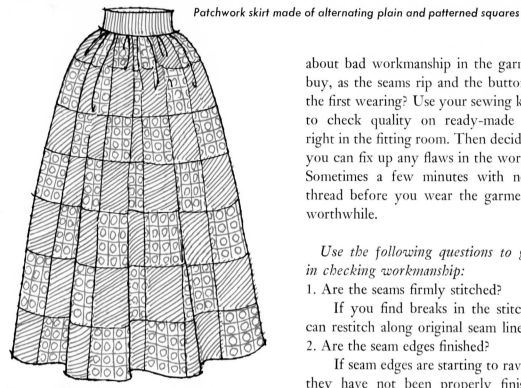

Patchwork skirt made of alternating plain and patterned squares

skirt floor length, plus a 3″ hem allowance.

To figure out how much material you will need, multiply waist measurement by 2½ and divide by 4. (A 24″ waist needs 60″ of material, or 15 of the 4″ squares.) Each row will be 15 squares wide, and you can make as many rows as you need to get the length. When your piece is finished, work under-lining with top-stitching as described above.

You may finish the skirt with waistband and zipper (page 90) or with an elastic in a casing (page 83) covered by a wide velvet or satin ribbon used as a belt. Face or hem lower edge.

Checking a Ready-made Garment

How many times have you complained about bad workmanship in the garments you buy, as the seams rip and the buttons pop on the first wearing? Use your sewing know-how to check quality on ready-made garments, right in the fitting room. Then decide whether you can fix up any flaws in the workmanship. Sometimes a few minutes with needle and thread before you wear the garment can be worthwhile.

Use the following questions to guide you in checking workmanship:
1. Are the seams firmly stitched?

If you find breaks in the stitching, you can restitch along original seam line.
2. Are the seam edges finished?

If seam edges are starting to ravel because they have not been properly finished, you can pink or overcast the edges.
3. Are buttonholes firmly finished?

If the buttonholes look as though they will start to fray almost instantly, you can use Buttonhole Twist to work over the machine stitching for reinforcement.
4. Are buttons, hooks, snaps, and other fastenings securely attached?

If not, it's easy to give them a little extra stitching.
5. Are children's clothes sturdy and practical?

Play clothes should have a reinforced section at the knee. Dresses should have generous hems.

Good workmanship is one of the things you pay for in expensive clothes. You can use your sewing skill to bring a little missing workmanship to a bargain buy.

SEWING FOR OTHERS

You have had the experience of sewing for yourself and now you are probably ready and eager to put your skill and know-how to use to make things for your family and other special people in your life. A few extra hints will help you give these things the professional look you want them to have. You will be proud of what you make and you will find that you are saving a lot of money, too.

Sewing for Men

Men of all ages love to have things made especially for them. Check through the pages of your big pattern catalog; you'll find patterns aplenty for sport shirts, vests, bathing suits with matching tops, surfer shorts, bathrobes, even costumes. Togetherness has crept into the men's sections of the catalogs. You will find a good selection of his-and-hers styles in matching vests and shirts to make up in the newest colors and fabrics you can find.

Now that men no longer feel that navy blue is the only color in the world, it's more fun to sew for them. Pick bright plaids, stripes, paisleys, motif prints, polka dots, and swinging solids for shirts or beachwear. Choose crisp Dacron®/cotton combinations that require little or no maintenance time from you, or look to such traditional favorites as corduroy or washable wool. Even the polyester double knits brighten a male wardrobe.

PATTERN SIZES

Pattern sizes for boys and men reflect shirt sizes. If you've been buying a 15½/34 ready-to-wear shirt for him, select a medium pattern size with a 36″ waist and a 40″ chest. Men's clothes are built to fit at the neck and shoulder.

Unless your man is exceptionally heavy or slim, you won't have to worry about pattern alterations. Boys' patterns come in straight sizes, up to 14.

MAKE A SHIRT

Patterns for menswear are very specific, and give you exact directions for handling yokes and linings. There are, however, some details which require explanation. If the shirt is of heavy material, or a slightly transparent print, the lining can be a light, firm, solid-color fabric. As in women's clothing, the lining should be as washable as the fabric.

A man's shirt demands a flat felled seam. If you've never made one before, practice before tackling a shirt. It is used to give a trim, flat seam finish with no raw edges at all. To make

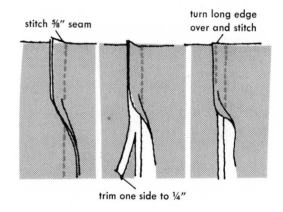

stitch ⅝″ seam

turn long edge over and stitch

trim one side to ¼″

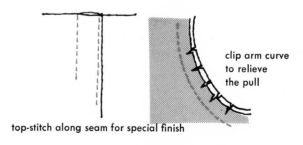

top-stitch along seam for special finish

clip arm curve to relieve the pull

A flat felled seam

a sample, place two pieces of fabric right sides together, and sew a ⅝″ seam. Trim one side to ¼″. Turn the raw edge of the long side over to cover the short side. Press or baste and stitch down to the shirt. If you want a double-stitched finish for the shirt (a sign of quality in a ready-to-wear shirt) run another row of stitching near the actual seam. Around the curve of the arm, it may be necessary to clip the seams a little to relieve the pull when you press the seam over. Finish all the collar and cuff top-stitching to match seams (double or single row). As with most top-stitching, use a slightly longer than usual machine stitch, about eight or ten to the inch.

Be sure to follow your pattern instructions exactly; men's shirts have a definite order of assembly. Do all finishing on the machine, even buttonholes (which run up and down) and hems. And be sure to get the buttonholes on the left side; men's shirts button left over right.

OTHER GIFT IDEAS FOR MEN

Vests made of napped suede cloth fall into the instant-sewing category, since they are unlined and present no fitting or finishing problems. Regular vests may be made of contemporary materials. If you do needlepoint or crewel embroidery, you may use these skills to decorate a man's vest, either by embroidering appropriate motifs directly onto the fabric, or by making a separate pocket patch which may be stitched to the garment.

If you are making something for a man, make it very specially his by adding a monogram. Some of the newest sewing machines have attachments that produce monograms automatically. If your machine isn't that talented, you can make very tidy straight letters with a standard satin stitch (see your machine instruction manual). It's a good idea to work monograms on pockets rather than on the garment itself. If you make a mistake, you can always cut out another pocket.

A man's necktie has long been the most original, imaginative, and colorful part of his wardrobe. With a good pattern, you'll find it fairly easy to make a tie, using good heavy tie silk, cotton, or a synthetic blend. It is very important to cut the fabric on the true bias, and you'll find one of the new cutting boards with bias markings very helpful. Use an all-bias non-woven interfacing. You can make a tie from ⅝ yard of 45″ fabric, plus ½ yard of 25″ interfacing and ¼ yard of lining. There's very little machine stitching involved in making a tie. It's mostly pressing and hand stitching, so be prepared to put a little time in on the project. A matching pocket handkerchief makes a nice gift set.

Sewing for Babies and Children

There is nothing, absolutely nothing, as enchanting as sewing for babies. Here's where delicate detailing and careful workmanship really show up. You'll find, too, that sewing for babies carries with it a certain built-in mystique. You work with special care to be sure that the tiny garment will be as perfect as the baby who wears it, to be sure that no lumpy seams or raw edges chafe that tender skin, and you work an extra measure of love and special wishes into every seam. After all, this just might be the baby who grows up to change the world, and you want to do your part in getting him off to the right start. This may seem a foolish way to feel when sewing baby clothes, but just try it. You'll see.

CHECK THE PATTERN BOOKS

You'll find plenty of traditional layette patterns available in a single layette size. Pretty christening dresses, slips, kimonos, wrappers, caps, and bootees are there for you to make from sheer lawn or batiste. Organdy, though pretty, is a tiny bit scratchy. Very fine Dacron®/cotton blends, in soft solids and dainty prints, are especially good. Decorative details, done with lace edging, hand or machine embroidery, tucking and dainty appliqué, are all suitable for baby clothes.

If a baby is going to star at a traditional church christening, he will require a traditional christening gown. Most babies today, however, spend a lot of time in practical little jump suits which zip or snap from neck to toe. These are comfortable, allow the baby plenty of kicking ease, and keep tiny toes from getting cold. They are much more sensible than the usual baby kimono. Make several in fine stretch terry, cotton jersey, or even a lightweight polyester knit. Be sure to use a cotton/Dacron® thread if you are sewing with a synthetic, and a zigzag stitch if you are sewing on a knit. Be sure, too, that anything you sew is thoroughly and completely washable and requires no ironing.

GIFT STITCHERY

If you are gift-making, it's more sensible to stitch your baby clothes in the six-month size rather than the layette size. By six months, a baby is big enough to wear bright little appliqués, stronger colors, and more definite designs. Then, too, there's a little more fashion choice in the older size range, which usually goes up to a toddler size 3, and the patterns include plenty of trimming suggestions.

There are also chubby sizes for the fat-baby set. So measure your child carefully and often; they seem to grow faster and faster!

When sewing for little girls, be sure to take full advantage of the new synthetics and synthetic blends. Be sure the fabrics you buy are pre-shrunk and colorfast, and your tapes and trimmings as well. If you are in any doubt, it's no trouble to toss the dress ingredients in with a load of laundry, or to soak them in the sink. If necessary, press before cutting.

A young girl often has very strong fashion preferences, and it's wise to take these into consideration. Let her go fabric shopping with you; let her study pattern books; let her help decide the kind of garment she wants. You'll be rewarded by her enthusiasm and her pride.

MAKE IT FIT

Well-fitting clothes are important to a child. It's far better to make stitched-in allowances for growth than to make a garment too big in the first place. Clothes that are too big make a child especially conscious of his own small-ness, and make him feel clumsy and ill-at-ease.

After checking measurements to get the right pattern size, check the pattern itself, as described on page 21, to see whether altera-tions are needed. If so, alter it just as you would an adult pattern.

GROWTH ALLOWANCE

There are several ways to provide built-in growth allowance in children's clothes. A jumper can be made with adjustable shoulder straps, or extra buttonholes to drop the gar-ment from the shoulder. A deep hem is im-portant in children's clothes. Plan for a good four inches in a straight or gathered skirt, two inches in a gored or flared skirt.

Growth allowance in skirt and waistline tucks

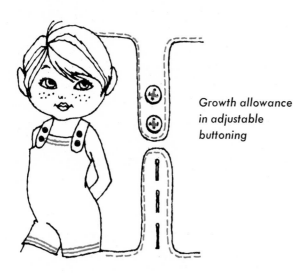

Growth allowance in adjustable buttoning

It's possible to provide for growth through tucks in strategic places. A tuck may be in-serted just above the waistline in a fitted dress, to be let down when the child needs the extra length. To do this, cut all sections of the bodice, including any neck-to-waist facings, 1″ to 1½″ longer than the pattern calls for. Sew facings in place. Then lay in your tuck just above the waistline seam. A decorative tuck is pressed upward on the right side, and serves as a waistline accent. Hand-tack it in place at intervals. If the tuck is to be covered by a belt or sash, it should be on the inside of the garment and pressed down.

Tucks may also be put in a skirt, just above the hem, and are very attractive when done in groups. A fairly long stitch is fine for tucks, though chain stitching is even easier to rip out. Some machines are equipped with a chain stitch feature.

Since children's clothes are subject to more wear and tear than grownup clothes, be sure your workmanship is up to the situation. French seams (see page 142) offer a neat, strong finish for lightweight fabrics. Heavier fabrics, such as corduroy, should have the seam edges overcast by machine. Play clothes should be built for active duty, but good clothes and night clothes may be stitched more lightly.

After a little boy gets out of the pre-school category, it's better to buy his rough play clothes, such as blue jeans and khakis, and use your sewing skills on shirts, beachwear, and night clothes.

Special Finishes for Children's Clothes

Children's clothes offer all kinds of possibilities for interesting touches; and how they love those special effects! It's possible to add different trims to a basic dress, make it in different materials, and have a set of dresses that look entirely different.

SCALLOPS

A scalloped hem is feminine, dainty, and fun to do. You may make the scallops with a separate hemmed facing, or line the whole dress. This is very easy to do with the help of a simple pattern. Measure the hem edge of the dress and mark into equal sections. Using a cup, glass, or special scalloping ruler, trace scallops onto wrong side with chalk or pencil. Lay facing or lining against fabric, right sides together, and stitch along marked lines. Bridge the space between each scallop with one stitch across. Trim seam to ¼", less if your fabric is *very firm*. Notch out every ½" or less, and clip at the point between. Turn right side out and smooth with fingertips and a blunt rounded implement such as a table knife. Press smoothly.

If you have an automatic zigzag sewing machine, you can set it to make small scallops completely automatically. These scallops are fine for collars, neck and sleeve edges, and front facings.

RUFFLES

Little girls and ruffles just naturally seem to go together. Ruffles may be applied to a plain edge, such as a hem; they may be inserted in a seam; or they may be stitched on with a heading. While ruffles may be cut on the bias, they are usually cut on the straight cross grain for children's clothes, to give a crisper, perkier effect.

Cut fabric two to three times as long as the finished ruffle will be. Finish the outer edge before gathering, using a narrow machine-stitched hem. To gather the ruffle, set your sewing machine for its longest stitch (not a basting stitch) and sew as described in gathering directions, page 39. Pull bobbin threads to gather. While your sewing machine probably has a ruffler, short lengths can be done as easily without it.

To attach a ruffle to a raw edge, pin ruffle in place on garment with right sides together and stitch as shown. Trim the seam, overcast the edge, and press. The raw edge of a curved seam may be finished with a shaped or bias facing (see page 77).

To make a ruffle with a heading, finish both edges before gathering. Run gathering thread

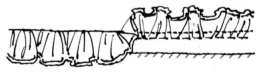

Press ruffle down to cover overcast edge.

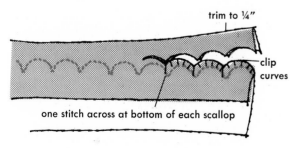

trim to ¼"

clip curves

one stitch across at bottom of each scallop

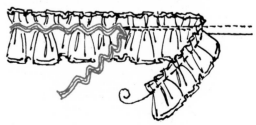

Ruffle with heading and rickrack trim

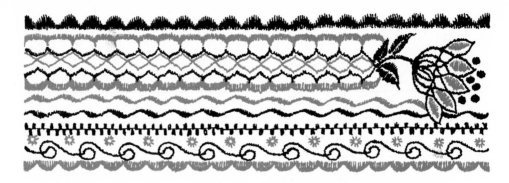

1″ from top edge. Pin in place, and top-stitch to hem of garment. Cover stitching with rick-rack or a narrow trim if desired. This type of ruffle may be on the edge of the garment which will be finished as usual with hem or facing, or rows may be used around a skirt or sleeve.

FRENCH SEAMS

Children's clothes are sometimes made with French seams, both for durability in light-weight fabrics and for the sake of appearance. The French seam is also useful in lingerie, and in any fine-fabric sewing.

To make a narrow French seam, lay fabric wrong sides together. Stitch a plain seam a scant ⅜″ from raw edges. Trim seam allowance to ⅛″. Press seam allowances to one side. Fold work on stitched line, wrong sides out and right sides together. Stitch again, ¼″ from fold. This stitching will be on regular marked seam line.

Decorative Stitching

If you've been wondering what to do with all those fancy stitches your sewing machine can turn out, here's your answer. Decorative stitching, in different thread colors and different designs, can make marvelous bands of Mexican-like embroidery. You can alternate rows of decorative stitching with bright ribbons, embroidered trim, or rickrack, for extra decorative punch.

There are two approaches to putting bands of trim on a garment; you can stitch it directly

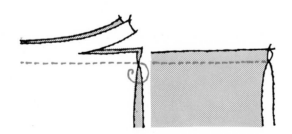

Trim to ⅛″.   Turn and stitch ¼″ from fold.

A separate band trims a skirt.

onto the cutout section of the garment before it is assembled, or you can make a separate band to be stitched on. If you are making a band of trimming to circle a full skirt, for example, you might find it easier to put the work on a separate band. For yoke and sleeve treatments, work with the cutout dress sections.

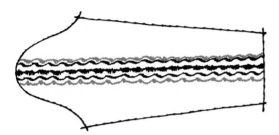

Use decorative stitching to trim a sleeve.

To insure straight rows, mark lines of stitching lightly with a yardstick and pencil. The presser foot makes a handy spacing guage, if you let the left edge of it follow the previous row of stitching. Make your designs in a nice close satin stitch; use scallop motifs for outer edges, other designs for inside rows. Let an embroidered ribbon have the very center. Use your twin needle to make the stitching go twice as fast.

FUN WITH APPLIQUÉ

If you like to sew, you'll love doing decorative appliqués to add whimsy to your children's clothes, and your children will be enchanted by this sort of loving extra. All kinds of designs can be adapted to appliqué work, and you will find this a very satisfying and creative decorative approach.

Patches can be decorative as well as utilitarian, and are especially fun on knees of little trousers. Decorative patchings by machine re-

quires you to open a leg seam on pants to get the work flat under the needle.

Where can you find ideas for appliqué? Your child's coloring book, for one place. A beginning coloring book will have plenty of strong, simple drawings which are just right. Using dressmaker's carbon, trace the design onto the fabric. Back the fabric with a layer of thin Pellon® or with crisp organdy, to give extra body.

Coloring books offer ideas for appliqué designs.

To Appliqué by Hand

Staystitch appliqué and backing together with your sewing machine exactly on the appliqué outline. Cut out design, leaving ¼″ seam allowance. Turn this allowance under, clipping if necessary, and press flat. Stitch on any cutout sections that are part of the appliqué

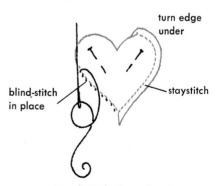

turn edge under

blind-stitch in place

staystitch

Hand-stitched appliqué

design. Pin complete appliqué in position, and blindstitch in place.

To Appliqué by Machine

Cut out design with fabric and backing together, leaving wide margins. Staystitch along the outline, joining base fabric, backing, and appliqué fabric. This will discourage slipping. Make a test swatch, using the same materials, and test all stitches before doing actual work. Set machine for a close satin stitch, and work along your basted lines. With small, sharp scissors, trim away excess fabric of appliqué close to line of stitching.

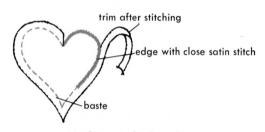

Machine-stitched appliqué

If your machine has a built-in buttonholer, you can use buttonholes for some of your decorative sewing. The eyelet buttonhole, for instance, makes fine eyes. Longer buttonholes may be used as leaves, long windows, chain links, or flower petals.

Bias tape is useful for decorative work, and makes magnificent initials. Just top-stitch it in place, using straight or decorative stitching.

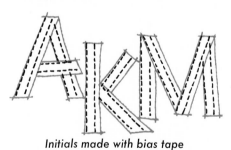

Initials made with bias tape

If you do a lot of decorative sewing, you will soon develop a special appliqué box, with odd lengths of ribbon, rickrack, and buttons, plus design ideas, so you'll always have the ingredients handy for original and imaginative appliqués.

Halloween Costumes and Special Outfits

If you are not too busy, you will enjoy making Halloween costumes for your children. The ready-made outfits cost several dollars, and are rarely well made. Since playing dress-up is such an important part of a child's development, it's nice to have Halloween costumes that are worn on the big night, then tucked into the dress-up box to offer rainy-day entertainment for the rest of the year. Also, like other children's clothes, Halloween costumes may be handed down from one child to the next.

Pattern books offer basic costume silhouettes with suggested variations. Almost any kind of animal can be made from a jump-suit pattern, using fake fur, flannel, or terry.

An all-purpose cape of terry, felt, cotton, or corduroy offers all kinds of possibilities including Batman, Superman, Snow White's wicked stepmother, a witch, a magician, a king,

Dracula, a goblin, Mighty Mouse—the list is as long as a youngster's imagination. Use colored stick-on tape to make appropriate symbols.

Little girls love full, swirling skirts with lots and lots of fabric. In a long skirt, she is an instant princess, queen, bride, old-fashioned lady, or good witch. If you have some white ruffled sheer curtains which have served their turn on the home decorating front, take an hour to convert them to a glamorous dress-up skirt. Save an extra curtain for a bridal veil or the princess's train.

Never overlook fabric sources—any drapery, bedspread, or lightweight blanket will convert to a costume. Rather than buy new fabric, check Goodwill and Salvation Army centers; they are usually loaded with cast-off household linens, to give you yards and yards of good fabric at minimal cost. Always run these items through the washer before using.

The fine art of make-over is especially useful when applied to costumes, for there's plenty of material in bathrobes, evening gowns, and the like. Costumes offer a good way to clean out your remnant drawer, too—consider a Coat of Many Colors, a Horse of a Different Color, or the Patchwork Girl of Oz.

Dancing classes often require ballerina costumes for their young performers. Patterns are available for these. You can simplify the pattern instructions by sewing the bodice onto a pair of dyed-to-match cotton panties. Re-read the section on gathering, page 39, before gathering the net.

Halloween costumes, dancing costumes, and other outfits are good fun for you and for the children. Use your imagination to create them inexpensively, and use the many talents of your sewing machine to make them extra special. Your youngsters will remember their costumes far, far longer than they will remember whether the beds got made or the rugs vacuumed on the big day.

Make a Decorative Wall Hanging for a Special Child

Materials needed:
1¾ yards crisp cotton fabric
12 1" black buttons for wheels
Fabric scraps in assorted colors
Thread to match fabrics
Black thread
Bias tape
Spool of pink thread for smoke
Graph paper in 1" squares*
Carbon paper
Pencil and ruler

* Or mark 1" squares on a 10" x 48" strip of shelf paper.

Instructions:
Enlarge pattern pieces onto 1" graph paper, or on paper marked into 1" squares. Each small square in the diagram equals one 1" square. Cut out paper pattern pieces. Pin pattern pieces to fabric, matching grain lines. Cut out, leaving ¼" seam allowance all around each piece. Use carbon paper to transfer pattern markings to fabric.

Pin and press under seam allowances. Thread machine with black thread and set for straight stitch, twelve to fifteen to the inch. Stitch roof line on caboose roof (5B), roof line and windows on boxcar (3) rounded line on engine (1B) and lines on cowcatcher (1A). To make lines for boxcar ladder (3), set machine for wide zigzag stitch. Run zigzag line from lower edge of boxcar to ½" above roof line. Reset

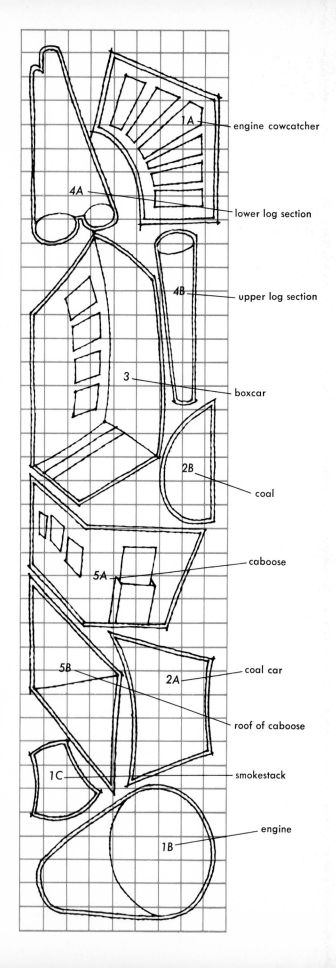

engine cowcatcher

lower log section

upper log section

boxcar

coal

caboose

coal car

roof of caboose

smokestack

engine

machine for satin stitch at medium width. Run line of satin stitching on each side of wide zigzag to form ladder. Leave machine set on medium-width satin stitch and black thread.

Cut background fabric piece 57″ by 12″.

Cut lining fabric strip 57″ by 9″. On lower edge of background fabric, press under ½″ seam allowance. Along right side, from top to bottom, draw fold line lightly with pencil 1½″ in from raw edge. Starting 1″ from lower edge, measure and mark for ruler lines at 1″ intervals. Make inch marks 1″ long. Make foot marks 2″ long. Note that markings begin at 6″, so that first foot mark is 6″ from lower edge.

With machine set for satin stitching, stitch over marked lines. Work from inside edge toward raw edge, extending stitching just slightly beyond fold line for seam allowance. This insures a neat finished edge.

Pin pieces in position as shown in photograph (following page 132): engine pieces 1A, 1B, 1C; coal car pieces 2A and 2B; boxcar 3, log sections 4A and 4B; and caboose 5A and 5B.

Top-stitch pieces in place, working close to pressed edges. Stitch contrast log (4B) to log base (4A) and pin bias strips in position before stitching log unit and bias strips (see color photograph). Stitch coal in place first, and stitch coal car over lower edge of coal.

Stitch main engine section first, then cowcatcher, then smokestack. Make "smoke" as follows: with sharp razor blade or Stanley knife, cut completely through spool of thread so pieces of thread may be removed in one section. Tie at center and fluff threads. Handstitch in position over smokestack.

Sew buttons in place for wheels as shown.

With right sides together, pin long edges of lining section to long edges of hanging. Stitch as pinned. Press seam allowances open. Turn hanging right side out and press, centering lining section. Make narrow hem in lower edge. Turn and stitch a 1" casing on the upper edge. Put narrow wood dowel through casing and tie a cord on ends of dowel for hanging.

To use individual cars for decorative patching or appliqué, you may wish to make the cars on a smaller scale. In this case, enlarge them onto paper marked in ½" squares. For use on garments, back each car with a layer of interfacing for extra body. Appliqué in place by hand or machine. (See pages 143–144.)

A SEWING GRAB BAG OF HELPFUL HINTS AND TIPS

Your Sewing Calendar

Women who sew a lot eventually find themselves following a time plan. If you are always just a little late with your sewing, maybe you need a schedule to help you get organized.

January: Shop clearance sales to pick up bargains in wools, fake furs, and winter fabrics. Make a bright wool dress to get you through the winter blahs, and a terrific at-home thing for snowy nights.

February: Spring fabrics are in! Pick a gloomy day, and brighten it by spending it at your favorite fabric spot. Get the ingredients for your important spring costume. If you sew for your daughters, shop for them at the same time. Double check everyone's measurements. Diet now?

March: Turn off the phone and sew up a storm for spring.

April: Feeling a little broke? Sewing is good for the budget. Make summer cottons for yourself and the girls.

May: Now's the time for casual wear—playsuits, shorts, maybe even a swimsuit. Try a pair of surfer shorts for your son, a quickie project.

June: Last chance for summer sewing! Finish it up with a beach bag and a gay summer print. Put away winter clothes; weed out the closets. Check fabric shop for bargains in light spring wools and blends.

July: This is your relaxing month. Read the new pattern books on the beach. Prowl the stores, and watch for special summer promotions in the world of sewing. Think about fall fashions.

August: Summer is running out. Check over fall clothes, fix hems, make minor repairs. Sew transition cottons for the school set, a snappy slacks-and-vest outfit for yourself, and a good wool skirt in the latest length.

September: Put away summer clothes, and sort out give-aways for your favorite charity or thrift shop. Sign up for a course in advanced dressmaking or even tailoring. Check your sewing supplies and clean your sewing machine. If you aren't up to making a winter coat yet, make a terrific poncho.

October: If you have kids in the trick-or-treat league, Halloween costumes head the list. Find a specialty for this year's church bazaar, and make a dozen of them. Get started on gift stitching for Christmas—a filmy peignoir for your mother-in-law and bright granny gowns for the girls.

November: Are there some sewing enthusiasts on your Christmas list? Give them snowy-Sunday packages: fabric, pattern, trims, and notions, all ready to sew. Needlework kits are nice, too. There's still time for a little handwork to make your gifts special. Try a whimsical appliqué, a graceful monogram.

December: Home stretch! Finish the gift stitching, and make something sensational for holiday parties. Think glitter. It's available by-the-yard, to add glamour to simple patterns in soft fabrics. And make up your own Dear

Santa list: a length of marvelous fabric, a subscription to your favorite pattern magazine, a new sewing book, a set of sewing lessons, even a new sewing machine. Best gift of all—more time to sew!

Tips from the Sewing Experts

Sewing is fun, creative, and exciting. For some women, it's even more; it's a glamorous, fast-moving, full-time profession. Women who love to sew work as fashion directors, educators, designers, writers, artists, stylists. They are the real sewing experts.

A few of the most important women in the sewing industry were asked to contribute a good-and-easy sewing tip that they use in their own sewing. They were delighted to share their know-how, so more women could share their enthusiasm for sewing.

From Pat Perry, Technical Sewing Director of Vogue Patterns: "Please . . . follow the instructions on the pattern guide sheet. Many sewing errors happen because a sewer is in too much of a hurry and is negligent about following directions. For truly professional results, *no* step should be omitted no matter how insignificant it may seem."

From Virginia Mann, Editor of Famous Features Newspaper Pattern Syndicate: "Be sure all your sewing tools (thread, needle, scissors, etc.) and all your dress ingredients (fabric, pattern, zipper, buttons, etc.) are together before you start, so you won't lose time and concentration by jumping up and looking for missing items. In other words, get off to a well-organized start."

From Frances Gutman, Educational Director for Coats and Clark: "For successful sewing on knits, use a polyester-core thread, a fresh needle, and tension slightly looser than usual."

From Jessie Hutton, Educational Director, The Singer Company: "To avoid puckers in permanent press fabrics, select patterns with seams that are just slightly bias, to provide extra give. Avoid a tailored set-in sleeve, and use the finest needle for your thread."

Miss Hutton offers a second tip on working with plaids: "Avoid patterns with diagonal bustline or shoulder darts, or with shaped joinings in the bodice or skirt."

From Mildred G. Ryan, Vice-President, McCall's Pattern Company: "Choosing a pattern in the correct figure type and size is the key to perfect fit and to a more successful sewing experience. Extensive pattern adjustments are avoided. Construction time is shortened. Sewing is easier. It often makes the difference between a garment with a smart, professional look, and an amateurish one."

And here are a few general tips that may be helpful to you:

Sewing seems to go more smoothly if the house, or at least the sewing room, is neat and your mind is clear to concentrate.

Don't sew when you are overtired, and don't sew too far into the night. You are too apt to make mistakes.

Assembly-line stitching speeds the job. If you are joining several little pieces such as facing sections, join them one right after the other, pulling the thread through without cutting. The sections will be strung together like beads on a necklace. Just clip them apart.

Always be sure your bobbin is full before starting to sew, and have an extra one ready if your machine doesn't have an automatic bobbin winder.

Don't agonize over rethreading your sewing

machine. Tie your new thread to your old thread up near the spool pin; pull the old right through all the threading mechanisms, except the needle, smooth as silk. Cut the knot, at the needle, and thread the needle.

When you finish sewing for the day, clean up sewing litter and plan your sewing for the next session.

The more you sew, the easier it gets! If you have a hard time with some of the finer details, just keep doing them. Before you know it, you'll be a real artist at show-off sewing.

Finally—don't be shy about asking for advice. Everyone was a beginner once.

Take It Easy—Let the Professionals Give You a Hand

Did you know that a good fabric shop has all sorts of helpful services to assist you with some of the more time-consuming sewing details? Here are the things they can have done for you.

Belts and/or buckles can be made and covered to your specifications.

Buttonholes can be made, sometimes even handmade ones for tailored garments.

Buttons can be covered, and much more elegantly than you could manage at home.

Purses can be made to match your dress.

All sorts of odd-size-and-shape zippers are available through special order, including double-ended ones for ski clothes, extra-heavy separating zippers, and zippers with reversible slides for reversible jackets.

You can have fabric tucked, so that you can cut out a whole tucked blouse front.

You can have hemstitching done in rows, like tucking for decoration, or to be cut

through for a picot edge on chiffons, and other delicate fabrics.

You can have pleating done for skirts. Consult with the company doing it for the amount of fabric needed and preparation of fabric prior to pleating.

Questions and Answers About Your Sewing Machine

All new sewing machines and most second-hand ones come with a complete and thorough instruction book. Read it carefully; it was written by experts to help you. There are many adjustments and some simple repairs you can do yourself to keep your machine out of the repair shop. If it's not sewing properly, see if you can't find the difficulty and its remedy in this section.

1. Why does the thread keep breaking?
   Most likely, your machine is threaded wrong. Other possibilities are too-tight tension, a bent needle, or poor-quality thread with slubs. The thread may be snagging on the spool as it unwinds.
2. What makes the fabric pick and pull, sometimes making a line across?
   Try a new needle. You may be trying to sew with a dull or bent needle.
3. Why are my stitches all different lengths even though I have the machine set for the right stitch length?
   You're controlling your fabric too much, pulling from behind and holding in front. Relax! And be sure your fabric is supported, so the fabric weight doesn't pull too much.
4. My machine seems to be skipping stitches. What can I do?

Try a finer needle or a new needle. For synthetic knit fabrics try a ball-point needle.

5. My zigzag stitching looks fine on the right side, but resembles loose featherstitching on the wrong side. How can I make the stitching even?

Make your stitch a little finer and check your upper tension setting. It may need to be adjusted.

6. My machine is completely jammed. What is wrong?

This indicates tangled threads in the bobbin. Turn hand wheel away from you to break or cut threads jammed in the bobbin case. Use tweezers to remove loose threads.

7. Why does my needle keep breaking?

Change to a heavier needle size, and be sure you are using the right needle for your machine. If the screw is loose on your presser foot, it may be out of position so the needle strikes it. Make sure the needle is tight in its clamp.

8. How often should I clean my machine?

Under normal use, once a week. Clean away lint and fluff with your lint brush. Wipe tension discs, takeup lever, thread guides, presser bar, needle bar, bobbin case, and machine arm with a soft cloth. Apply one drop of machine oil to spots indicated in your instruction book. After oiling, stitch scrap material to absorb extra oil. Leave a fabric blotter under the needle when the machine is not in use, to absorb excess oil.

9. How often is major cleaning needed?

About three times a year, you should clean, oil, and lubricate your machine, according to the instructions in your book. Regular care will prolong the life of your machine, and will keep it stitching smoothly.

10. Any normal precautions to remember?

Keep the machine covered when not in use, to keep out children, pets, and dust. Always check the settings before starting to sew; you may have left your machine on a zigzag or buttonhole setting last time. Unplug the machine, and put the foot control where it won't be stepped on by mistake. And keep your instruction manual handy!

Caring for Your Clothes

Once you have learned to make attractive clothes, you will find that they are worth a little special care to keep them looking lovely with regular cleaning and thoughtful daily handling.

Try to replace buttons, snaps, and hooks, and stitch up snagged hems as soon as you notice them. Otherwise, it is far too easy to let these minor chores accumulate till they add up to a major job.

Your clothes should be hung carefully. Invest in a group of good hangers; wire ones from the cleaner's put nasty creases in the shoulders of dresses and jackets. Fold knits and keep them in a drawer or over a padded hanger so they don't stretch. A velvet-covered stole hanger is perfect if you have one. Bias-cut dresses fare well on these hangers, too.

Try to develop a critical eye for closet clutter. Too often, closets are filled with clothes that need mending or alteration, and these non-wearables take free-hanging space from good clothes. Be strong and get rid of them, or at least get them off into another closet where they can only crowd each other. Maybe, some snowy weekend, you will really do something about those old clothes.

Never store clothes in a hot attic, or in a closet with hot pipes in it. Natural fibers, such as wool or silk, lose their life completely in such an atmosphere.

Never put anything away dirty. If you've picked up a spot on an otherwise clean dress, spot-clean it with one of the many preparations available for this purpose. If your fabric is a sensitive one, such as pure silk or fine wool, have the spot removed professionally. A good dry cleaner is a friend indeed. He will handle your clothes with even more consideration if he knows you sew your own, and if you can tell him the fiber content of your garments.

Winter coats should always be cleaned before summer storage, as should suits, slacks, and other cold-weather garments.

If you suspect a style change is in the air, take the hem out of a skirt before having it cleaned. It's the only way to get rid of the dark streak and the crease that mark a let-down hem.

Coin-operated cleaning machines are great for knits and for pile fabrics such as velvet and corduroy, or any clothes that do not need hard pressing. They are an aid to the clothes-care budget, too.

Naturally, you will be washing your polyester garments and some of your cottons, as well as practically everything you make for the children. The polyesters, knit or woven, respond beautifully to machine washing. Be sure to use a cycle for delicate fabrics; to prevent snags, put knits in a mesh bag. Knits may be tumble-dried on a setting for delicate fabrics, but toss in a couple of towels to absorb the moisture and cushion the tumbling action.

Keep laundering in mind when you make cottons that are going to be put into the washing machine. Zippers, seam bindings, and other ingredients, as well as the fabric itself, should be pre-shrunk before sewing. The seam edges should be finished so that the washing action won't cause fraying. And if your dress material is permanent press, the bindings should be no-iron also.

When your closet is full of lovely outfits you've made yourself, you will find it's no chore to care for them. You have put in time to make then just right in the first place, so give them the little extra time needed to keep them that way.

FOR EASY REFERENCE

On the following pages you will find valuable reference material to aid you in each of your sewing projects.

Your own PERSONAL MEASUREMENT CHART is on page 155. It is yours alone; fill it in carefully, revise it if you gain or lose weight, and use it both for pattern-size selection and for accurate pattern alteration.

The STANDARD PATTERN INDUSTRY CHARTS (page 156) give the basic measurements used by all pattern companies for figure types and pattern sizes, and will help you determine your correct pattern size.

The FABRIC CONVERSION CHART (page 158) gives you yardage equivalents in different fabric widths. If you've fallen in love with a 32" import, and the pattern envelope lists yardage requirements only as narrow as 36", this chart will tell you how much more of your fabric to buy. Also, it will help you decide how much 45" lining material to buy for a 60" wool.

The FABRIC, THREAD, AND NEEDLE CHART (page 159) will tell you what size needle and what type thread to use for various fabrics, including knits and polyesters.

Your Personal Measurement Chart

Take your measurements honestly, and fill
in the chart in the spaces provided.

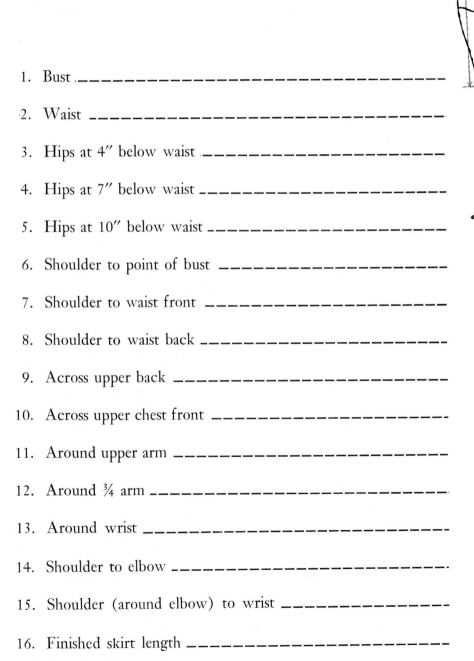

1. Bust _____

2. Waist _____

3. Hips at 4″ below waist _____

4. Hips at 7″ below waist _____

5. Hips at 10″ below waist _____

6. Shoulder to point of bust _____

7. Shoulder to waist front _____

8. Shoulder to waist back _____

9. Across upper back _____

10. Across upper chest front _____

11. Around upper arm _____

12. Around ¾ arm _____

13. Around wrist _____

14. Shoulder to elbow _____

15. Shoulder (around elbow) to wrist _____

16. Finished skirt length _____

STANDARD PATTERN INDUSTRY CHARTS

WOMEN'S

Women's patterns are designed for the larger, more fully mature figure; about 5'5" to 5'6" without shoes.

Size	38	40	42	44	46	48	50
Bust	42	44	46	48	50	52	54
Waist	34	36	38	40½	43	45½	48
Hip	44	46	48	50	52	54	56
Back waist length	17¼	17⅜	17½	17⅝	17¾	17⅞	18

MISSES'

Misses' patterns are designed for a well proportioned, and developed figure; about 5'5" to 5'6" without shoes.

Size	6	8	10	12	14	16	18
Bust	30½	31½	32½	34	36	38	40
Waist	22	23	24	25½	27	29	31
Hip	32½	33½	34½	36	38	40	42
Back waist length	15½	15¾	16	16¼	16½	16¾	17

JUNIOR PETITE

Junior Petite patterns are designed for a well proportioned petite figure; about 5' to 5'1" without shoes.

Size	3jp	5jp	7jp	9jp	11jp	13jp
Bust	30½	31	32	33	34	35
Waist	22	22½	23½	24½	25½	26½
Hip	31½	32	33	34	35	36
Back waist length	14	14¼	14½	14¾	15	15¼

JUNIOR

Junior patterns are designed for a well proportioned, shorter waisted figure; about 5'4" to 5'5" without shoes.

Size	5	7	9	11	13	15
Bust	30	31	32	33½	35	37
Waist	21½	22½	23½	24½	26	28
Hip	32	33	34	35½	37	39
Back waist length	15	15¼	15½	15¾	16	16¼

YOUNG JUNIOR/TEEN

This new size range is designed for the developing pre-teen and teen figures; about 5'1" to 5'3" without shoes.

Size	5/6	7/8	9/10	11/12	13/14	15/16
Bust	28	29	30½	32	33½	35
Waist	22	23	24	25	26	27
Hip	31	32	33½	35	36½	38
Back waist length	13½	14	14½	15	15⅜	15¾

HALF-SIZE

Half-size patterns are for a fully developed figure with a short backwaist length. Waist and hip are larger in proportion to bust than other figure types; about 5'2" to 5'3" without shoes.

Size	10½	12½	14½	16½	18½	20½	22½	24½
Bust	33	35	37	39	41	43	45	47
Waist	26	28	30	32	34	36½	39	41½
Hip	35	37	39	41	43	45½	48	50½
Back waist length	15	15¼	15½	15¾	15⅞	16	16⅛	16¼

CHILDREN'S

Size	1	2	3	4	5	6	6X
Breast	20	21	22	23	24	25	25½
Waist	19½	20	20½	21	21½	22	22½
Hip				24	25	26	26½
Back waist length	8¼	8½	9	9½	10	10½	10¾
Approx. Heights							

GIRLS'

Girls' patterns are designed for the girl who has not yet begun to mature. See chart below for approximate heights without shoes.

Size	7	8	10	12	14
Breast	26	27	28½	30	32
Waist	23	23½	24½	25½	26½
Hip	27	28	30	32	34
Back waist length	11½	12	12¾	13½	14¼
Approx. Heights	50"	52"	56"	58½"	61"

TODDLERS'

Size	½	1	2	3	4
Breast	19	20	21	22	23
Waist	19	19½	20	20½	21

Figure Types

Misses'   Junior   Junior Petite   Young Junior Teen   Girls'   Half-size   Women's

FABRIC CONVERSION CHART

FABRIC WIDTHS	32"	35"-36"	39"	41"	44"-45"	50"	52"-54"	58"-60"
	1 ⅞	1 ¾	1 ½	1 ½	1 ⅜	1 ¼	1 ⅛	1
	2 ¼	2	1 ¾	1 ¾	1 ⅝	1 ½	1 ⅜	1 ¼
	2 ½	2 ¼	2	2	1 ¾	1 ⅝	1 ½	1 ⅜
	2 ¾	2 ½	2 ¼	2 ¼	2 ⅛	1 ¾	1 ¾	1 ⅝
	3 ⅛	2 ⅞	2 ½	2 ½	2 ¼	2	1 ⅞	1 ¾
	3 ⅜	3 ⅛	2 ¾	2 ¾	2 ½	2 ¼	2	1 ⅞
	3 ¾	3 ⅜	3	2 ⅞	2 ¾	2 ⅜	2 ¼	2
	4	3 ¾	3 ¼	3 ⅛	2 ⅞	2 ⅝	2 ⅜	2 ¼
	4 ⅜	4 ¼	3 ½	3 ⅜	3 ⅛	2 ¾	2 ⅝	2 ⅜
	4 ⅝	4 ½	3 ¾	3 ⅝	3 ⅜	3	2 ¾	2 ⅝
	5	4 ¾	4	3 ⅞	3 ⅝	3 ¼	2 ⅞	2 ¾
	5 ¼	5	4 ¼	4 ⅛	3 ⅞	3 ⅜	3 ⅛	2 ⅞

(YARDAGE)

FABRIC, THREAD, AND NEEDLE CHART

FABRIC TYPE	FIBER	THREAD	NEEDLE SIZE Hand	Machine
SHEER, SOFT: net, chiffon, georgette	Cotton	Mercerized 50	8-9	9-11
	Silk	Silk A or mercerized 50		
	Synthetic	Poly or poly/cotton		
SHEER, CRISP: batiste, lawn, dotted swiss, lace, organza	Cotton	Mercerized 50	8-9	9-11
	Silk	Silk A, mercerized 50		
	Synthetic	Poly or silk		
	Blend	Poly/cotton, mercerized 50		
SOFT: crepe, challis, satin, light synthetic knits, silk jersey	Cotton, wool	Mercerized 50	7-8	11
	Silk	Silk A, mercerized 50		
	Synthetic	Poly, poly/cotton, mercerized 50		
CRISP, LIGHT: shantung, voile, pongee, gingham	Cotton	Mercerized 50	7-8	11-14
	Silk	Mercerized 50, silk		
	Synthetic, blend	Poly, poly/cotton, mercerized 50		
MEDIUM FIRM: knits and double knits, suitings, faille, pique, broadcloth	Woven natural fibers	Mercerized 50	7-8	11-14
	Knit natural fibers	Poly/cotton, mercerized 50		
	Woven or knit synthetics	Poly/cotton, mercerized 50		
SOFT, MEDIUM HEAVY: velvet, velveteen, tweed, fleece, sweater knits, corduroy	Cotton, wool	Mercerized heavy duty	5-7	16
	Synthetics and blends	Poly/cotton, mercerized heavy duty		
CRISP, MEDIUM HEAVY: damask, brocade, ottoman, matelassé	Cotton, wool, natural fibers	Mercerized heavy duty	5-7	16
	Synthetics, blends	Poly/cotton, mercerized heavy duty		
HEAVY: fake fur, sailcloth, upholstery materials, leather, suede, fabric-backed vinyl	Cotton, wool	Heavy-duty mercerized	5-7	16
	Leather, vinyl	Heavy-duty mercerized, poly/cotton		
	Synthetics	Poly/cotton		

Note: For decorative top-stitching (usually on medium to heavy fabrics) use silk buttonhole twist with a size 4-5 needle (hand) or size 16 needle (machine).

A Glossary of Sewing Terms

ALLOWANCE: Extra fabric outside the seam line, usually ⅝″.

ALTERATION: Adjusting pattern for fit before cutting; also fitting finished garment.

APPLIQUÉ: Fabric applied as decorative trim, usually contrasting in color.

ARMHOLE: Opening in a garment for the arm. (Sometimes called armscye.)

ARROWHEAD TACK: Small, triangular hand-embroidered motif used as reinforcement at strain points.

ASSEMBLE: Joining major pieces of garment.

BACKSTITCH: 1. Small, firm hand stitch. 2. A few reverse machine stitches to anchor the beginning or end of a seam.

BALL-POINT NEEDLE: Needle with rounded end for use on knits.

BAR TACK: Close stitching used as reinforcement at ends of buttonholes or pleats.

BASTING STITCH: Temporary stitch made by hand or machine.

BELTING: Stiff banding used inside waistline, or covered by fabric for a belt.

BIAS: True diagonal of a fabric. Diagonal strips of fabric used as a seam finish.

BLANKET STITCH: Similar to buttonhole stitch but more widely spaced.

BLINDSTITCH: Hand stitch used to hold a finished edge invisibly.

BODKIN: Long, blunt needle used for threading cord or elastic.

BOUND BUTTONHOLES: Buttonholes finished by fabric binding.

BOX PLEAT: Two pleats which turn away from each other to form a box shape on the right side.

BUTTONHOLE STITCH: A hand stitch used to finish a raw edge such as buttonholes, eyelets, scallops.

CASING: A stitched channel for ribbon or elastic.

CATCH-STITCH: A cross-stitch used to hold a raw edge in place.

CHAIN STITCH: A hand-embroidery stitch and an interlocking machine stitch.

CLIP: A short cut into a seam allowance, made to shape the garment.

CORDING: A cord encased in a bias fabric strip.

CROSSWISE GRAIN: The selvage-to-selvage grain.

DART: A stitched fold of fabric, used to shape the garment to the body. Can be straight, tapered, or shaped.

DRESSMAKER'S CARBON: Special carbon paper used with a tracing wheel to transfer pattern markings to fabric.

DECORATIVE STITCHING: Zigzag stitching done for decorative effect; embroidery.

EASE: Process of fitting two pieces of fabric together in a seam when one is slightly fuller than the other.

EASE ALLOWANCE: Extra width in a pattern to give room for movement in a garment.

EDGE-FINISH: Finish applied to a raw edge.

EDGING: A trim with one straight edge.

EDGE-STITCHING: Stitching placed close to the finished edge of a garment.

EMBROIDERY: Decorative stitching done by hand or by machine.

EMERY BAG: Small bag filled with powder, to sharpen and remove rust from pins and needles.

EYELET: A small hole in a garment, finished to hold lacings. (See Fabric Glossary, page 167.)

FACING: A piece of fabric used to finish a garment opening such as a neckline.

FASTENINGS: Zippers, hooks and eyes, snaps, buttons, frogs, etc., used to fasten a garment.

FEATHERBONING: A flexible strip of fabric-covered boning used as stiffening.

FINDINGS: Small supplies used in garment construction; also notions.

FLAP POCKET: A pocket with a top edge which folds over to the outside.

FLAT-FELL: A seam finish used on men's clothing, tailored blouses, and sportswear.

FOOT: Any of several sewing machine attachments used to hold fabric firmly in place.

FRENCH SEAM: A small, neat, double-stitched seam used on sheers and in children's clothes.

FROG: Decorative closing formed by braid shaped into intricate loops.

GATHERING: Rows of stitching pulled through fabric to control fullness.

GORE: Skirt section that is fuller at the bottom than at the top.

GRADING: Trimming seam allowances to different widths to eliminate bulk.

GRAIN: Direction of fabric threads.

GUSSET: Small piece of fabric set into a slash, as at underarm, to give added ease.

HEM: An edge finish, usually at the lower edge of a garment, which is folded up and stitched in place.

HEMLINE: The marked line at the bottom of a garment.

HEMSTITCHING: A decorative open stitch done by hand or machine. Not stitching used to hold a hem.

INSERTION: A piece of decorative material such as lace set into a garment for trim.

INTERFACING: A fabric stitched between the garment and the facing for added shape, body, and firmness.

INTERLINING: A fabric placed between the garment and its lining to give warmth.

INVERTED PLEAT: Pleats pressed toward each other.

IRON-ON: Seam bindings, patches, fusing agents, and interfacing fabrics which are pressed rather than stitched in place.

KICK PLEAT: A short pleat at the lower edge of a skirt to give walking room.

KIMONO SLEEVE: Bodice and sleeve cut in one piece.

KNIFE PLEATS: Series of pleats that turn in the same direction.

LAPPED SEAM: Made when one seam allowance is laid over the other and top-stitched.

LAYOUT: The way the pattern pieces are laid on the fabric for cutting, indicated by diagrams on the pattern instruction sheet.

LENGTHWISE GRAIN: Yarns running perpendicular to the cross grain.

LINING: A fabric constructed along the lines of the original garment, and set inside it, to present an attractive inside finish, prevent raveling of seams, and hold the shape of the garment.

MARKING: Transferring pattern symbols to fabric.

MATCHING: Joining construction markings, as at notches.

MITER: Diagonal joining of fabric pieces which meet at a corner.

MUSLIN: In fashion terms, a garment made of inexpensive fabric, usually muslin, as an alteration and cutting guide for a fashion fabric.

NAP: Short fibers on the fabric surface, which influence pattern layout.

NEEDLE BOARD: A board, covered with fine steel wire, used for pressing napped fabrics.

NOTCH: A diamond-shaped marking on pattern edge to indicate where fabric edges are to be joined.

NOTIONS: Supplies used in dressmaking, such as thread, tape, zippers, etc. Also findings.

OFF-GRAIN: Fabric is called off-grain when cutting or printing is not on true grain, or when fabric is pulled out of shape from careless rolling on the bolt.

OVERCASTING: Stitch worked over the raw edge of fabric, usually at seam allowances, to prevent raveling.

PATCHING: A mending technique using extra fabric to cover a hole.

PATCHWORK: Joining of different patches of fabric to make a piece of material.

PIECING: Sewing pieces of fabric together to make a single larger piece.

PIN BASTING: Placing pins at right angles to the seam as a form of basting for machine stitching (using hinged presser foot). When pinning for fitting only, pins are placed parallel to the seam.

PINKING SHEARS: Scissors used to cut a non-ravel, saw-toothed edge.

PIPING: A fold of bias fabric, ribbon, or fine covered cording inserted in a seam.

PIVOT: A method of stitching around a sharp corner by turning the fabric on the needle with the presser foot raised.

PLACKET: An opening in a garment, closed by a zipper, snaps, or hooks and eyes.

PLEATS: Folds of fabric used to control fullness in a garment.

PRE-SHRINK: Home or professional treatment of fabric to prevent shrinkage.

PRESS MITT: A heavily padded mitt used in pressing and shaping a garment section.

QUILTING: A stitched design used to hold together two layers of fabric and a padded lining.

RAGLAN: A sleeve with slanted seam extending to collar or neck edge.

RAVEL: Fray, as the edge of a seam, or to deliberately pull crosswise threads to straighten an edge or make a fringe.

RICKRACK: A saw-toothed decorative braid.

RUFFLE: A band of fabric gathered and applied as a trim.

RUNNING STITCH: Basic hand stitch.

SADDLE STITCH: A trimming stitch, usually applied by hand to a completed garment in a continuous even running technique. Often done in Buttonhole Twist or embroidery floss in a contrasting color.

SATIN STITCH: An embroidery stitch, by hand or machine, made of rows of closely spaced stitches.

SCALLOP: Series of stitched semicircles, used as an edge finish.

SEAM: The stitching line formed by sewing two pieces of fabric together.

SEAM ALLOWANCE: The fabric edge that extends beyond the stitching line, usually ⅝".

SEAM FINISH: A finish applied to the raw edge of a seam allowance to prevent fraying.

SELVAGE: Narrow woven border on the lengthwise edges of the fabric.

SHIRRING: Two or more rows of gathering stitches.

SHRINKING: Contracting of fabric when washed.

SLASH: An even cut in a fabric, longer than a clip.

SLEEVEBOARD: A small padded board for pressing sleeves and pant legs.

SLIPSTITCH: Tiny, almost invisible hand stitches.

SMOCKING: A decorative way of gathering fabric into folds for controlled release of fullness.

STAY: Tape or fabric used in garment construction for reinforcement at key points.

STAYSTITCH: A line of stitching done before garment assembly to prevent stretching of curved or bias edges.

STRAIGHTENING: In dressmaking, the process of working fabric to correct grain line; pulling cross threads.

STRAIGHT OF GOODS: Lengthwise fabric grain.

TACK: Hand stitching used to hold fabric pieces together.

TAILOR'S TACK: Temporary stitches used for transferring pattern markings to two layers of fabric.

TAILORING: Technique of construction for making suits and coats.

TENSION: Degree of looseness or tightness for bobbin and needle threads in a sewing machine.

TOP-STITCHING: Line of stitching on outside of fabric, usually decorative.

TRIM: To cut away excess fabric in seam allowance.

TRIMMING: A decorative braid, lace, etc.

TUCKS: Straight folds of fabric, evenly stitched.

TWILL TAPE: Woven cotton tape, used as a stay.

UNDERLINING: A fabric used to back a garment section, stitched in one with the outside fabric.

UNDERSTITCHING: Machine or hand stitching through facing and seam allowance to hold facing flat.

VELVET BOARD: See needle board.

WEIGHTS: Metal discs sewn into hemlines and some necklines for proper hang.

WELT: A strip of fabric used to finish the lower edge of a pocket with a slashed opening.

WORKED BUTTONHOLE: Buttonhole finished with rows of stitching, made by hand or by machine.

WHIPPING STITCH: A hand stitch used for hemming and overcasting.

YARDAGE: Length of fabric needed to make a garment.

ZIGZAG: A machine stitch made by a sideways needle movement; has many variations.

ZIPPER: A closing of metal or nylon teeth or nylon coil, stitched into a placket, or seam line.

ZIPPER ADHESIVE: A strip of adhesive applied to the zipper tape to keep it in position for stitching.

ZIPPER FOOT: Machine foot for stitching zippers.

A Fabric Glossary

ACETATE: Any of a class of synthetic fibers made from cellulose acetate. See Cellulose acetate.

ACRYLIC: A synthetic fiber used to make wool-like fabrics.

ALPACA: Fiber made from long, fine hair of Alpaca sheep; fabric made from alpaca and cotton.

ANGORA: Fibers from Angora sheep or rabbits, usually blended with wool.

ARGYLE: Plaid design with diagonal stripes.

BARATHEA: Closely woven fabric with pebbly weave.

BASKET WEAVE: Plain-woven fabrics. See Hopsacking, Monk's cloth, Oxford.

BATIK: Javanese process of dyeing, producing rich and intricate designs. Imitated by machine printing.

BATISTE: Soft, sheer plain-woven fabric; usually of cotton, but may be of silk or wool.

BENGALINE: Woven fabric with crosswise ribs. See Faille.

BIRD'S EYE: A cotton fabric with a small, diamond-shaped woven figure. See Piqué.

BLEND: Combination of two or more fibers in one yarn.

BONDING: Joining of two fabrics by an adhesive process to stablize sheer and stretchy fabrics for easier handling. See Laminated fabric.

BOUCLE: A woven or knitted fabric with looped or slubbed yarns or fibers adding textural interest.

BRAID: A novelty trim in attractive colors and designs. See Rickrack, Soutache, Gimp.

BROADCLOTH: In cotton or silk, a plain, closely woven fabric with lustrous finish. In wool, a brushed finish gives a napped effect.

BROCADE: A fabric woven on a Jacquard loom with all-over interwoven raised design. See Jacquard.

BROCATELLE: An extra-heavy brocade with the pattern raised on the right side. See Brocade.

BURLAP: Coarse, plain-weave fabric of jute, hemp, or cotton. See specific fibers.

BUTCHER LINEN: Originally a coarse linen; now imitated in other fibers. See Linen.

BYRD CLOTH: Fine cotton twill, windproof and water repellent; used in windbreakers, etc. Named for Admiral Byrd.

CALICO: Plain-weave cotton similar to percale, usually with small all-over print. See Percale.

CAMBRIC: Fine solid-color cotton fabric.

CAMEL'S HAIR: Soft underhair of the camel woven into fabric, sometimes combined with wool. Classic coating fabric, varying in quality with the fineness of the camel hair. Also a descriptive term for a color.

CANVAS: Strong, firm fabric, usually of cotton.

CASHMERE: Luxury coating fabric woven from hair of Kashmir goat. Now usually blended with wool for durability.

CELLULOSE ACETATE: A chemical compound of acetic acid and cellulose (a plant material) used in making synthetic yarns and fibers, notably rayon.

CHALLIS: Originally a silk and worsted made in Norwich, England; now a soft, lightweight fabric of wool, cotton, or blends in solid colors or printed with delicate floral patterns.

166

CHAMBRAY: Plain-weave cotton or silk with colored warp and white fill.

CHENILLE: Fabric woven with soft tufts.

CHEVIOT: Wool fabric in twill weave, heavier than serge.

CHIFFON: Soft, sheer plain weave in silk or synthetic. See Georgette.

CHINA SILK: Thin fabric used for linings. Synthetics now substitute.

CHINCHILLA: Heavy coating material with nubbed surface, usually wool.

CHINO: Cotton sportswear fabric in twill weave.

CHINTZ: Used more in home decorating than in dressmaking; a glazed or unglazed, plain or printed cotton.

CIRÉ: A finish applied to fabric to produce a sleek, watery shine.

CLOQUÉ: A single-woven fabric with raised surface. See Matelassé.

COMBED COTTON: Cotton yarn that has been cleaned to remove impurities.

CORDUROY: Woven cotton fabric with lengthwise wales of cut pile. Pinwale, medium wale, heavy wale, wide wale describe weight and wale widths. Also without wale. See Wale.

COTTON: Fabric made from the boll of the cotton plant. Available in many grades and weaves. See Batiste; Bird's eye; Broadcloth; Burlap; Byrd cloth, Calico; Cambric; Canvas; Chambray; Chintz; Chino; Combed cotton; Corduroy; Crinoline; Denim; Dimity; Doeskin; Duck; Faille; Flannel; Flannelette; Lawn; Madras; Moire; Monk's cloth; Muslin; Organdy; Percale; Piqué; Pima; Plissé; Polished cotton; Sailcloth; Sateen; Satin; Seersucker; Sharkskin; Terry; Velveteen.

CREPE: Plain-woven fabric with high-twist filling yarns which produce a crinkled surface.

CREPE DE CHINE: Plain-weave crepe, usually of silk.

CRINOLINE: Stiff, highly sized plain cotton with open weave. Used for stiffness in interlining or skirt linings.

DAMASK: A Jacquard-woven fabric which originated in Damascus, similar to brocade but flatter. See Jacquard.

DENIM: A sportswear fabric of cotton in a twill weave, often with white fill yarns.

DIMITY: Sheer cotton with a fine woven design.

DOESKIN: A heavy, short-napped woolen fabric; also made in cotton.

DONEGAL: A rough tweed with slubs of color.

DOTTED SWISS: Sheer cotton fabric ornamented with raised woven dots.

DOUBLE KNIT: Knit fabric made on two sets of needles, in wool or synthetics.

DRIP DRY: The first of the no-care finishes. Most often applied to cottons. See Permanent press and Wash and wear.

DUCK: Similar to canvas: tightly woven cotton with plain or rib weave.

DUVETYN: Smooth twill-weave fabric with velvety finish, usually of wool.

ELASTIC FABRICS: Made from yarns of rubber covered with cotton or synthetic; often called spandex.

EYELET: Fabric with decorative cutouts, edged in stitching.

FABRIC: A cloth knitted, woven, or felted (matted under heavy pressure) of natural, synthetic, or blended fibers or yarns.

FAILLE: Light fabric of silk, rayon, or cotton with pronounced horizontal rib. Lighter than bengaline, heavier than poplin.

FAKE FUR: Woven or knitted fabric with pile surface to resemble fur.

FELT: A dense fabric created by matting fibers under heat and pressure; also process by which fibers are matted under heat and pressure.

FIBER: Basic unit of textile yarns, natural or synthetic.

FIBERGLAS®: Fabric made from glass yarns; not used in dressmaking.

FILLING: Crosswise yarn in weaving; also called fill, weft, and woof.

FLANNEL: A plain- or twill-weave of wool, cotton, or rayon fabric, lightly napped.

FLANNELETTE: Plain-woven cotton fabric, napped on one side. See Outing flannel.

FLAX: Fibers from which linen is made. See Linen.

FLEECE: Coating fabric with deeply napped surface.

FLOCKING: The process of applying small particles to a fabric with adhesive to form a raised design.

FOULARD: Silk or silk-look fabric, lightweight, plain-woven or twilled, usually printed.

FUSIBLE: An agent used in joining two fabrics by heat and pressure.

GABARDINE: Tightly woven twill with diagonal rib. Available in stretch fabric.

GALLOON: Narrow tape or braid; also a double-edged lace.

GEORGETTE: Sheer, dull-textured fabric, heavier than chiffon with crepe-like surface.

GIMP: Also Guimpe. A flat, ornamental trimming.

GINGHAM: Yarn-dyed plain-woven cotton fabric in stripes, checks, plaids, or solids.

GROSGRAIN: Firm, closely woven ribbed fabric, woven in narrow widths for ribbons and belting.

HAND: Refers to the "feel" of a fabric.

HARRIS TWEED: A rough, durable homespun and hand-woven tweed, originally made on the island of Harris in the Outer Hebrides, northwest of Scotland.

HEMP: Coarse fiber from hemp plant, used in making burlap.

HERRINGBONE: A zigzag design produced by weaving.

HOPSACKING: Rough-textured basket-weave fabric.

HOUNDSTOOTH: A check design in a twill weave.

IRISH LINEN: Linen actually woven in Ireland. See Linen.

JACQUARD: A loom with a mechanism to produce intricate woven designs in damasks and brocades.

JERSEY: Plain knitted material, made from all kinds of yarns and blends.

JUTE: A glossy fiber used in burlap.

KNIT: Any fabric that is made by single- or double-needle knitting, as opposed to weaving.

LACE: Openwork fabric.

LAMÉ: A variety of metallic cloth.

LAMINATED FABRIC: Two or more layers of cloth fused together and handled as a single layer. Also, a foam-backed fabric. See Bonding.

LAWN: Thin, lightweight plain-woven cotton.

LEATHERETTE: Imitation leather made of cloth or plastic.

LINEN: Fabric made from flax fibers. See Butcher linen; Flax; Irish linen.

LISLE: Smooth cotton yarn, used mainly in knits.

LODEN: A thick woolen cloth, wind and water resistant.

LYONS VELVET: Stiff velvet with thick pile, usually silk.

MACKINAW: Heavy outerwear fabric, often double-faced.

MADRAS: Soft cotton shirting fabric with woven design.

MARQUISETTE: Fabric in a sheer, fine, open weave.

MATELASSÉ: A double-woven fabric with a quilted look.

MATTE: Dull, non-lustrous as matte finish, jersey.

MELTON: Thick, smooth wool twill.

MERCERIZED: Process applied to cotton thread to make it stronger and more lustrous.

MESSALINE: High-luster silk satin.

MOHAIR: Fibers from Angora goat blended with other wool fibers in weaving or knitting.

MOIRÉ: Watery pattern produced on silk, cotton, or rayon by embossed rollers.

MONK'S CLOTH: Coarse basket-weave fabric, usually of cotton.

MUSLIN: Plain, strong cotton in several weights, bleached or unbleached.

NAP: Soft fabric finish, produced by brushing.

NATURAL FIBERS: Fibers which occur in nature. See Cotton; Linen; Silk; Wool.

NYLON: Synthetic material used alone or in blends to make textiles. Extremely strong and abrasion resistant.

OMBRE: A rainbow-colored effect in fabrics.

ORGANDY: Crisp, sheer cotton in plain weave.

ORGANZA: Silk organdy, also of rayon or nylon.

OTTOMAN: Heavy corded fabric of silk or synthetics, also of wool.

OUTING FLANNEL: Soft lightweight woven fabric with nap on both sides.

OXFORD: Cotton fabric done in basket weave, used for shirtings. Also a descriptive term for a color blended with black yarns, as oxford gray, oxford blue.

PAISLEY: Made of or similar to a printed woolen fabric originally woven in Paisley, Scotland.

PATCHWORK: Patches of different fabrics sewed together.

PEAU DE SOIE: Rich, smooth silk dress material. Copied in rayon and blends.

PERCALE: Fine, lightweight cotton fabric.

PERMANENT PRESS: A description of fabric performance in wrinkle resistance and washability. See Drip dry; Wash and wear.

PIECE-DYED: Fabrics dyed after weaving. See Yarn-dyed.

PILE FABRIC: Cloth woven with deep furry surface.

PIMA COTTON: High-quality fabric woven from Egyptian cotton.

PIQUE: Firm cotton fabric with wale, waffle, or diamond woven in. See Bird's eye.

PLAID: Pattern of colored blocks and/or intersecting stripes.

PLISSÉ: Cotton fabric with alternating plain and puckered stripes.

POLISHED COTTON: Cotton finished with glossy face, usually in satin weave.

POLYESTER: Generic term for synthetic fiber with superior easy-care properties. Used alone or in blends.

PONGEE: Plain-woven silk fabric.

POPLIN: Fine ribbed fabric of natural or synthetic yarns.

QUILTING: Fine stitching in a design joining two outer fabrics with inner layer of padding.

RAYON: First of the synthetics, now produced in many versions. See Cellulose acetate.

REP: Fabric with pronounced cross rib.

RIBBON: Narrow strip of woven fabric.

RICKRACK: Flat woven braid in zigzag pattern.

SAILCLOTH: Heavy cotton in a plain weave.

SATEEN: Satin weave in mercerized cotton.

SATIN: Basic weave which produces a lustrous surface. Also fabric in this weave of silk or synthetic.

SEERSUCKER: Cotton fabric with plain and puckered stripes.

SERGE: Crisp, flat twill-weave fabric.

SHANTUNG: Plain-woven silk originally made in Shantung Province in China; made with thick and thin yarns for nubbed surface.

SHARKSKIN: In wool, a twill weave with white and colored yarns. Also a smooth, lustrous, closely woven fabric of silk, cotton, or synthetics.

SHETLAND: Knitting yarn or fabric from the wool of the Shetland sheep.

SILK: Filament produced by silkworms, woven into luxurious fabrics. See China silk; Chiffon; Crepe de Chine; Faille; Foulard; Lyons velvet; Messaline; Moiré; Ottoman; Peau de soie; Pongee; Satin; Shantung; Surah; Taffeta.

SOUTACHE: Narrow flat braid.

SPANDEX: Generic term for synthetic fiber with elasticity, or fabric made of spandex fiber.

STRETCH TERRY: terry cloth woven with stretch yarns.

SUEDE CLOTH: Fabric woven or knitted to simulate suede leather.

SYNTHETICS: Man-made fibers. See Acetate; Acrylic; Cellulose acetate; Nylon; Rayon; Spandex; Triacetate.

TAFFETA: Crisp, plain weave of silk, cotton, synthetics, or blends, made in several weights.

TARTAN: Specific wool plaids associated with Scottish clans.

TATTERSALL: Simple overcheck design on contrasting ground.

TERRY: Cotton fabric woven with loops on both sides or knit with loops on one side. See Stretch terry.

TICKING: Strong woven twill fabric, usually with stripes.

TIE DYE: Hand dyeing by tieing off portions of cloth.

TRIACETATE: Synthetic fiber similar to acetate.

TRICOT: Type of knit material resembling jersey, most used for lingerie.

TULLE: A fine machine-made net of natural or synthetic fibers characterized by a hexagonal mesh.

TWEED: Rough fabric in plain, twill, or herringbone weave, or in plaids and checks. Usually of wool, but simulated in cotton, silk, and blends.

TWILL: Basic weave with diagonal rib.

VELOUR: General term for pile fabrics, generally used in reference to coatings or hat felt. A lighter version of this fabric is used in sportswear.

VELVET: Luxurious fabric with short, thick pile. In many weights and fibers.

VELVETEEN: An all-cotton pile fabric resembling velvet.

VICUNA: The most luxurious animal fiber, woven into expensive coating materials.

VINYL: A plastic material, usually with a fabric backing.

VISCOSE: A form of rayon.

VOILE: Plain-weave sheer crisp fabric.

WALE: One of a series of ribs or cords in a woven fabric. See Corduroy.

WARP: Lengthwise threads in a woven fabric.

WASH AND WEAR: Refers to wrinkle resistance of fabric after laundering. See Permanent press; Drip dry.

WEFT: Crosswise threads in a woven fabric. Also called fill and woof.

WOOL: Soft fiber from sheep and other animals —camel, alpaca, angora, vicuña. Also fabrics woven from these fibers. See Angora; Batiste; Broadcloth; Camel's Hair; Cashmere; Challis; Chinchilla; Duvetyn; Flannel; Loden; Melton; Ottoman; Sharkskin; Shetland; Tartan; Tweed; Vicuña; Worsted; Zibeline.

WORSTED: Woolen fabric made by twisting yarns before weaving for crispness and durability.

YARN: Strand of textile fibers.

YARN-DYED: Color applied to yarn before weaving. See Piece-dyed.

ZIBELINE: Coating fabric with shaggy brushed nap.